FUNDAMENTALS OF CATHOLICISM
VOLUME III

D0843872

FUNDAMENTALS

OF

CATHOLICISM

VOLUME III

by

KENNETH BAKER, S.J.

IGNATIUS PRESS   SAN FRANCISCO

Imprimi Potest: Thomas R. Royce, S.J.
Provincial, Oregon Province
of the Society of Jesus
Portland, Oregon

Imprimatur: + Thomas J. Welsh
Bishop of Arlington, Virginia

Cover design by Riz Boncan Marsella

ISBN 0-89870-027-2
Library of Congress catalogue number 82-80297
Co-published by Ignatius Press, San Francisco
and Homiletic & Pastoral Review
86 Riverside Drive, New York, N.Y. 10024
Printed in the United States of America

CONTENTS

Part I: GRACE

Part II: THE CHURCH

Part III: THE SACRAMENTS

Part IV: ESCHATOLOGY

PART I

GRACE

I

THE MYSTERY OF DIVINE GRACE

Having completed our consideration of Jesus Christ in Volume 2, both with regard to who he is and what he did for us (redemption), we will now move on to an examination of the fruit of redemption itself, which is called "divine grace". The notion of "grace" is very common in Catholic thinking and practice. At an early age we learned that we gain the grace of God by praying, by attending Mass and going to confession, by performing acts of penance and by saying the Rosary.

Every Catholic schooled in catechism knows that one must die in the state of sanctifying grace in order to be saved and to go to heaven. Many will recall the definition of grace that they learned from their catechism: "Grace is the supernatural life of the soul that makes us children of God and heirs of heaven." What I propose to do in the following essays is to explain the fundamental ideas and teachings of the Church on this very important subject of grace.

In the course of history many errors and heresies have arisen which are contrary to the true doctrine of the Church on grace. In order to steer one's way safely through these treacherous theological waters, it is absolutely essential to adhere to the certain, clear teaching of the Magisterium of the holy Roman Catholic Church.

The Catholic doctrine of grace is intimately connected with the doctrine of original sin. You may recall that in previous essays I explained the Church's teaching on the Fall of our first parents. Briefly, God created Adam and Eve and placed them in the Garden of Paradise; in addition to their natural and preternatural gifts, he bestowed on them sanctifying grace or original justice which made them children of God and heirs of heaven. This meant that they were eventually destined for the Beatific Vision of God for all eternity.

Adam and Eve sinned against God; they rebelled against him. As punishment they were cast out of Paradise. They lost sanctifying grace; they lost their preternatural gifts of immunity from suffering and death. From Adam until Christ the state of man was one of alienation from God. The gates of heaven were closed and man's state was desperate.

The point of Jesus' death on the cross on Calvary is that he reconciled man with God in principle. After Christ, his objective redemption must be accepted and appropriated by each man and woman so that it may come to fruition in the subjective redemption of each person. The application of the fruits of the redemption to the individual person is called in Catholic theology "sanctification" or "justification".

Because God has endowed human nature with the exceptional gifts of reason and free will, the process of justification requires the free cooperation of each person. God's grace is offered freely to each human being (see 1 Tim 2:4), but grace works together with man's freedom—not in opposition to it. Because God made us free he does not force our wills; he wants us to love him freely in return, but he will not force us. The impenetrable mystery of divine grace is located in the mutual cooperation of God's power and human freedom. In the course of these essays I will try to explain as clearly as I can what the Church says on this difficult and important matter, but please do not expect everything to be perfectly clear. After all, we are dealing with a divine mystery. Through revelation and the teaching of the Church we know a great deal about it, but we cannot explain everything; if we could, the mystery would no longer be a mystery.

In the working out of the salvation of each human person God helps man not merely by the interior principle of divine grace, but also by exterior helps, such as the life of Christ, revelation, the teaching of the Church and the dispensing of the sacraments. The ultimate goal of grace and all subjective redemption is the face-to-face Beatific Vision of God.

In the language of the Bible grace is the condescension or special benevolence and favor shown by God to the human race. In the objective sense, grace is the unmerited gift that proceeds from this benevolent disposition.

As the Church understands it, grace is something more than the gifts of nature, such as creation and the fertility of the soil. For grace is a *supernatural* gift of God that he bestows freely on rational creatures so that they can attain personal union with him. Grace is totally supernatural; it surpasses the being, powers and claims of nature and includes sanctifying grace, actual grace, the infused virtues and the gifts of the Holy Spirit. By grace we become sharers in trinitarian life.

The essence of grace is its gratuity, since no creature has or can have a right to the Beatific Vision. And the purpose of divine grace is to bring us to the face-to-face vision of God.

2

SPEAKING OF GRACE

In Catholic theology the word "grace" is used in many different ways. It usually carries the connotation of *supernatural* and *gratuitous*, but we should pay close attention to how it is used in each case. As we saw in the last essay, "Grace is the supernatural life of the soul that makes us children of God and heirs of heaven."

The most basic division of grace is between sanctifying grace and actual grace. We will have much to say about these two terms shortly. Sanctifying or habitual grace is an *abiding*, supernatural and personal quality of the soul which sanctifies man intrinsically and makes him holy and pleasing to God.

Actual grace (or helping grace) is a *temporary* supernatural intervention by God by which the powers of the soul (especially intellect and will) are influenced to perform a salutary act which is directed to the attaining or preservation or increase of sanctifying grace.

The person who possesses sanctifying grace is pleasing to God; one who dies in the state of sanctifying grace will go to heaven and enjoy the face-to-face vision of God for all eternity.

Actual grace is a *temporary* help from God; it is wholly supernatural. It is given gratuitously by God to pagans and unbelievers to move them toward faith, hope and charity; it is given to Christian sinners to help bring them to repentance and to the reception of the sacraments; it is given to good Christians to help them become better— to help them become saints.

Another way of looking at grace is to consider whether it is *uncreated* grace or *created* grace. As one might suspect from the word itself, "uncreated" grace refers to God himself insofar as he dwells in the souls of the justified and insofar as he gives himself to the blessed in heaven for possession and enjoyment in the Beatific Vision.

What is given by God and possessed by the creature is God himself; therefore, this aspect of grace is called "uncreated". The actual indwelling in the hearts of the faithful and the personal enjoyment of the Beatific Vision, considered as acts of a finite, created person, are called "created graces" because they have a beginning in time.

In other words, "uncreated grace" is God himself, while "created grace" is a supernatural gift or operation in the creature which is really distinct from God.

It is important to remember that all grace, whether sanctifying or actual, is the grace of Christ. For God bestows his grace on us in view of the infinite merits of Christ's Passion and death. Moreover, the grace of Christ elevates us into a higher, supernatural order of being and activity. This means that the person in the state of sanctifying grace can perform good acts that merit an increase in divine life.

We may also consider grace as either *external* or *internal*. External grace is any activity of God for the salvation of men which is external to man and which affects him in a moral way only. Thus, divine revelation, the life of Christ, the Gospels, the sacraments and the good example of the saints are all external graces. Internal grace affects the soul and its powers intrinsically and operates on it immediately. Thus, sanctifying grace, the indwelling of the Holy Spirit, and the infused virtues of faith, hope and charity are internal graces. The purpose of external graces is to dispose men for the acceptance of inner graces.

The purpose of sanctifying grace is the personal sanctification of the one who receives it. Some graces, however, are conferred on particular persons for the sanctification of others. In this class belong the extraordinary charismata (e.g., prophecy, gift of miracles, etc.) and the priestly power of consecration. The possession of these gifts is independent of the personal moral qualities of their possessor, precisely because they are *for others*.

Grace is not a thing; it is not something static or impersonal; it is not like more or less milk in a bottle. Grace is God himself; it is dynamic and personal. It is a perpetual outpouring of divine love, mercy and benevolence.

Grace is gentle; it is an invitation from God to man; it is not dictatorial and it is not coercive. Actual grace can be resisted by man's free will and sanctifying grace can be lost through mortal sin. Our free cooperation with grace, therefore, is our proper response to the prior love of God.

3

ACTUAL GRACE ENLIGHTENS THE MIND AND STRENGTHENS THE WILL

The notion of divine grace has been and is a very important part of Catholic teaching. In the previous essay we considered some of the ways in which the Church speaks about grace, especially the division into sanctifying grace and actual grace. My present concern is to explain what is meant by "actual grace".

Before getting into that, let me remark that the Church's teaching on grace is based on her belief that the end or goal of each human person is eternal life with God in heaven: that is, a participation in the divine life that produces supreme happiness and that will never come to an end. It is a personal sharing in the life of God himself. No mere creature, by the fact that it is a creature, has a right to such intimacy with its Creator.

Now we know from revelation that God has destined all men for eternal life. The end of man, therefore, completely surpasses his natural powers. It is for this reason that the Church uses the word "supernatural" to describe man's end, the Beatific Vision. Since man's end is supernatural, the means to arrive at that end must also be supernatural. This is where the need for grace comes in.

A related notion is that of "elevation". In order to be on the same "plane" as eternal life, man's soul and faculties must be elevated by God to the supernatural level. That is what grace does. Sanctifying grace imparts a permanent elevation of the soul and faculties, while actual grace elevates the intellect and will temporarily, in order to assist them to posit salutary acts: that is, good acts such as acts of faith, hope and charity that are conducive to eternal life.

Looked at from another point of view, what this means is that man all by himself, purely on the natural level and without the special assistance of God, is incapable of doing anything that is meritorious of eternal life. Of course, we do not now live in a purely natural order, because Christ died for all and his salvific grace is offered to all (see I Tim 2:4). But just because the grace of God is now offered to all men, it does not follow that it is "natural"; it is and remains wholly supernatural.

Now to the main point. What is actual grace? It is a temporary supernatural help from God that influences the spiritual powers of man for the purpose of moving him to perform salutary acts, such as praying, making an act of faith, attending an extra Mass, going to confession and so forth. By reason of its *temporary* character, actual grace is distinguished from sanctifying or habitual grace, which inheres as a permanent quality in the soul. By reason of its *supernatural* character, actual grace is distinguished from God's natural or ordinary cooperation in the activities of his creatures (= divine concursus).

Although you will not find the words "actual grace" in the Bible, the reality to which they point is certainly expressed there in a number of different places. The Second Council of Orange in the year 529 rejected the theory of the Semi-Pelagians that man can perform some salutary acts, such as praying, without the grace of God. In support of this position it cited many texts of the Bible, especially St. Paul in Philippians 2:13, "It is God who of his good pleasure works in you both the will and the performance."

By his actual grace God can effect the direct internal enlightenment of the intellect and the strengthening of the will. We can distinguish this internal activity from his indirect enlightenment of the intellect which takes place by external means such as reading the Bible, hearing a sermon or being influenced by a very holy person.

The existence of internal divine enlightenment of the mind and its necessity for the performance of salutary acts is affirmed repeatedly in Holy Scripture: "Before God we are confident of this through Christ: not that we are qualified in ourselves to claim anything as our own work: all our qualifications come from God" (2 Cor 3:4–5).

St. John says that God illumines every man born into this world, and he quotes the words of Jesus about the divine internal call that must precede any following of the Lord: "No one can come to me unless he is drawn by the Father who sent me" (Jn 6:44). Likewise, St. Luke recounts the conversion of Lydia, the seller of purple clothes. A good woman, she listened carefully to St. Paul and "the Lord opened her heart to accept what Paul was saying" (Acts 16:14).

It is clear, therefore, that we need the grace of God to

perform supernatural acts. In support of this, let us conclude with the testimony of Paul that the apostolic preaching remains unfruitful if not accompanied by the inner enlightenment of God: "I did the planting, Apollos did the watering, but God made things grow. Neither the planter nor the waterer matters: only God, who makes things grow" (1 Cor 3:6–7).

4

KNOCKING AT THE DOOR

So far in this series we have seen what grace is, and we have seen that it is distinguished into sanctifying and actual grace, depending upon whether grace inheres permanently in the soul or whether it is a fleeting, temporary elevation of the powers of the soul in order to assist them to posit a salutary act.

Because man is destined to a supernatural end—one that wholly surpasses his natural powers—he is in constant need of God's assistance. Since there exist a number of basic situations in which a person can find himself or herself, it follows that God's grace will have to be looked at a bit differently, according to its different forms and functions.

Let us consider some of the differences. Those who do not believe in Christ and who lack Baptism need the grace of Christ in order to move toward faith. In this state grace calls them, invites them. Here we encounter spontaneous, nondeliberate acts that gently lead a person to faith. It is God's actual grace which accomplishes this. Grace in this sense is called by theologians "antecedent grace" because it precedes the free and deliberate act that leads to faith and salvation. In this case God works alone "in us and without us", and produces spontaneous, indeliberate acts of knowledge and love.

God's antecedent grace is also involved in the process of repentance in the case of the Christian who has fallen into mortal sin. For the mortal sinner has lost the grace of God and cannot regain it without the antecedent help of God. In other words, he needs God's (actual) grace in order to regain sanctifying grace. The sinner may abandon God, but God, like Francis Thompson's "Hound of Heaven", never abandons the sinner. He pursues him, calls him, invites him, bothers him until he returns.

The official teaching of the Church in the Council of Trent is that "In adults the beginning of justification must proceed from the antecedent grace of God acquired by Jesus Christ." The New Testament speaks about the reality of antecedent grace in the metaphors of the Lord standing and knocking at the door of our hearts (Rev 3:20) and of the Father "drawing" men to Christ by touching their hearts internally (Jn 6:44).

Actual grace in the above sense precedes all super-natural, salutary acts that are meritorious of eternal life. But what about the salutary acts themselves? Can man perform them on his own, without the help of God? Or does man need God's actual grace to perform salutary acts such as faith, hope, charity, prayer, self-sacrifice, penance and so forth? The Church says that in all salutary acts God and man work together. In these cases God works "in us and with us" so that our salutary acts are the common work both of God's grace and of our own free activity. Grace in this sense is called "consequent" or "helping" grace. Here we are dealing with deliberate free acts that are co-produced by the grace of God and man's free will.

Acts of faith, hope and love that lead to salvation are free deliberate salutary acts in this sense. This grace is necessary to achieve justification or sanctifying grace in the first place. It is also necessary for all the meritorious acts that are performed by those already in the state of habitual grace.

The Church says that there is a supernatural influence of God on the faculties of the soul which coincides in time with man's free act of the will. Thus, the Council of Trent says that the sinner returns to justification "by freely assenting to and cooperating with grace" (Denzinger 797). The same Council also says that "God's goodness towards all men is so great that he wants his gifts to be their merits" (Denzinger 810).

St. Paul stresses the importance of grace in performing salutary human acts. Thus, he writes: "By the grace of God I am what I am, and the grace that he gave me has not been fruitless. On the contrary, I, or rather the grace of God that is with me, have worked harder than any of the others" (1 Cor 15:10).

St. Augustine has been called the Doctor of Divine Grace. Here is what he says about antecedent and consequent grace: "God works in man many good things to which man does not contribute; but man does not work any good things apart from God since it is from God man receives the power to do the good things which he does."

What is actual grace? Is it an activity of the soul itself? Or is it a real gift of God added to the soul for a specific purpose? The common view of theologians is that it is a supernatural gift or power which precedes the vital act of the soul and by which our faculties of intellect and will are elevated and moved into action. Thus, actual grace is a supernatural power given by God to the soul; it unites itself with the faculties of intellect and will and with them forms one united principle from which the supernatural act proceeds.

Accordingly, actual grace is a calling, an enlightening, a knocking, a strengthening, a drawing—in short, a touching by God.

5

THE NECESSITY OF GRACE

It has been pointed out that God has destined man to a *supernatural* end, namely, the face-to-face vision of God which involves a share in the divine life itself. Such an end completely surpasses the natural ability of man to attain it. Just as a man is not able to fly by flapping his arms the way a bird flaps his wings, so also is man not able, solely on the basis of his natural resources, to do anything that is meritorious of eternal life.

In theological language, acts that are meritorious of the Beatific Vision are called "salutary acts": that is, acts that lead to eternal salvation. The question has been raised often in the history of the Church: Can man, unaided by divine grace, posit any salutary acts? Some early heretics, whom St. Augustine opposed for twenty years, said that he could. Following the teaching of Augustine, the Church has said since at least the sixth century that the internal supernatural grace of God (= elevating grace) is absolutely necessary for every salutary act.

In opposition to the heretics, called "Semi-Pelagians", the Second Council of Orange decreed in 529: "As often as we do good God operates in us and with us, so that we may operate", and "Man does no good except that which God brings about that man performs" (*Denzinger* 182, 193). In 1547 the Council of Trent reaffirmed this same doctrine in its famous Decree on Justification: "If anyone says that, without divine grace through Jesus Christ, man can be justified before God by his own works, whether they were done by his natural powers or by the light of the teaching of the (Mosaic) Law: let him be anathema" (*Denzinger* 811).

The doctrine of the absolute necessity of divine grace for all salutary acts is solidly grounded on Holy Scripture. In the parable of the vine and the branches Jesus vividly describes the power of grace going out from him to others so that they can perform salutary acts: "I am the vine, you are the branches. Whoever remains in me, with me in him, bears fruit in plenty; for cut off from me you can do nothing" (Jn 15:5). The fruit in this case is acts that are meritorious of eternal life. In the same regard, St. Paul says: "No one can say 'Jesus is Lord' unless he is under the influence of the Holy Spirit" (1 Cor 12:3).

According to St. Thomas Aquinas, the absolute necessity of supernatural grace for every salutary act follows logically from the supernatural character of man's final end, namely, the Beatific Vision. The reason for this is that the act must be proportioned to the end. The natural by itself can never attain the supernatural.

The Semi-Pelagian heretics conceded to St. Augustine that man needs divine grace in order to be saved. But they erred in saying that the first steps in the process of attaining faith in Jesus Christ come from man himself, without the help or grace of God. Both of the Councils mentioned above firmly rejected that view and declared that supernatural grace is also necessary for the very beginnings of faith and salvation. We come back to the same point: By his own unaided efforts man cannot do anything to merit eternal life.

Thus the Second Council of Orange decreed: "If anybody says that the . . . beginning of faith and the act of faith itself . . . is in us naturally and not by a gift of grace that is by the inspiration of the Holy Spirit, he is opposed to apostolic teaching" (*Denzinger* 178). And Trent said: "In the case of adults, justification must begin with God's prevenient grace through Jesus Christ" (*Denzinger* 797). In the previous essay we considered the reality of antecedent grace—a point that is again referred to here.

The New Testament teaches us that faith is a gift of God. For example, consider these words of St. Paul: "It is by grace that you have been saved, through faith; not by anything of your own, but by a gift from God; not by anything you have done, so that nobody can claim the credit" (Eph 2:8–9).

In support of this doctrine St. Augustine cites a number of the important Fathers of the Church. He also makes reference to the prayer of the Church for the conversion of unbelievers. If the conversion depends solely on themselves, then why pray for them? Augustine says: "If faith is simply a matter of free will and is not given by God, why then do we pray for those who do not wish to believe, that they might believe?" In her liturgy the Church often prays that God will grant his grace that sinners repent and that unbelievers accept faith in Jesus Christ.

Thus, even the beginning of faith requires the grace of God and grace is a wholly gratuitous gift of God. When a person begins to consider the possibility of accepting Christ, the first grasp of the credibility of revelation and the readiness to believe are under the influence of God's immediate enlightening and strengthening actual grace, as we saw in the previous essay.

6

FINAL PERSEVERANCE

The grace of God is required in order to be able to posit a salutary act, that is, one that leads to eternal life. Thus, the grace of God is absolutely necessary in order to be able to make an act of faith in God.

Once a person has attained faith and sanctifying grace, what then? Does that mean that he or she is confirmed in grace for the remainder of life? Does it mean that one is certain of eternal salvation?

Questions such as these are treated in Catholic theology under the title of "final perseverance". The precise point is this: Can the justified person persevere to the end of his life without some special help from God? The Church says that he cannot.

Final perseverance means to live and die in the grace of Christ. Please note that here two points are especially important: 1) continuance in grace—this depends on a special help from God; 2) death in the state of grace—this also depends on God's special protection. Thus, the Council of Trent said that final perseverance is "a great gift" from God; it also taught that those in the state of grace cannot long persist in grace without the special help of God: "If anyone says that without God's special help it is possible for a justified man to persevere in the justice he has received, or says that with God's special help it is impossible: let him be anathema" (*Denzinger* 832).

The "special help" the Council talks about is composed of actual graces given to the justified person to enable him to overcome temptations and to avoid mortal sin.

It is helpful to distinguish between "perseverance" and "final perseverance". For many are baptized and receive grace but then do not persevere in grace until the end of their life; they persevere for a time and then fall away for one reason or another.

Another distinction is made between the power to persevere in grace and actual perseverance. For every justified person receives the grace of potential perseverance. But it does not follow from this that every justified person actually dies in the state of grace. Here we run into the mystery of the relationship between the freedom of the human will and the grace of God. God's grace is necessary, but it can be resisted by the perverse human will. There is much about this that we do not understand because it is a mystery. There have been many theological battles in past centuries over this question.

The New Testament attributes the successful completion of the work of salvation to God: "I am quite certain that the One who began this good work in you will see that it is finished when the Day of Christ Jesus comes" (Phil 1:6).

Final perseverance in the grace of God is indeed a great gift, for it means entrance into heaven and eternal life. God so influences the events in a person's life that the moment of death comes while he is persevering in the grace of Christ. Dying in the state of grace is not an accident; it is a special grace because it is distinct from all others and because it is had only by those who are saved.

We know that God is infinitely just and merciful. If a person dies in the state of grace, the thanks belong to God. If he dies in mortal sin, it is his own fault. God does not damn anyone—he desires the salvation of all (see 1 Tim 2:4).

We are all concerned about dying in the state of grace. The Good Thief "stole" heaven at the end of his life; Judas perhaps perished because of his betrayal of Christ, his refusal to hope and then his suicide. It should be noted that final perseverance is a supernatural gift of grace. As such it cannot be merited—it is a gift. Can we not have any certainty about our final perseverance? Yes we can. It is a kind of conditional certainty. God has promised that those who keep his commandments and remain faithful in prayer will persevere to the end; they will be granted the grace of final perseverance.

That our prayer will be heard is founded on the promise of Jesus: "I tell you most solemnly, anything you ask for from the Father he will grant in my name" (Jn 16:23). Because of original sin, and the ensuing weakness of intellect and will, the possibility of a fall from grace always remains for us. Since we are not immovably anchored in goodness and virtue, no one can know for certain, without a special revelation from God, whether he will actually persevere to the end.

The need for a special grace of final perseverance is rooted in the fact that the human will, because of the constant revolt of the flesh against the spirit, does not have the power within itself to stand fast in virtue. So it exceeds the power of the individual to provide that the moment of death coincides with being in a state of grace.

7

IS IT POSSIBLE TO AVOID ALL SINS?

We have already considered that the actual grace of God, a temporary supernatural enlightening and strengthening help, is necessary in order to perform salutary acts. Persevering in grace and dying in the state of sanctifying grace also result from a special gift from God.

A related question is this: Can the justified or "graced" person avoid all sins, even venial sins, for his whole life long without a special privilege of grace from God? On this point the Church teaches explicitly, basing herself on the revealed Word of God, that no just person can go through his whole life without committing at least some venial sins, unless that person has been granted a very special privilege from God.

Our Lord was totally sinless. He is the Lamb of God who takes away the sins of the world. The devil never at any time had power over him. Also, the belief and teaching of the Church is that the Blessed Virgin Mary, Mother of the Church and Co-Redemptrix of the human race, never committed any sins, either mortal or venial. Mary is the woman of Genesis 3:15 who, through her offspring, crushes the head of Satan. The Council of Trent in 1547 declared the following to be a dogma of Catholic faith: "If anyone says . . . that a man once justified can avoid all sins, even venial sins, throughout his entire life without a special privilege of God, as the Church holds in regard to the Blessed Virgin: let him be anathema" (*Denzinger* 833).

Church teaching on this delicate point was occasioned by the error of the fifth century Pelagian heretics, against whom St. Augustine fought for over twenty years. They claimed that the human will of its own natural power, without any supernatural help from God, is able to avoid all sin, not only mortal but also venial.

Sin is an offense against God, who is man's last end. A *mortal* sin is committed when a person, by a deliberate act, turns away from God completely. Examples of such acts would be serious violations of the Ten Commandments, such as blasphemy, fornication, adultery, murder, robbery.

An offense against God which does not involve a complete turning away from him, a complete rejection of man's final end, is termed a *venial* sin. Examples of venial sins include lies of convenience, dishonesty in small things, impatience, uncharitableness, immodesty and so forth.

The doctrine of the Church quoted above refers primarily to what are known as semi-deliberate venial sins. These include many unpremeditated faults that we fall into—anger, impatience, unkind remarks, selfishness, uncharitable thoughts about others and the like. Because of the pull of concupiscence, the war of the flesh against the spirit, we cannot always be in full control of these inclinations or movements.

It should be noted, on the other hand, that the justified person always has sufficient grace to avoid mortal sins. What we are saying here is that it takes a very special gift of many actual graces, such as Our Lady had, in order to avoid all venial sins for one's whole life.

The above teaching is based squarely on the Bible, which says that no one is entirely free from all sin. The apostle St. James says, "In many things we all offend" (3:2). Our Lord himself teaches sanctified Christians to pray in the "Our Father": "forgive us our trespasses" (Mt 6:12). St. Augustine and the Council of Carthage (418 A.D.) rejected the Pelagian interpretation of the "Our Father", in which the saints ask for forgiveness not for themselves, but for others. St. John says clearly that we are all sinners: "If we say that we have no sin, we deceive ourselves, and the truth is not in us" (1 Jn 1:8). Obviously he is speaking here about venial sin.

In the same regard, St. Thomas Aquinas says that in our present state of fallen nature, that is, as a result of original sin and concupiscence, we can, through the power of God's sanctifying grace, avoid all mortal sins, but not all venial sins. He says that man cannot avoid all venial sins because of the disorder that entered into his sensual appetite as a result of original sin. We can, he says, control some of the disordered movements of our lower appetites, but not all of them. For this he gives two reasons: 1) while we are resisting one temptation we may be afflicted by another, and 2) the human mind is not capable of being constantly alert to avoid such temptations (see *Summa Theologica* I–II, 109, 8).

The basic reason for this situation is the weakness of the human will which results from the Fall of Adam. Also, God, in the infinite wisdom of his Providence, permits lesser faults in order to keep us humble and in order to remind us constantly that we depend totally on him.

8

MAN WITHOUT GRACE

It is precisely in the teaching on divine grace that one discovers how different the Catholic view of the world is from that of Protestants and contemporary atheistic secular humanists.

The Catholic doctrine of grace stands between the two extremes of naturalism and exaggerated supernaturalism. Thus, against the Pelagians and rationalists of all times the Church affirms the absolute necessity of grace to attain faith, to perform any salutary act and to gain the Beatific Vision. Likewise, against the exaggerated supernaturalism of the Protestant Reformers (Luther, Calvin, etc.) and certain Catholic heretics (Baius, Jansenius and their followers) the Catholic Church defends the natural capacity of man to know about God and some divine truth, and to perform some morally good actions.

Consider, for example, the following points. It is a dogma of the Catholic faith that even in his fallen state man can, by his natural intellectual power, know religious and moral truths. That might seem very obvious to you, but it really is not. When you consider the effects of original sin on man's intellect and will, it is not so far-fetched to come to the conclusion that his natural powers were destroyed in the Fall of Adam and Eve. As a matter of historical fact, that is exactly what the Protestant Reformers, Baians and Jansenists said. This proposition has been repeatedly condemned by various popes, including St. Pius V and Clement XI.

In the nineteenth century the First Vatican Council declared: "The same holy Mother Church holds and teaches that God, the origin and end of all things, can be known with certainty by the natural light of human reason from the things that he created; 'for since the creation of the world his invisible attributes are clearly seen, being understood through the things that are made' (Rom 1:20)" (*Denzinger* 1785).

So man in his fallen state does not need grace to know at least some truth about God. But can he perform any morally good actions without being in the state of sanctifying grace? The Church replies that he can, and with the help of actual grace he can also perform some good actions that prepare him for justification. Thus, not all the actions of the person in the state of mortal sin are sins.

Listen to what the Council of Trent said: "If anyone says that all works performed before justification, regardless of how they were performed, are truly sins or merit God's hatred . . . let him be anathema" (*Denzinger* 817). Our Lord himself urged sinners to repent and prepare themselves for justification (Mt 3:2). It is impossible that he would urge his listeners to that which is sinful. The Church's penitential practice and all the preparation for Baptism would be meaningless, if all the actions performed without sanctifying grace were sins.

Given man's supernatural end, the question arises of whether or not unbelievers can perform morally good acts. In the sixteenth century Michel de Bay (Baius, 1513–1589) said: "All the actions of infidels are sins, and the virtues of philosophers are vices." This proposition was condemned by Pope St. Pius V. So the Church teaches that not all the works of unbelievers are sins.

St. Paul says that pagans are able to act morally: "For instance, pagans who never heard of the Law but are led by reason to do what the Law commands, may not actually 'possess' the Law, but they can be said to 'be' the Law" (Rom 2:14).

Accordingly, unbelievers can perform some good acts by their natural powers alone—without the help of actual grace. For Pope Pius V also condemned the following proposition of de Bay: "Without the help of God's grace, free will can do nothing but sin" (*Denzinger* 1027).

There are severe limits, however, on what fallen man can know about God. Thus, it is morally impossible for him, without supernatural revelation, to know easily, with absolute certainty and without admixture of error, all religious and moral truths of the natural order. From Vatican I (*Denzinger* 1786) we know that this is a dogma of Catholic faith. And the Council of Trent said that, without the help of grace, one cannot keep the whole moral law and avoid all serious sin for a long period of time (*Denzinger* 806, 832).

Without grace, therefore, man can know something about God and can accomplish some good, but he is very vulnerable to error and sin. He cannot possibly save himself without the supernatural help of God.

9

THE GRATUITY OF GRACE

Many people find it hard to accept the truth that faith, justification and salvation are wholly dependent on God and the gift of his grace. It is natural to think that man must do something by his own power and initiative that induces God to look favorably on him and so grant him the grace of justification.

While this view might *seem* correct, still it is contrary to the word of revelation and the teaching of the Church. Thus, the Second Council of Orange declared in 529 against the Pelagians and Semi-Pelagians that no supernatural merit, based on natural good works, precedes the gift of grace. And the Council of Trent taught, as we have seen, that faith and justification in adults begin with God's free gift of antecedent grace. These teachings are based on the words of the Lord: "No one can come to me unless he is drawn by the Father who sent me" (Jn 6:44), and "without me you can do nothing" (Jn 15:5).

The official teaching of the Church on this point is that grace cannot be merited by any natural works that deserve a reward from God. Nothing man can do, by his own natural powers, can oblige God to communicate his grace to him.

It might be helpful to recall what is meant by "grace" and "merit". Grace means "favor" or "gift" of God; it is the free personal communication of his life and love to the human person. Just as love cannot be demanded from another, so also God's grace is and remains a free gift. In theological language "merit" means a work completed for the benefit of another on whom it establishes a claim for reward. So you can see from these definitions that mere human effort, no matter what it might be, is not sufficient to "merit" God's grace. The reason is that there is a basic lack of proportion between nature and grace. In this regard St. Paul says, "There is a remnant chosen by grace. By grace, you notice, nothing therefore to do with good deeds, or grace would not be grace at all" (Rom 11:6).

When God grants his grace to the unbeliever and brings him to faith and justification, that grace is not granted as a reward for human effort; rather, it was God's grace that moved him in the first place. On this very point the Council of Orange taught: "If anyone says that the grace of God can be conferred because of human prayer, but that it is not grace that prompts us to pray, he contradicts the Prophet Isaiah or the Apostle who says the same thing: 'I was found by those who did not seek me; I appeared openly to those who made no inquiry of me' (Rom 10:20; see Is 65:1)."

According to St. Paul, right prayer proceeds from the grace of the Holy Spirit: "The Spirit too comes to help us in our weakness. For when we cannot choose words in order to pray properly, the Spirit himself expresses our plea in a way that could never be put into words" (Rom 8:26).

We have seen that the initiative in the work of salvation comes from God; it depends on his antecedent grace. It follows, then, that salutary prayer can be uttered only with the help of a grace that precedes our prayer.

In order to receive grace a person must be properly disposed. Because of the absolute gratuity of grace, here also we find that man, by his own unaided efforts, cannot acquire any positive disposition for grace. Again, the reason for this is that there is no inner proportion between nature and grace. Thus, the Council of Orange again said that "even the desire to be cleansed is accomplished through the infusion and the interior working of the Holy Spirit." St. Paul expresses the same truth in the words: "It is God who of his good pleasure works in you both the will and the performance" (Phil 2:13).

St. Thomas Aquinas insists on the necessity of antecedent actual grace to prepare the soul for the reception of sanctifying grace (see *Summa Theologica*, I–II, q. 109, art. 6).

In this regard, the scholastic theologians in the twelfth century developed an axiom that all priests learned in the seminary: "God does not deny his grace to the one who does what he can." St. Thomas explained this axiom in the sense of cooperation with the actual grace of God. It means that whoever does with the help of grace that which lies in his power will not be denied further grace by God (ibid.).

The axiom may also be understood in the sense of a negative disposition for grace, that is, the avoidance of serious sin. The connection between the avoidance of sin and the communication of grace, however, is not a causal connection; it is a factual one based on God's universal will for salvation. Accordingly, God does not give his grace because man avoids sin, but because he earnestly desires the salvation of all mankind.

10

GOD DESIRES THE SALVATION OF ALL

We have seen that the grace of justification is a wholly free, unmerited gift or grace of God. It is worth the time and effort to consider whether or not God offers his grace to all men or just to some. Moving in this direction raises the very difficult theological problems of predestination and final reprobation.

Revelation and the Magisterium of the Church teach us that God's grace is offered to all. St. Paul said in I Timothy 2:4 that "God desires the salvation of all men and that all come to a knowledge of the truth." But since in fact not all men attain eternal salvation, that is, since some go to hell, it follows that God's will of salvation is conditioned in some way. For if it were not, then it would be impossible for anyone to lose his soul.

Thus, theologians distinguish two aspects of the divine salvific will: 1) God's universal will of salvation which wishes the salvation of all men on the condition that they die in the state of sanctifying grace. This can be called his *antecedent* and *conditioned* will; it requires and presupposes the free cooperation of men. 2) God's particular will of salvation which unconditionally desires the salvation of all those who die in the state of sanctifying grace. This can be called his *consequent* and *unconditioned* will and actually coincides with what is meant by divine "predestination".

The Church teaches that God earnestly desires the salvation of all men. The Council of Trent in the sixteenth century rejected the claim of the Calvinists and Jansenists that God's salvific will is restricted just to the predestined: "If anyone says that only those who are predestined to life have the grace of justification, and that all others who are called, are indeed called, but do not receive grace, inasmuch as they are predestined to evil by the divine power: let him be anathema" (*Denzinger* 827). So it is heretical to say that only the predestined receive grace from God.

Moreover, in the Nicene Creed that we pray each Sunday we say: "For us men and for our salvation he came down from heaven." There are no limitations put on the Incarnation—Christ came to save all. That credal statement is based on the teaching of Holy Scripture which is contained in passages like this: "Yes, God loved the world so much that he gave his only Son, so that everyone who believes in him may not be lost but may have eternal life. For God sent his Son into the world not to condemn the world, but so that through him the world might be saved" (Jn 3:16–17).

The Second Vatican Council taught the same doctrine. In the Constitution on the Church we read the following: "Through her [the Church] he [God] communicates truth and grace to all" (no. 8), and "All men are called to salvation by the grace of God" (no. 13). The same idea is expressed by the Council again and again. So it is very clear that God's salvific will is universal—he desires the salvation of all men and that all come to a knowledge of the truth.

It is one thing to consider God's universal salvific will in itself, as we have just done; it is something else to consider how it works in the practical order. For here it requires the cooperation of man, who is and remains a free creature. Part of the mystery of man is his ability, as a free person, to reject God's grace—to say No to God.

It is a dogma of the Catholic Church that God gives sufficient grace to all of the just in order to keep the commandments of God. Thus, the Council of Trent declared: "If anyone says that the commandments of God are impossible to observe even for a man who is justified and in the state of grace: let him be anathema" (*Denzinger* 828). The contrary teaching of Cornelius Jansen was rejected by Pope Innocent X in 1653 as heretical (cf. *Denzinger* 1092).

Our Lord himself said that his commandments can be kept by the just: "My yoke is sweet and my burden is light" (Mt 11:30). In the same vein we read in 1 John 5:3, "This is what loving God is—keeping his commandments; and his commandments are not difficult."

"Sufficient grace" is a technical theological expression for actual grace as considered apart from the supernatural effect for which it was given; it can also mean that grace which gives one the power to accomplish a salutary action, as distinguished from an efficacious grace, which secures that the salutary act is accomplished.

We know from Scripture that God does not entirely withdraw his grace from hardened sinners. "I desire not the death of the wicked, but that the wicked turn from his way and live" (Ezek 33:11). So the Church teaches that baptized sinners "can always be restored by true contrition" (*Denzinger* 430). This means that God gives sufficient grace to sinners for their conversion. He also gives all unbelievers sufficient grace to attain their eternal salvation, for he really desires the salvation of all men. But, still, they always remain free to reject his grace.

II

THE PERPLEXING PROBLEM
OF PREDESTINATION

The revealed truth that God desires the salvation of all men, which we considered in the last essay, inevitably raises the question of predestination and reprobation. Now we will treat predestination; in the following essay we will examine the notion of reprobation or eternal damnation.

What is meant by "predestination"? The word signifies the ordination of God by which certain men are led efficaciously to the attainment of eternal, supernatural salvation. This divine ordination involves two acts on the part of God. First, there is an act of divine intellect by which God infallibly knows which men are to be saved and the precise means whereby they will attain this salvation. Second, it includes an act of the divine will by means of which he decrees to save these men in the very fashion that he himself has planned. Thus, St. Thomas Aquinas defines predestination as "a plan existing in the divine mind for the ordering of some persons to eternal salvation" (*Summa Theologica* I, q. 23, art. 2).

Predestination, therefore, formally exists in the divine mind and will. As it is carried out in human history, predestination is distinguished into either incomplete or complete depending on whether it is to grace only or also to glory. According to St. Thomas, complete predestination is the divine preparation of grace in the present life and of glory in the life to come.

The traditional doctrine that God has predestined certain men to eternal salvation is proposed by the ordinary and universal teaching of the Church as a truth of revelation. This doctrine has been taught by numerous councils of the Church, including the Council of Trent. The reality of predestination is clearly attested to by St. Paul: "God cooperates with all those who love him, and with all those he has called according to his purpose. They are the ones he chose specially long ago and intended to become true images of his Son, so that his Son might be the eldest of many brothers. He called those he intended for this; those he called he justified, and with those he justified he shared his glory" (Rom 8:28–30).

St. Paul presents all the elements of complete predestination: the activity of God's mind and will, and the principal stages of its realization in time.

The problem of divine predestination is a great mystery. On the one hand, we know that God knows all things—past, present and future. Before he creates each one of us he knows infallibly whether we will be saved or lost for all eternity. We also know from divine revelation the goodness and mercy of God. St. Paul says that "He desires the salvation of all men and that all come to a knowledge of the truth" (1 Tim 2:4). On the other hand, there is the reality of man's freedom—even with regard to God's grace. The momentous truth about man is that he can say No to God. Thus, God offers his grace of justification to all, but man has the freedom to reject that grace and to go his own way. Since God created man free, he will not violate that freedom by forcing man to be saved.

The sad truth is that not all men attain the glory of heaven—some go to hell for all eternity. We cannot say for certain that any particular individual is in hell, but we do know that the fallen angels or devils are there and it would seem that some men are there. That is what the Church teaches based on these and similar words of Our Lord: "Enter by the narrow gate, since the road that leads to perdition is wide and spacious, and many take it; but it is a narrow gate and a hard road that leads to life, and only a few find it" (Mt 7:13–14).

The main difficulty in the doctrine of predestination is whether God's eternal decree has been taken with or without consideration of human freedom. If it is taken in view of his foreknowledge of a person's merits or free response to grace, it seems to make God dependent on the actions of creatures. If it is taken independently of the preknown merits of a particular person, then it seems to imply that God not only positively wills the salvation of the elect, but also that he positively wills the damnation of certain persons—a false doctrine that was taught by John Calvin and has been repudiated by the Church as heresy.

Numerous theories have been worked out by Catholic theologians in the attempt to reconcile God's goodness and omnipotence with human freedom. All of them admit, however, along with St. Paul, that predestination is an unfathomable mystery (see Rom 11:33).

God alone knows the number and identity of the predestined. But in view of the known goodness of God, of his universal desire for salvation, and of the superabundance of the grace of Christ (see Rom 5:12–21), one is encouraged to assume that the kingdom of God is greater than the kingdom of Satan.

Trent declared against Calvin that certainty with regard to one's predestination can be attained only by special revelation. St. Paul urges us to work out our salvation "in fear and trembling" (Phil 2:12). In spite of the uncertainty about one's salvation, there are certain signs that indicate a high probability of predestination. These signs include a persevering practice of the virtues, frequent reception of Holy Communion, active love of one's neighbor, fidelity to the Church, devotion to the Sacred Heart of Jesus and to his Blessed Mother.

12

WHY DOES GOD ALLOW SOME
MEN TO BE LOST FOREVER?

In the last essay I offered a brief introduction to the difficult theological problem of divine "predestination". If you found that difficult, don't be surprised—so have many Christian thinkers since the time of the Apostles, including the great St. Paul. What we will consider now is equally, and perhaps even more, difficult to understand, namely, divine reprobation of the damned or those who are lost for all eternity. Most people, I suspect, would prefer not to think about this. I must confess that I too would prefer to think about something more pleasant. But the truth is often unpleasant and eternal damnation is a truth of revelation.

For our own good we must think about it, especially if we want to have some understanding of the whole truth of faith. Pope John Paul II has often stressed that bishops and priests must proclaim "the faith in its entirety" and not just those parts of it that may appeal to them.

"Reprobation" as understood in Catholic theology is the eternal resolve of God's will to exclude certain rational creatures from eternal happiness. St. Thomas points out that both predestination to glory and reprobation are aspects of divine Providence, that is, the eternal plan for the world that exists in the divine mind and that he wills to execute. So the word "reprobation" designates God's foreknowledge of the sinner's evil deeds and his will to allow someone to fall into sin and to die in that state. The result is that the sinner rejects God's grace, chooses his own will over the will of God and therefore condemns himself to hell. The all-wise God permits this for a greater good, namely, free acts of love which merit the Beatific Vision.

With regard to the content of God's resolve of reprobation, we must always hold fast to the constant teaching of the Church that God does not positively and antecedently condemn any human person to hell. Wycliffe, Huss and Calvin taught that God does antecedently condemn some persons to hell, but the Church has always rejected that opinion as heretical. Theologians make a distinction between positive and negative reprobation, depending on whether the divine resolve has for its object condemnation to hell or exclusion from heaven. Considering the reason for reprobation, they also distinguish between *conditioned* and *unconditioned* reprobation, insofar as the divine resolve of reprobation is dependent on or independent of the prevision in the divine mind of future mortal sins.

Thus, the general teaching of the Church is that, by an eternal resolve of his will, God predestines certain men, on account of their foreseen sins, to eternal rejection. What this means is that there is in God a conditioned positive reprobation which is based on foreseen future mortal sins. Reprobation in this sense does not contradict God's universal will of salvation for all rational creatures. He creates all men free; he offers his grace to all, but some misuse their freedom and say No to God; these he allows to go their own way so that they end up in hell. Their reprobation therefore is conditioned by their foreseen future sins.

By contrast, Wycliffe, Huss and Calvin taught that God positively predetermines some men to sin; he does not give them sufficient grace to save themselves. In this view, God unconditionally predestines certain persons to the eternal punishment of hell without even considering their future sins. Such a view has been rejected by the Church as false. Thus, the Second Council of Orange in 529 said, "We do not believe that some are predestined to evil by the divine power; and, furthermore, if there are those who wish to believe in such an enormity, with great abhorrence we anathematize them" (*Denzinger* 200).

Against John Calvin the Council of Trent decreed: "If anyone says that only those who are predestined to life have the grace of justification, and that all the others who are called, are indeed called, but do not receive grace, inasmuch as they are predestined to evil by the divine power: let him be anathema" (*Denzinger* 827).

The conditional nature of positive reprobation is required by the universality of God's salvific will. This excludes God's willing in advance of foreseen future sins the damnation of certain persons. Such teaching is based on the Bible. Thus St. Peter tells us in his Second Letter (3:9) that the Lord "is being patient with you all, wanting nobody to be lost and everybody to be brought to change his ways" (see also 1 Tim 2:4; Ezek 33:11).

In this same vein St. Augustine says: "God is good, God is just. He can save a person without good works, because he is good; but he cannot condemn anyone without evil works, because he is just."

God has not seen fit to reveal to us who is lost or whether the number of the damned is great or small. In writing on this mysterious and troubling subject, St. Thomas Aquinas says that our own predestination to eternal life can be helped by prayer—by our own prayer and by the prayers of others. The reason for this is that God's providence, of which predestination is a part, takes into account the whole course of one's life—not just isolated incidents, either good or evil. Hence, fervent prayer and the frequentation of the sacraments of the Church are valid signs of being included in the numbers of those predestined to eternal life.

13

GRACE DOES NOT DESTROY HUMAN FREEDOM

I have been explaining various aspects of the Catholic doctrine on divine grace. At the present time theologians, interested in other topics, are not writing much about grace and the supernatural. In the past, however, there were intense debates among Catholics and between Catholics and Protestants about the exact nature of grace, especially actual grace, which is what we are now examining.

In the sixteenth and seventeenth centuries, for example, the Dominicans and Jesuits argued with each other on the relationship between grace and freedom. The problem, though clarified considerably by the debates, was never resolved and so still remains. Here I will try to show you what the problem is and then indicate how the various Catholic scholars attempted to resolve it.

In previous essays I have shown that God really desires the salvation of all men; to this end he offers his grace to all, with no exceptions. On the other hand, we are confronted with the fact that not all human persons achieve eternal salvation. This means that some people resist and reject God's offer of grace. In the exercise of their freedom, they say No to God. We must conclude, therefore, that some of God's graces achieve their purpose or are effective, while other graces do not achieve their purpose and so are ineffective.

Theologians call the first type of grace "efficacious grace" and the second type "sufficient grace". God offers his grace as a real help to the human will for the performance of salvific acts. The graces we cooperate with are therefore efficacious because they result in good acts; the graces we reject or do not cooperate with are called "sufficient" because they truly enable us to act but we resist them by our free will.

We find here a very mysterious interplay between God's grace—which functions in virtue of his omnipotence and of his omniscience or absolute knowledge of all things past, present and future—and the human free will.

The fact is that some grace is successful and some is not. The obstacle is the perverse human will. But, one might ask, if God is omnipotent and if he knows all things, why does he not give only efficacious grace and so bring it about that no one goes to hell and all go to heaven? I cannot give a clear answer to that question; I wish I could. The reason is that it involves the mystery of human free will. Another way of forming a related unanswerable question is the following: Given God's omnipotence, how can he create a creature that is free and can say No to him? The fact is that he has done it. We know this from our own personal experience of free choice, from the testimony of the Bible in many places (see Dt 30:19; Sir 15:18; Mt 23:37; Acts 7:51), and from the official teaching of the Church.

We can rightly conclude, therefore, that there is a difference in efficacy between efficacious grace and sufficient grace. Given the difference, theologians then ask whether the difference is found in the grace itself or in human freedom. If it is found in the grace it would mean that grace is efficacious by its own intrinsic power; if it is found in human freedom, it would mean that it becomes efficacious by the extrinsic activity and assent of the will.

When confronted with this difficulty, the Reformers and the Jansenists in the seventeenth century tried to resolve it by denying the freedom of the human will. These views were condemned by the Church. Any valid solution to the problem must respect and affirm both God's absolute omnipotence and the freedom of the will.

In the dispute between the Dominicans (Báñez, 1528–1604) and the Jesuits (Molina, 1525–1600), there was no mutual agreement on what precisely makes an actual grace efficacious. In the Báñezian theory the efficacy of such grace depends on the character of the grace itself. In the Molinist theory grace is given to each individual under circumstances that God foresees to be congruous with the dispositions of the one receiving the grace.

In every Catholic theory, however, the theologians agree that efficacious grace does not force the will nor destroy human freedom. In fact, it is a defined teaching of the Church that the human will remains free under the influence of efficacious grace and that therefore efficacious grace is not irresistible. For Trent declared: "If anyone says that the free will of man, moved and awakened by God, in no way cooperates with the awakening call of God by an assent by which man disposes and prepares himself to get the grace of justification; and that man cannot dissent, if he wishes, but, like an object without life, he does nothing at all and is merely passive: let him be anathema" (*Denzinger* 814).

In 1653 Pope Innocent X condemned as heretical the proposition of Bishop Jansenius that "in the condition of fallen nature interior grace is never resisted" (*Denzinger* 1093). As Catholics we must hold fast to the truth that the human will remains free under the influence of grace. This is also a necessary presupposition for the meritoriousness of good works.

14

EFFICACIOUS AND SUFFICIENT GRACE

Before moving on to the consideration of sanctifying grace, I would like to make a few final observations about efficacious and sufficient grace. The subject may seem abstruse and obscure to you, but a knowledge of this is important for some understanding of the Catholic doctrine on divine grace. And it is the doctrine on grace that explains the Catholic position on predestination and reprobation—subjects which we have already covered.

In the previous essay we reflected on the distinction between actual graces that are *efficacious* and *sufficient*. The former result, with man's free cooperation, in good or salvific acts; the latter, though truly giving one the power to perform some salvific act, do not terminate in a good act—they remain inefficacious because they are rejected by human free will.

The Protestant Reformers and the Catholic Jansenists denied the existence of purely sufficient grace because, according to them, grace exercises a necessitating influence on man's will. Thus, in their view, "sufficient grace" is always efficacious and therefore terminates in a good act.

According to official Catholic teaching, however, there is such a thing as grace which is truly sufficient and yet remains inefficacious: that is, a grace which does not obtain a good, free act, but gives sufficient power to produce one. Thus, the Council of Trent teaches that man can prepare himself for the grace of justification with the help of antecedent grace, which is truly sufficient; and that he can also refuse his assent if he wills to, and so the grace remains merely sufficient (*Denzinger* 814, 797).

In confirmation of the above the Bible witnesses to the fact that men often reject God's grace and so leave it unused. Thus, we read in Matthew 23:37, "How often have I longed to gather your children, as a hen gathers her chicks under her wings, and you refused!" In the same vein St. Stephen, before he was stoned to death, said, "You stubborn people, with your pagan hearts and pagan ears. You are always resisting the Holy Spirit, just as your ancestors used to do" (Acts 7:51).

Once we have understood what is meant by efficacious grace and sufficient grace, we can proceed to the problems that have occupied theologians for about four centuries. Thus, with them we can ask: How does efficacious grace secure salvation with infallible certainty for the person who receives it? Does this efficacy reside in the grace itself or in the free assent of the human will foreseen by God?

The Thomists or Báñezians said that efficacious grace, by its own inner power, infallibly brings about that the elect freely consent to perform the salutary acts which merit eternal salvation. Thus, for them efficacious grace is intrinsically different from sufficient grace. This solution safeguards the omnipotence of God, but it leaves unanswered the question as to how sufficient grace can be truly sufficient; and it seems to imply that the human will loses its freedom in the face of efficacious grace.

The Molinists, most of whom were Jesuits, taught that there is no intrinsic difference between efficacious and sufficient grace. According to them the difference is external and accidental, depending upon whether or not man's free will assents to and accepts the proffered grace. If the free will assents to grace, it becomes efficacious; if it refuses assent, the grace remains purely sufficient. According to Molina, God from all eternity, by reason of his foreknowledge which Molina calls "middle knowledge", foresees the free assent of the will in particular circumstances to specific graces. On the basis of that foreknowledge he imparts various graces.

The Molinistic system supports and defends the freedom of the human will in the face of grace and in performing salutary acts. It seems, however, to diminish the omnipotence of God and make him in some sense dependent on the finite human free will. Furthermore, the explanation of God's infallible foreknowledge of the outcome of man's free choice by the so-called "middle

knowledge", and the resulting infallible efficacy of efficacious grace remains very obscure in this system.

There were other attempts in the seventeenth and
eighteenth centuries to explain the mysterious relationship between divine grace and human freedom—by some
Augustinians, by St. Robert Bellarmine and by St.
Alphonsus Liguori. But they are all reducible, in one
way or another, to the position of Báñez or to that of
Molina—or to a syncretistic combination of the two.

Although neither position explains the problem satis-
factorily, either one can be safely held by a Catholic. In
1748 Pope Benedict XIV stated that all three views of
grace, the Dominican, the Jesuit and the Augustinian,
could be held (*Denzinger* 2564–2565).

15

JUSTIFICATION: FROM DEATH TO LIFE

In Catholic theology God's grace is distinguished into
actual and *sanctifying*, depending upon whether it is a
passing supernatural help from God or a permanent
modification of the soul. In our consideration of grace
thus far we have concentrated on actual grace. Now let
us move on to examine Church teaching on the nature of
sanctifying grace. The same reality is also often referred
to as "habitual grace" because it resides in the soul

permanently, like a habit, such as the ability to speak the English language.

Holy Scripture and theologians speak of the sanctity or holiness of God as his "justice". In reference to men, the word "justice" is often used interchangeably with "grace" or "sanctifying grace". According to the Council of Trent, justification of a human person is "a passing from the state in which man is born a son of the first Adam, to the state of grace and adoption as sons of God through the second Adam, Jesus Christ our Savior" (*Denzinger* 796).

In other words, justification is the process by which a person, through faith in Jesus Christ and sorrow for his sins, receives the gift of the Holy Spirit and so becomes a child of God and an heir of heaven.

Now there was a major dispute in the sixteenth century between the Protestant Reformers, especially Luther and his followers, and orthodox Catholics on the precise meaning of justification. Luther thought that human nature was substantially corrupted by original sin and that it consists in concupiscence. In previous essays I have explained how the Catholic Church understands these terms. Briefly, original sin means that Adam lost sanctifying grace for himself and for his descendants; he also incurred an inclination toward evil which we call "concupiscence". Through faith and Baptism we can now recover the sanctifying grace that Adam lost for us, but concupiscence remains. It is not itself sin, but it comes from sin and leads to sin, as Trent said. In the Catholic view, man's nature is not wholly corrupt, as Luther thought; rather, it is weakened by sin and inclines toward sin.

As a consequence of his view of man's nature as corrupt, Luther said that justification is a juridical act by which God declares the sinner to be justified, although he remains interiorly sinful and unjust. For Luther, justification does not destroy sin; it just covers it over or disregards it. Thus, there is no inner renewal and sanctification of the sinner, but merely an external imputation of the justice of Christ.

The Catholic understanding of justification is diametrically opposed to that of Luther. In the Catholic view, justification involves the complete removal of all sin and, on the positive side, results in the sanctification and renewal of the inner man. Thus, the Council of Trent officially declared: "Justification is not only the remission of sins, but sanctification and renovation of the interior man through the voluntary reception of grace and gifts, whereby a man becomes just instead of unjust and a friend instead of an enemy, that he may be an heir in the hope of life everlasting (see Titus 3:7)" (*Denzinger* 799).

The Bible portrays the forgiveness of sins as an eradication of evil, not just a "covering over" of something that remains. Thus, St. Peter says in Acts 3:19, "Now you must repent and turn to God, so that your sins may be wiped out." John the Baptist said of Jesus, "Look, there is the lamb of God that takes away the sin of the world" (Jn 1:29). In reference to the forgiveness of sins, the Bible often uses words like wash away, take away, remove and remit.

From a positive point of view, Holy Scripture presents justification as a "rebirth" from God: "Unless a man is born through water and the Spirit, he cannot enter the kingdom of God" (Jn 3:5). St. Paul speaks of justification or spiritual regeneration as an "inner renewal" (Eph

4:23 ff.), and sanctification: "Now you have been washed clean, and sanctified, and justified through the name of the Lord Jesus Christ and through the Spirit of our God" (1 Cor 6:11). Justification involves going from a state of death to one of life (1 Jn 3:14), from darkness to light (Col 1:13). St. Peter goes so far as to say that God, by giving us his gifts of grace, has made us "partakers in the divine nature" (1 Pet 1:4).

The Fathers of the Church often spoke of man's sanctification through grace as a type of "deification", basing themselves on various biblical statements, such as that of St. Peter quoted above. Moreover, it would be contrary to God's truthfulness if he should say, as he does through his prophets and Apostles, that the sinner is sanctified, if he actually remained steeped in sin.

16

PREPARATION FOR SANCTIFYING GRACE

Because justification of adults is such a tremendous gift, the question was raised by some of the Reformers in the sixteenth century about whether or not one can prepare himself for justification. Luther's followers said that it was not possible to prepare oneself for the reception of sanctifying grace because man's nature, corrupted by original sin, is incapable of performing any good acts that would help him in God's eyes.

The Council of Trent rejected that view and declared: "If anyone says that a sinful man is justified by faith alone, meaning that no other cooperation is required to obtain the grace of justification, and that it is not at all necessary that he be prepared and disposed by the action of his will: let him be anathema" (*Denzinger* 819). Thus, the Council said that the sinner can and must prepare himself by the help of actual grace for the reception of the grace by which he is justified.

In support of its position the Council quoted the following passages from the Holy Bible: "Turn to me and I will turn to you" (Zech 1:3), and "Convert us, O Lord, to you, and we shall be converted" (Lam 5:21). The first text stresses the freedom of movement of our will toward God; the second stresses the necessity of God's antecedent grace.

In this regard, we might also reflect on the many passages in the Bible that urge sinners to repent and convert themselves to God before it is too late.

A further indication of the need for personal preparation is the Church's requirement of adequate instruction before admitting adults to Baptism. On the same point, St. Thomas Aquinas says that the sinner must freely embrace God's grace. The reason for this is that God moves all things toward their end according to their own nature. Because he created man as a free, rational creature, he owes it to himself to respect that freedom. It is certainly true that actual grace is operative in the process, but still the human will must accept that grace and cooperate with it.

It is the defined, dogmatic teaching of the Catholic Church that an adult cannot be justified without faith. The Council of Trent said that "faith is the beginning of man's salvation, the foundation and source of all justification, 'without which it is impossible to please God' (see Heb 11:6)" (*Denzinger* 801).

But what did the Council mean by "faith"? It certainly rejected the Lutheran notion of "fiducial faith", which is a confident trust in God through the saving merits of Jesus Christ. In Luther's view, that was all that was required. In the Catholic view, faith, in addition to being an act of trust in God, also has a dogmatic content that the mind must give assent to. Thus, for Catholics faith consists in the firm acceptance of the divine truths of revelation on the authority of God who has revealed them. And Trent declared that fiducial faith alone is not sufficient to justify the sinner.

Revealed truth is most important. That is why the Lord instructed his Apostles to teach and proclaim the Gospel throughout the world. "Preach the Gospel to every creature. He that believes and is baptized shall be saved. He that believes not shall be condemned" (Mk 16:16). St. John says at the conclusion of chapter 20 of his Gospel: "These are recorded so that you may believe that Jesus is the Christ, the Son of God, and that believing this you may have life through his name" (verse 31).

Another error of the sixteenth-century Reformers was that fiducial faith *alone* is sufficient for justification and eternal salvation. The Catholic Church in the Council of Trent rejected that position. The Church teaches that, even though faith (properly understood) is indispensable, still other virtuous acts are required for justification. The other needed dispositions of soul are spelled out by Trent: fear of divine justice, hope in the mercy of God, beginning to love God, hatred for sin and the intention to receive Baptism. This is very much in accord with the

Bible which requires other acts of preparation for the coming of God's grace: the fear of God (Prov 14:27), hope (Sir 2:9), love of God (Lk 7:27), sorrow for sin and penance (Acts 2:38; 3:19).

So faith is absolutely essential, but it must be accompanied by other acts, such as hope and love. For this reason, the Church requires a period of instruction, testing and prayer (catechumenate) before conferring Baptism on adults.

17

WHAT IS SANCTIFYING GRACE?

Justification is the spiritual *process* by which a person, through faith in Jesus Christ, receives the sanctifying grace of God. We have already considered the major aspects of actual grace. In this essay we will look into the nature of sanctifying grace.

The question we want to answer here is this: What is sanctifying grace? The Baltimore Catechism says that it is "that grace which confers on our souls a new life, that is, a sharing in the life of God himself" (question 111). What is this "new life"? Is it a created gift of God to man? Or is it the communication of God himself? These are very difficult questions that cannot be fully answered here, but we can make a start on them.

The most common opinion among Catholic theologians is that sanctifying grace is a created supernatural gift, conferred on the believer, that is really distinct from God. The Council of Trent said that sanctifying grace is "God's justice, not by means of which he is himself just, but by which he makes us just" (*Denzinger* 799). This excludes the possibility of identifying grace with the Holy Spirit. For the Holy Spirit is the efficient cause of grace, not the formal cause. St. Paul says in Romans 5:5 that "the love of God has been poured into our hearts by the Holy Spirit which has been given to us." Thus, the Holy Spirit is the mediator of the love of God and is therefore distinguished from sanctifying grace, just as the gift is distinguished from the giver.

In addition, sanctifying grace is a supernatural state of being, which is infused by God, and which permanently inheres in the soul. A person in the state of grace *is* or *exists* in a way different from a person who is not in the state of sanctifying grace. Grace is not just an attitude of good will on the part of God so that he "overlooks" man's sinful state without actually removing it. No. Grace really changes man from a "child of wrath" to a "child of God". The Council of Trent says that God's grace is "poured" into us and that it "inheres" in us. These expressions indicate that the grace by which we are justified is a permanent state in us.

The Roman Catechism, which was issued at the direction of the Council of Trent and which is the basis of the Baltimore Catechism, says that sanctifying grace is "a divine quality inhering in the soul".

That grace is a permanent quality inhering in the soul is alluded to in many texts of the New Testament. Thus, the Bible refers to justification as a *divine seed* in man: "No one who has been begotten by God sins, because God's seed remains inside him" (1 Jn 3:9); as the *anointing* or *seal* of the Holy Spirit (2 Cor 1:21ff.); as a *participation* in the divine nature (2 Pet 1:4). It also speaks of grace as a *rebirth* (Jn 3:5; Titus 3:5) and as a *new creation* (2 Cor 5:17; Gal 6:15).

These various statements about how God transforms the believer imply a permanent supernatural state of being that inheres in the soul. Thus, the God-given supernatural life in the justified person presupposes a permanent life principle that is also supernatural.

The Council of Trent said that sanctifying grace "inheres" in the soul. This means that it is a permanent quality that modifies the being or existence of the human person. In philosophical language it is called an "accidental mode of being", since it enhances the being of the human person but does not change it substantially. Perhaps we could say that it resembles what happens when a person studies Spanish and learns the language. After studying Spanish he possesses a talent he did not have before; he is still basically the same person but now he also knows a new language. He has undergone an accidental change, but one that remains.

Sanctifying grace is called by theologians an entitative habit of the soul because it perfects the very substance of the human soul. We can acquire some habits, such as learning how to swim or play tennis, but the supernatural habit of sanctifying grace is infused into the soul directly by God.

18

SHARING IN GOD'S LIFE

All living things strive to protect their lives. As human beings we seek to preserve our life, to expand it as much as possible and to make it more secure. There is in us an innate desire to secure a life that is more permanent than the fragile, fleeting life we experience in our day-to-day existence. Scientists are trying to prolong life as much as they can; some of them think that human life can eventually be stretched out over centuries. But since life on this earth depends on a body and since a body is composed of parts that must at length be separated, they are doomed to failure. There can be no such thing as perpetual, eternal life for a body in the condition we know it.

We know from revelation, however, that through faith in Jesus Christ we can attain eternal life—beginning here and to be consummated in the next life. For Jesus himself says, "Anyone who eats my flesh and drinks my blood has eternal life, and I shall raise him up on the last day" (Jn 6:54).

It is sanctifying grace that makes it possible for us to have "eternal life" because grace is a "sharing in", a "participation in" the very life of God or the divine nature. We saw in the previous essay that the Catechism defines sanctifying grace as "a sharing in the life of God himself". What this means is that God, out of his great love for us, confers on us believers a share in his own divine life.

The notion of sharing or participating in the life of God is perhaps difficult to grasp. It is not the same as sharing a chocolate bar with someone else, because God does not lose anything by conferring his grace on us. It is more like sharing knowledge and love with another. Thus, the mother and father who impart knowledge to their children do not lose anything in the process. For knowledge and love are not diminished by being shared with others.

Similarly, by his grace God communicates himself to the believer in a most intimate way. This communication is in fact so intimate that we can truthfully say that the faithful Christian "participates" in the divine life.

The notion of participation is enshrined in the liturgy of the Mass. Thus, as the priest pours a little water into the wine at the Offertory he says, "By the mystery of this water and wine may we come *to share in the divinity of Christ*, who humbled himself to share in our humanity." And St. Peter writes in his Second Letter, "Through them [God's power and glory] you will be able *to share the divine nature* and to escape corruption in a world that is sunk in vice" (1:4).

There is also a relationship between being born from God and participating in his nature. Thus, when the New Testament speaks of justification as a form of "generation" or "birth" from God (see Jn 3:5; Titus 3:5), it is indirectly teaching the participation of man in the

66

divine nature, because, as we have seen, the act of generation consists in the communication of the nature of the generator to the one generated. So, if we are "born of God" (and we are) then it can truthfully be said that we participate in the divine nature.

In speaking of this astonishing reality some of the Fathers of the Church, such as St. Athanasius, spoke of grace as a type of "deification" or "trinification" of man. Thus, in one of his writings Athanasius says, "The Word became man, so that we might become God." We should not think of this "deification", however, in any pantheistic sense, since the soul is not absorbed into the divinity by losing its own identity and creatureliness.

What is involved here is a real communion of man with God. This consists in an accidental unification of the two by means of the created gift of God's grace. Grace thus assimilates the soul to God and unites it with him in a way that transcends all created activity.

According to his human nature, man is created in the image and likeness of God—especially with regard to his spiritual soul; by sanctifying grace he is elevated to a much higher grace of assimilation to God. St. Thomas Aquinas says that grace is "a certain likeness of the divinity that man participates in" (*Summa Theologica* III, q. 2, art. 10, ad 1). Just as God's being is the principle of his life, knowledge and love, so also is sanctifying grace, as our participation in the divine being, the source of divine and eternal life in us.

Man's supernatural assimilation to God by sanctifying grace will be completed in the next life by the Beatific Vision. Thus grace in this life and glory in the next are related to each other as the caterpillar is related to the butterfly. Grace is the beginning of glory and glory is the fulfillment of grace. The basic identity of grace and glory were already taught by Our Lord when he said, "Anyone who believes in the Son *has* eternal life" (Jn 3:36).

19

CHILDREN OF GOD

We have been investigating the nature of sanctifying grace and we have seen that this mysterious, supernatural reality means that the Christian believer shares, or participates, in the very life of God—Father, Son and Holy Spirit. Now we will move on to consider some of the effects of sanctifying grace on the soul of the justified person.

One of the major effects of sanctifying grace, as its very name indicates, is the *sanctification* or making holy of the soul. Holiness in the proper sense belongs to God. So the closer one comes to him, the more one increases in holiness. According to the Council of Trent, the conferral of grace that takes place in justification is a "sanctification and renovation of the interior man". Thus the baptized person really becomes holy through the reception of grace.

In the opening verses of his letters St. Paul addresses the Christians as "saints", that is, they are holy because they are "in Christ" and endowed with his grace. To the

Corinthians he wrote, "Now you have been washed clean, and sanctified, and justified through the name of the Lord Jesus Christ and through the Spirit of our God" (1 Cor 6:11). In the same vein he admonished the Ephesians, "Put on the new man, who according to God is created in justice and holiness of truth" (Eph 4:24).

Another effect of sanctifying grace is that it makes the graced person *a friend of God*. We are touching here on a truly astonishing reality—that the creature could be called, and actually be, a friend of his Creator! But that is what the Bible and the Church say. Thus, Trent says that by justification one is changed "from an unjust person into a just person and from an enemy into a friend (of God)" (*Denzinger* 799). Jesus said to his Apostles, and through them to us: "You are my friends, if you do what I command you. I shall not call you servants any more, because a servant does not know his master's business; I call you friends, because I have made known to you everything I have learnt from my Father" (Jn 15:14–15).

As St. Thomas Aquinas shows, friendship is a mutual love of benevolence or goodwill which, in turn, is based on a similarity of nature or something shared in common. So the basis of the Christian's fellowship with God is his or her possession of sanctifying grace. For we have already seen that grace makes us partakers of the divine nature, as St. Peter said in his Second Letter (1:4). The mutual love based on grace is called "charity". The theological virtue of charity, which always accompanies divine grace and inheres in the will, enables the sanctified person to love God in return for his many gifts and his great goodness.

A third effect of sanctifying grace is that it makes the justified person a *child of God* and an *heir of heaven*. Trent puts it this way: "Justification is a passing from the state in which man is born a son of the first Adam, to the state of grace and adoption as sons of God through the second Adam, Jesus Christ our Savior"; the same Council says that the just person is "an heir according to the hope of life everlasting" (*Denzinger* 796, 799). St. Paul testifies to the same truth: "The spirit you received is not the spirit of slaves bringing fear into your lives; it is the spirit of sons, and it makes us cry out, 'Abba, Father!' The Spirit himself and our spirit bear united witness that we are children of God. And if we are children we are heirs as well: heirs of God and coheirs with Christ" (Rom 8:15–17). Because God, through grace, communicates to us a share in his divine nature, we truly become his adopted children and heirs of his kingdom, namely, eternal life and the Beatific Vision.

A fourth effect of sanctifying grace is that it makes the graced person a *temple* of the Holy Spirit. By "temple" here is meant a holy dwelling place or residence. Thus, the Holy Spirit dwells personally in the souls of the just, not merely because of the created gifts of grace that he imparts, but in his uncreated divine nature. The New Testament attests to this truth in a number of places: "Do you not know that you are the temple of God and that the Spirit of God dwells in you?" (1 Cor 3:16; see also Rom 5:5; 1 Cor 6:19).

The personal indwelling of the Holy Spirit effects an accidental union between the Spirit and the soul of the graced person. Since the indwelling of the Holy Spirit is an external activity of God (i.e., outside the inner divine life), and since such activities are common to all three Persons of the Trinity, it follows that the indwelling of the Holy Spirit implies an indwelling of the three divine

Persons. Because this indwelling is a manifestation of God's love for man, it is usually appropriated to the Holy Spirit, even though it is equally true of the Father and the Son. St. John expresses this truth beautifully: "If any one love me, he will keep my word. And my Father will love him: and we will come to him and will make our abode with him" (14:23).

20

A BRILLIANT ARRAY OF GIFTS

In addition to making us children of God, heirs of heaven and temples of the Holy Spirit, sanctifying grace also confers upon us a brilliant array of virtues and gifts that enable us more easily to live out our Christian commitment and to respond to the promptings of the Holy Spirit. I am referring here to the infused theological virtues of faith, hope and charity, to the infused moral virtues and to the gifts of the Holy Spirit.

The Church teaches infallibly in the Council of Trent that, when a person attains sanctifying grace, God infuses into him or her the three theological virtues of faith, hope and charity. Here is what Trent said: "In the very act of being justified, at the same time that his sins are remitted, a man receives through Jesus Christ, to whom he is joined, the infused gifts of faith, hope and charity" (*Denzinger* 800). These virtues are conferred on the soul as habits or dispositions that remain in the soul permanently—or at least as long as one remains in the state of grace. This teaching of the Church is based on a number of statements in the New Testament, especially the testimony of St. Paul in Romans 5:5, "The charity of God is poured forth in our hearts by the Holy Spirit who is given to us."

The three theological virtues are a permanent state or condition in the justified person according to St. Paul who writes in another passage, "And now there remain faith, hope and charity" (1 Cor 13:13).

If one falls into mortal sin and so loses sanctifying grace, what happens to the theological virtues? The Church teaches that love is infused at the same time as grace and is lost with the loss of grace. Faith and hope, however, are separable from grace. This means that they are not lost by every mortal sin, as grace and charity are, but only by those sins that are directed against them. Thus, the sin of unbelief drives out faith and the sin of despair drives out hope. Therefore, one who commits a serious sin of impurity against the Sixth Commandment loses sanctifying grace and divine charity; but that same person retains faith and hope and so, with the help of actual grace, through repentance can recover the grace which has been lost.

Theologians commonly teach that the four cardinal moral virtues of prudence, justice, temperance and fortitude are also infused into the soul along with sanctifying grace. This doctrine cannot be explicitly proved from the Bible, but it is suggested in a few passages. Thus, we read in Wisdom 8:7, "If one loves justice, the fruits of her works are virtues; for she teaches moderation and prudence, justice and fortitude, and nothing in life is more useful for men than these." The same virtues are mentioned by St. Peter in his Second Letter (1:4–9).

In favor of the infusion of the four cardinal virtues St. Thomas Aquinas argues that they are required by the theological virtues of faith, hope and charity. For just as natural virtues proceed from the natural principles of intellect and will, so also must there be supernatural moral virtues that proceed from the new supernatural principles of faith, hope and charity (see *Summa Theologica*, I–II, q. 63, art. 3).

There is also an ancient tradition among Catholics, based on the Bible, that along with sanctifying grace God infuses into the soul of the justified person what are called the "gifts of the Holy Spirit". The seven gifts of the Holy Spirit are: wisdom, understanding, knowledge, counsel, fortitude, piety and fear of the Lord (see Is 11:2–3). Our Lord tells us in John 14 to 16 that the Holy Spirit dwells in the souls of the just; the Holy Spirit is never present without his gifts.

In the passage referred to above Isaiah says that these gifts characterize the coming Messiah. Fathers of the Church and many theologians argue from this that the gifts must be bestowed on all of the just, because they are shaped after the image of Christ (see Rom 8:29).

According to St. Thomas the gifts of the Holy Spirit are supernatural dispositions or habits of the faculties of the soul by means of which a person is enabled easily and joyfully to respond to the suggestions and inspirations of the Holy Spirit.

Some of the gifts (wisdom, understanding, knowledge, counsel) aid man's intellect, while others (fortitude, piety and fear of the Lord) aid his will. They are different from

73

the infused virtues (theological and moral) because the motivating principle of the gifts is the Holy Spirit himself. The infused virtues enable a person to lead an ordinary life of Christian virtue, whereas the gifts of the Holy Spirit enable one to perform extraordinary and heroic acts.

The gifts of the Holy Spirit have a definite effect on us. Some of the effects are the "fruits of the Holy Spirit" and the Beatitudes. The Beatitudes were announced by Jesus in his Sermon on the Mount (see Mt 5:3–10). The fruits of the Holy Spirit, good works performed under his inspiration and with a certain delight, are: charity, joy, peace, patience, benignity, goodness, long-suffering, mildness, faith, modesty, continency and chastity.

21

GRACE CAN BE LOST

The Protestant Reformers in the sixteenth century fell into many errors about the nature of justification or sanctifying grace. At that time they sowed much confusion in the minds of good Catholics. In order to clarify traditional Catholic teaching and to set the minds of the faithful at rest, the Council of Trent set forth in unambiguous terms what the Church holds with regard to grace.

For example, the Reformers said that the justified have an absolute certainty about their justification that excludes all possible doubt. The point here is the degree of certainty that we can attain about whether or not we are in the state of grace. Luther and Calvin said that we have absolute certainty. That does not square, however, with the clear teaching of Holy Scripture on the subject. For St. Paul says: "Work out your salvation in fear and trembling" (Phil 2:12); and, "My conscience does not reproach me at all, but that does not prove that I am acquitted: the Lord alone is my judge" (1 Cor 4:4).

Accordingly, Trent made the following official declaration on the subject: "Whoever reflects on himself, his personal weakness, and his defective disposition may fear and tremble about his own grace, since no one can know with the certitude of faith, which cannot admit any error, that he has obtained God's grace" (*Denzinger* 802).

The difference between Protestants and Catholics on this subject is the level of certainty with regard to the possession of God's grace. The Church teaches that a divine revelation is required in order to know with the certainty of faith that one is in the state of grace. For without such a revelation no one can know with absolute certainty whether or not he has fulfilled all of the conditions which are necessary to achieve sanctifying grace.

Does this mean that we can never know whether or not we are in the state of grace? Not at all. We can easily have a high level of moral certitude that we are in the state of grace through the testimony of our conscience from certain clear signs such as joy in the love of God, rejection of sin and worldliness, and an awareness of being free from mortal sin.

Since the Reformers erroneously considered grace as a merely external imputation of the justice of Christ, they were forced to hold logically that it is identical in all men. The Catholic Church teaches that sanctifying grace is not identical in all the just. She also teaches that grace can be increased by good works—another point denied by many Protestants.

The Council of Trent declared that the measure of grace in each individual varies according to God's benevolence and to the disposition and cooperation of the recipient. Here are the precise words of the Council: "Not only are we considered just, but we are truly said to be just, and we are just, each one of us receiving within himself his own justice, according to the measure the Holy Spirit imparts to each one as he wishes, and according to the disposition and cooperation of each one" (*Denzinger* 799).

We find confirmation of this doctrine in the words of St. Paul: "Each one of us has been given his own share of grace, given as Christ allotted it" (Eph 4:7). In the same vein he says in 1 Cor 12:11, "All these [gifts] are the work of one and the same Spirit, who distributes different gifts to different people just as he chooses."

The basic reason for the possibility of different levels of sanctifying grace is found in the fact that grace is a real supernatural quality that inheres in the soul. Since that is so, it allows for more or less grace, just as some possess more knowledge than others.

Calvin taught that it is impossible for the justified to lose the state of grace; Luther said that it can be lost only by the sin of unbelief. In opposition to those erroneous views, the Council of Trent said that the state of grace is lost by every mortal sin, and not just by the sin of unbelief: "We must also assert . . . that the grace of justification, once received, is lost not only by unbelief, which causes the loss of faith, but also by any other mortal sin" (*Denzinger* 808).

The Bible states quite clearly that grace can be lost. Consider the examples of Adam and Eve, Saul, Judas, Peter. Our Lord warned his disciples in the Garden of Gethsemane, "Watch and pray that you do not enter into temptation" (Mt 26:41). And Paul told his converts, "The man who thinks he is safe must be careful that he does not fall" (1 Cor 10:12). He also said that he chastised his own body so that, while preaching to others, he might not be lost himself (1 Cor 9:27).

The sacrament of Penance and the constant practice of confessing one's sins presuppose that grace can be lost by mortal sin. Because man's will is free and changeable, it is always possible that a Christian will turn his back on God and embrace sin which is diametrically opposed to God and sanctifying grace.

22

MERIT AND REWARD

The idea of supernatural "merit" is an integral part of the Catholic doctrine on grace. We learned about it in our first catechism lessons and we encounter it regularly in Catholic books of devotion and theology. Common expressions in Catholic conversation include phrases like "meriting an increase of sanctifying grace" and "meriting heaven".

Both the idea and the word "merit" have a long theological history. In Catholic theology merit means a work performed for the benefit of another, on whom it establishes a claim to give a reward. As you can see, merit and reward are correlative terms. Merit is closely related to the notion of paying a just price for goods and services rendered. Thus, if a woman works in a store for eight hours and the boss has agreed to pay her $5.00 per hour, then she has a right to $40.00. We say that she deserves the $40.00 because she has earned it.

Merit therefore involves justice and equality. Similarly, if someone has done a great favor for us, like helping to paint the house, we are under a certain social obligation to reciprocate the favor in the future if we can or if we are asked. Merit is defined as the right one has to a reward—a right that is based on a work done. If it is a strict right in justice, then Catholic theology calls it *de condigno* merit (the English word is "condign", which means "deserved"). If it is a question simply of appropriateness or liberality on the part of the one giving the reward, it is called *de congruo* merit (the English word is "congruous" or "suitable").

The Catholic doctrine on merit is important because it was firmly denied by the Protestant Reformers in the sixteenth century. At first Luther said that all man's works are sinful, even his prayers; later he admitted that a just man can and must perform some good works, but he denied that these are in any way meritorious of grace and eternal life. Calvin taught that all of man's works are "impurity and dirt" in the eyes of God.

The teaching of the Catholic Church is that, by his good works, the person in the state of sanctifying grace really merits a supernatural reward from God. The Second

Council of Orange in the sixth century, basing itself on the Bible and on the teaching of St. Augustine and St. Prosper of Aquitane, said: "The reward given for good works is not won by reason of actions which precede grace; rather, grace, which is unmerited, precedes actions in order that they may be performed meritoriously" (*Denzinger* 191).

The Council of Trent teaches the same doctrine and stresses that, for the justified person, eternal life is both a grace promised by God and a reward for his own good works and merits (see *Denzinger* 809, 810). The point is that God's grace is required to perform any and all good works; in his goodness God makes these good works (which depend on his grace) also meritorious of further grace and of eternal life.

The word "merit" does not occur in the New Testament, but the idea is certainly there since the word "reward", which is related to merit, does occur. Thus, Jesus promises rich rewards to those who, for his sake, suffer persecution: "Be glad and rejoice for your reward is very great in heaven" (Mt 5:12). At the end of the world the Divine Judge will decree eternal reward for the just on the basis of their good works: "Come, you whom my Father has blessed, take for your heritage the kingdom prepared for you since the foundation of the world. For I was hungry and you gave me food . . ." (Mt 25:34ff.). St. Paul, who stresses the importance of grace, also mentions the meritorious nature of good works performed with the help of grace. Thus, Paul teaches that the reward is in proportion to the good works performed: "He will repay each one as his works deserve" (Rom 2:6); and, "Each will duly be paid according to his share in the work" (1 Cor 3:8).

When St. Paul refers to his own eternal reward as "a crown of justice which the Lord, the just Judge, will give to me in that day" (2 Tim 4:8), he shows that the good works of the just establish a claim on God for a reward. So grace gives man the power to perform works that deserve a reward from God.

Human philosophy cannot prove the reality of supernatural merit because it rests on God's free promise of reward for obeying his commandments. In this life we say that virtue is its own reward. We also know that good deeds performed for another deserve some kind of reward. Between man and God, however, there is an infinite chasm. Of himself man cannot do anything that would merit a reward from God. It is precisely the gracious gift of his grace that lifts us up to the supernatural level and makes us capable of performing works that are meritorious of eternal life. His is the gift and his is the reward, but we must freely cooperate with the gift.

23

THE CONDITIONS OF MERIT

Because of the importance of supernatural merit, which we briefly considered in the last essay, it will be helpful to examine this Catholic doctrine in more detail. After all, we are striving in this life for a full happiness that satisfies all our desires and cannot be lost: that is, heaven or eternal life. According to our faith, "heaven" means the reward that God bestows on us by virtue of the *merit* which we have accumulated by living a good life in accordance with his will and his commandments.

At this point we might well ask: What are the conditions of supernatural merit? We can answer this question by considering 1) the meritorious work, 2) the person meriting and 3) God who does the rewarding. Let us now examine each aspect.

1) *The meritorious work.* The work itself must be something that is morally good, that is, in full conformity with the moral law as established by God. For God, who is absolutely good and truthful, can reward good only, not evil under any pretext. It must also be a fully human act that is free from coercion, both internal and external. For only free acts merit reward or punishment. In this regard Our Lord himself said, "If you wish to enter into life, keep the commandments" (Mt 19:17).

Finally, a meritorious act must proceed from a supernatural motive and be accompanied by actual grace. We have already seen in a previous essay that every salutary act must proceed from divine grace. What we are saying here is the same thing, since meritorious works are salutary acts. Thus, Jesus promises a reward to those who do good for his sake: "If anyone gives you a cup of water to drink just because you belong to Christ, then I tell you solemnly, he will most certainly not lose his reward" (Mt 9:41).

In the same vein St. Paul says that we should do everything in the name of the Lord Jesus: "Never say or do anything except in the name of the Lord Jesus, giving thanks to God the Father through him" (Col 3:17); and again, "Therefore, whether you eat or drink, or whatever else you do, do all for the glory of God" (1 Cor 10:31). The most perfect motive for Christian action and virtue is the pure love of God, but this can be implicit in most actions because of the practical difficulty of thinking of it explicitly all the time.

2) *The person meriting*. The person meriting must be living in the body on this earth; so the souls in purgatory, those in heaven and assuredly those in hell cannot merit. Now is the only time to merit grace and eternal life. The fate of the human person is sealed for all eternity by the condition he or she is in at the moment of death. Thus, Jesus says, "The night will soon be here when no one can work" (Jn 9:4; see also Mt 25:34ff. and Lk 16:26). In the third century Origen thought it possible that souls in the next life could acquire merits; this view was rejected by the Fathers and by the teaching of the Church.

The meriting person must also be in the state of grace, at least as far as condign merit is concerned. For the teaching of Trent on the subject of merit refers only to those who are justified (see *Denzinger* 836, 842). Jesus demands that we live "in him" in order to bring forth supernatural results: "As a branch cannot bear fruit all by itself, but must remain part of the vine, neither can you unless you remain in me" (Jn 15:4).

3) *God who rewards*. As I tried to explain in the previous essay, merit depends on the decree of God that he will reward with eternal life those good works that are performed with his grace. Because of the infinite distance between the creature and his Creator, man, of himself, cannot make God his debtor unless God makes himself such by his own free will. But we know from revelation that God has done precisely that. Thus, Jesus says, "Everyone who has left houses, brothers, sisters, father,

mother, children or land for the sake of my name will be repaid a hundred times over, and also inherit eternal life" (Mt 19:29). Likewise, St. Paul speaks of "the hope of the eternal life that was promised so long ago by God who does not lie" (Titus 1:2).

Given the infinite distance between man and God, why are good works meritorious? Theologians who follow St. Thomas say that the reason for their meritoriousness is to be found in the intrinsic value of good works that are performed in the state of sanctifying grace. Man is elevated by grace to the supernatural level, so grace effects a certain inner equivalence between the good works and the eternal reward.

It should be noted here that the conditions for congruous merit (*meritum de congruo*) are the same as for condign merit (*meritum de condigno*), except for the state of grace and for God's promise of a reward. But more about this in the next essay.

24

MERIT, GRACE AND GLORY

In the two previous essays we have considered the reality of supernatural *merit* which, in virtue of the grace given, establishes a certain claim on God for a reward for good works performed in this life. Merit is of two kinds: 1) condign merit, which is a claim in justice; and

2) congruous merit, which establishes a claim for a reward out of graciousness or liberality on the part of the donor.

We have already reflected on the conditions of supernatural merit on the part of the good work itself, the person meriting and God who gives the reward. Our final consideration on merit will concentrate on the object of these two kinds of merit.

Let us look first at *condign merit* (*meritum de condigno*). The Church teaches through the Council of Trent that a person in sanctifying grace merits for himself through each good work an increase of sanctifying grace, eternal life (if he dies in the state of grace) and an increase of heavenly glory.

Increase of sanctifying grace: There is a direct relationship between grace and glory. Grace is the ticket to glory, its preliminary stage; glory is the fulfillment of grace, its consummation. Good works, performed in the state of grace and flowing from grace, effect an increase of grace and glory.

Eternal life: The Council of Trent clearly teaches as a doctrine of Catholic faith that the justified person, by the good works he performs by the grace of God, merits eternal life and actually attains to it if he dies in the state of sanctifying grace. According to the New Testament, eternal life is the reward for good works performed in this life (see Mt 19:29; 25:46; Jn 14–16 passim).

If a person lives a good Christian life for many years without mortal sin, performs many good works and acquires many merits in the eyes of God and then commits a mortal sin and loses grace—then what happens to all those merits? Suppose this individual, soon after his fall, repents of his sin, goes to confession and is restored to the state of grace again. Are the good works and merits of those many years lost forever in the sight of God?

While a person is in the state of sin his merits are in a sense dead. According to the common teaching of Catholic theologians, however, because of the goodness of God former merits revive when the sinner repents and begins again to walk in the way of the Lord. So in the case given above, the former merits are restored when the person repents of his sin.

Increase of heavenly glory: According to the Council of Florence (1438–45) the degree of heavenly glory varies from person to person depending on the difference in their merits (*Denzinger* 693). We may conclude therefore that an increase in merit results in an increase of heavenly glory. Thus, St. Paul says in 2 Corinthians 9:6, "Do not forget: thin sowing means thin reaping; the more you sow, the more you reap." And Our Lord says in Matthew 16:27, "For the Son of Man . . . will reward each one according to his behavior."

Now let us consider *congruous merit*, which does not establish a claim in justice; there is a certain "fittingness" or "suitability" about it. A person in the state of mortal sin can acquire congruous merit by cooperating with the actual graces that God sends him; this cooperation finally leads to regaining the state of grace. The truth of this is intimated by the psalmist when he sings, "My sacrifice is this broken spirit, you will not scorn this crushed and broken heart" (Ps 51:17).

The justified Christian cannot merit *de condigno* the great grace of final perseverance, but he can merit it *de congruo*. The reason for this is that it is appropriate that God bestow on the good man who cooperates with grace the actual graces necessary for perseverance in grace until death. But such a claim to the grace of final perseverance is not strong and is involved in uncertainty. The efficacy of humble, constant and persevering prayer is much more certain. Thus, Jesus says, "Ask and it shall be given to you" (Mt 7:7), and "If you ask the Father anything in my name he will give it to you" (Jn 16:23).

The justified person can merit congruously for others what he can merit for himself, for example, actual graces. So we can offer good works for others and also pray for them. St. James offers us good advice on this point: "Pray for one another, and this will cure you; the heartfelt prayer of a good man works very powerfully" (James 5:16). Only Jesus Christ, Head of the Church and Savior of mankind, can merit for others *de condigno*. It is only because of him and his merits before the Father that we are able to merit anything in the first place.

PART II

THE CHURCH

I

THE FAITHFUL OF THE WHOLE WORLD

For more than a century now popes, bishops and theologians have been reflecting, rather intensely, on the origin, nature, definition, structure and properties of the Holy Roman Catholic Church. In fact, the last two General Councils, Vatican I (1869–70) and Vatican II (1962–65), were largely concerned with these matters.

Having completed our consideration of grace, we will now proceed to a rather detailed analysis of the Church. The area in theology that deals with these questions is commonly called "ecclesiology", a word derived from the Greek *ecclesia* which means assembly, gathering, community, church.

Ecclesiology is one of the newer branches of theology, at least as a distinct area of study. It developed after the Council of Trent in the sixteenth century with the purpose of defending the authority of the hierarchy against the attacks of the Protestants. So from its inception it has been involved in polemics with a view toward defending the revealed truth and refuting errors.

Perhaps one reason for the special concern about the nature of the Church in the past century is the very complexity of the subject. As we shall see, the Church is both visible and invisible; it is both tangible and spiritual. In any treatment of the Church there is always the danger that one aspect or another will be short-changed. Thus, in the past some Catholic "legalists" have stressed the external, societal dimension of the Church almost to the exclusion of her spiritual nature. On the other hand, many Protestants, and now some Catholics, stress the "spiritual" nature of the Church to such an extent that her visible dimension more or less disappears.

In the Bible the word "church" (= *ecclesia* in Latin and Greek; *qahal* in Hebrew) means convocation or meeting of the people. In the New Testament the word occurs over a hundred times in order to signify either the individual Christian communities or, sometimes, the universal Church. In the Gospels the word appears only three times, all in Matthew (see 16:18 and 18:17).

In addition to the word "Church", other terms are also used in theology, such as Catholic Church, Mystical Body of Christ, People of God, Kingdom of God, Temple of God, House of God, Spouse of Christ and Mother Church. In due course we will consider these names.

It should be noted here that the word "catholic" means whole, total or universal. The expression "Catholic Church" does not occur in the Bible, but there is some basis for it in Matthew 26:13 and Mark 14:9 which refer to the Gospel being preached "throughout the whole world". It seems that St. Ignatius of Antioch in the early second century was the first one to use the expression. Its use was common in the third century; in the fourth century the name was introduced into various creeds and finally was incorporated into the Creed of the First Council of Constantinople in 381: "We believe in one, holy, *catholic* and apostolic Church."

According to the New Testament the Church is the community of the believers in Christ, either individual assemblies in various homes or cities (see Rom 16:5; Acts 8:1), or the totality of all believers (Mt 16:18; Gal 1:13; Eph 1:22).

From the various names we get a general notion of the Church as being an assembly of people and therefore some kind of *society*, *universal* in character and *spiritual* in nature. It is very difficult, however, to give a strict scientific definition because of the dual nature of the Church which is at once a social external reality and a spiritual invisible entity.

The broadest definition of the Church is: "the faithful of the whole world". Since the sixteenth century the Church has usually been defined as a union of human beings who are united by the profession of the same Christian faith, and by participation in the same sacraments under the direction of their lawful pastors, especially by the vicar of Christ of earth, the Bishop of Rome.

At the Second Vatican Council this concept of the Church was reaffirmed, but it was also qualified so as to include somehow all who are baptized in Christ and profess their faith in him. They are the People of God on whom he bestows the special graces of his providence. Thus, there is still a great deal of discussion among theologians about the proper relationship between the visible Church and the invisible Church, between the Roman Catholic Church and the kingdom of God. Many now think that the kingdom, at least in some sense, is more extensive than the visible Church.

2

JESUS PERSONALLY FOUNDED THE CATHOLIC CHURCH

Having seen that the Church is the community of the faithful of the whole world, we will now consider the origin or foundation of the Church. It is an article of the Catholic faith, declared by Councils and proclaimed officially by many popes, that the holy Roman Catholic Church was founded by the God-Man Jesus Christ.

Thus the First Vatican Council declared: "The eternal Shepherd and Guardian of our souls (1 Pet 2:5), in order to render the saving work of redemption lasting, decided to establish his holy Church that in it, as in the house of the living God, all the faithful might be held together by the bond of one faith and one love" (*Denzinger* 1821). Pope St. Pius X, in his 1910 Oath Against Modernism, said: "The Church was founded immediately and personally by the true and historical Christ during the time of his earthly life" (*Denzinger* 2145).

More recently the Second Vatican Council repeated the same truth: "The mystery of the holy Church is manifest in her very foundation, for the Lord Jesus inaugurated her by preaching the good news, that is, the coming of God's kingdom" (Constitution on the Church, no. 5). By the "foundation" of the Church what is meant is that Jesus Christ during his earthly life personally laid down the essential elements of her teaching, her sacraments and her visible structure.

It is necessary to stress the truth that the Church was founded personally by Christ because many so-called reformers and dissidents have said and do say that the Church is merely a human invention, or else they say that Jesus did not will some aspects of it, such as the Eucharist or the Sacrament of Orders or the primacy of the successor of St. Peter. For example, sixteenth century Reformers taught that Christ founded an invisible Church and that the visible, organized society is a purely human invention. Others, admitting the visible nature of the Church, deny the primacy of the Bishop of Rome. For over a hundred years various liberals and Modernists have claimed that Jesus, expecting the world to end soon, had no intention of founding a Church. They claim that the Church grew out of the "collective consciousness" of the faithful of the first century when they realized that Jesus erred about the near end of the world.

In opposition to all such false opinions, the Fathers at Vatican II repeated the constant teaching of the Church: "This Church, constituted and organized in the world as a society, subsists in the Catholic Church, which is governed by the successor of Peter and by the bishops in union with that successor" (Constitution on the Church, no. 8).

Jesus began his public ministry by preaching, "Repent, for the kingdom of heaven is close at hand" (Mt 4:17; Mk 1:15). By his many miracles he demonstrated that the Messianic era, promised by the prophets of old, had now dawned on the world (Mt 12:28). Jesus did not understand the kingdom as a reality to be established only at the end of the world. It is rather a kingdom founded on Peter and the Apostles, a kingdom that will continue to grow and develop as long as the world lasts and will be perfected in the future world. Many of Our Lord's graphic parables—the sower of the seed, the net cast into the sea, the leaven, the mustard seed—vividly portray the kingdom of God as already existing in this world.

Jesus established his new religious community on Peter, the "rock" (Mt 16:18). He gathered together disciples and chose from among them twelve who "were to be his companions and to be sent out to preach, with power to cast out devils" (Mk 3:14). Because of their mission he called them "Apostles", that is, ambassadors or "those who are sent". He instructed them over a long period of time, gave them the power of binding and loosing (Mt 18:17ff.), of offering the Eucharist (Lk 22:19), of forgiving sins (Jn 20:23), and the power of baptizing (Mt 28:19). He sent them out into the whole world with the mandate to preach the Gospel and to baptize (Mt 28:19ff.). Before he ascended into heaven he transferred to them his mission from the Father: "As the Father sent me, so am I sending you" (Jn 20:21). Finally, he appointed Peter to be the head of the college of Apostles and the supreme guardian of his Church (Mt 16:18ff.; Jn 21:15–17).

With Pope Pius XII we can distinguish three stages in the establishment of the Church: The Redeemer "began building the mystical temple of the Church when by his preaching he made known his precepts; he completed it when he hung glorified on the cross; and he manifested and proclaimed it when he sent the Holy Spirit as Paraclete in visible form on his disciples" (*Mystical Body of Christ*, no. 26). So the three stages include: preaching, suffering and promulgation.

3

WHY DID CHRIST ESTABLISH HIS CHURCH?

We know what a thing is from what it does; and what it does reveals to us its purpose. Having defined the Church and having shown that it was founded by Jesus Christ during his earthly mission, we may now ask about its specific purpose. Why did Jesus establish his Church? Tradition and the Magisterium reply that Jesus founded the Church in order to continue his work of redemption for all time.

Jesus was sent into this world by his Father to save us from our sins and to lead us to heaven. But he spent just a few years on this earth, and that was almost two thousand years ago. Jesus was sent for the salvation of *all men*, not just those who happened to be living during his lifetime and during the ministry of the Apostles. The First Vatican Council declared that Christ, "in order to render the saving work of redemption lasting, decided to establish his holy Church that in it, as in the house of the living God, all the faithful might be held together by the bond of one faith and one love" (*Denzinger* 1821).

By his life, death and resurrection Jesus merited for us all the fruits of the redemption; but they must be applied to each individual person in some way. The task of the

Church throughout history is to apply the graces of redemption to individuals. The Church does this and continues the redemptive work of Christ by exercising his threefold office—the teaching office, the pastoral office and the sanctifying office.

Jesus bestowed his mission from the Father on his Apostles: "As the Father sent me, so am I sending you" (Jn 20:21). For what purpose did the Father send Jesus into this world? He sent him to bring about the eternal salvation of mankind: "I have come so that they may have life and have it to the full" (Jn 10:10). Jesus also said, "The Son of Man has come to seek out and save what was lost" (Lk 19:10).

Jesus conferred on his Church, through Peter and the Apostles, all the means necessary to accomplish her task of saving mankind. Thus, he commanded his Apostles to preach the Gospel to all nations, to secure obedience to his commandments and to administer the sacraments— his instruments of saving grace (see Mt 28:19–20). He also bestowed on his Apostles the power of binding and loosing (Mt 18:18), the power to celebrate the Holy Eucharist (Lk 22:19), and the power to forgive sins (Jn 20:23).

Saints Peter and Paul and the other Apostles looked upon themselves as representatives of Christ and dispensers of the mysteries of God: "People must think of us as Christ's servants, stewards entrusted with the mysteries of God" (1 Cor 4:1). So the immediate purpose of the Church is the sanctification of men and women by the communication of the whole Gospel, of the commandments and of the grace of Christ in the sacraments.

It follows from the purpose of the Church and from the means she uses to attain her end that the Church is a supernatural and spiritual society. The ultimate goal of the Church lies not in this world but in the world to come. This truth is summarized by Jesus when he says, "Give back to Caesar what belongs to Caesar—and to God what belongs to God" (Mk 12:17). Moreover, that Jesus and his Church do not seek earthly power was stated clearly by Jesus to Pilate: "My kingdom is not of this world" (Jn 18:36). Jesus' kingdom is a spiritual and supernatural one. Pope Leo XIII said it very well: "Although this society [the Church] consists of men, just as civil society does, yet by reason of the purpose set for it, and by reason of the means with which it seeks to achieve this purpose, it is a supernatural and spiritual society: and for this reason it is essentially different from civil society" (*Immortale Dei*).

Since the purpose of the Church, then, is a purely religious one, she has of herself no direct political, economic, social or cultural tasks to perform. Vatican II says clearly: "Christ, to be sure, gave his Church no proper mission in the political, economic or social order. The purpose which he set before her is a religious one" (Constitution on the Church, no. 42).

According to Leo XIII the Church is also a perfect society: "The Church, according to her nature and her rights, is a perfect society, as she possesses in herself and by herself, by the will and goodness of her Founder, everything that is necessary for her existence and efficacy. Since the aim which the Church pursues is the most sublime, so also her power is the most eminent, and it cannot be considered as being less than the civil power or in any way subject to the civil power." Both the Church and the State are supreme in their own areas and should not interfere with each other; but there should be friendly cooperation in those areas that overlap, such as marriage laws and the education of children.

The Church must always resist the intrusion of the State into her affairs in such things as the appointment of bishops, restrictions on religious freedom and free communication with the Holy Father in Rome.

4

THE MYSTICAL BODY OF CHRIST

The Roman Catholic Church, as the community of the faithful of the whole world which was personally founded by Jesus Christ for the salvation of all mankind, is essentially a supernatural mystery. With regard to her general characteristics, she is both external and internal; she is both physical and mystical because she is a visible society whose head is Christ and whose soul is the Holy Spirit. Since her goal or purpose is the eternal salvation of men and women, she is not primarily a this-worldly organization. At the same time, she is ordered to the life of grace in Christ for persons in the present.

With regard to her intimate nature, the Church is most aptly and clearly defined as "the Mystical Body of Christ". That means that she is a supernatural union of men in Christ, which is based on the vital influence of the Holy Spirit and the external bonds of the same faith, sacraments and government.

The most penetrating analysis of this idea of the Church was given by Pope Pius XII in 1943 in his encyclical letter entitled *The Mystical Body of Christ*. There he declared in no. 13: "If we would define and describe this true Church of Jesus Christ—which is the One, Holy, Catholic, Apostolic Roman Church—we shall find nothing more noble, more sublime or more divine than the expression 'the Mystical Body of Christ'—an expression which springs from and is, as it were, the fair flowering of the repeated teaching of the Sacred Scriptures and the holy Fathers."

St. Paul says clearly that the Church, as the community of the faithful, is the body of Christ, and that Christ is the head of that body. Under the images of body and head he vividly portrays the spiritual or "mystical" connection between Christ and his Church. Thus he writes: "He (the Father) has put all things under his feet and made him . . . the head of the Church which is his body" (Eph 1:22); "Now the Church is his body, he is its head" (Col 1:18); "Now you together are Christ's body; but each of you is a different part of it" (1 Cor 12:27).

It should be noted that the word "mystical" does not appear explicitly in Scripture, as applied to the body of Christ. The idea is there, but not the word. The expression developed during the Middle Ages, and became quite common by the end of the twelfth century. The word "mystical" (= hidden) is meant to indicate the spiritual, transcendent or "hidden" character of the union of grace between Christ and all the faithful. "Mystical", however, does not mean that the Church is a spiritual body only—one that is united only by the internal bonds of faith, hope and charity (Pius XII, nos. 14, 70–76). On the contrary, the body of the Church is also concrete and visible; it is endowed with the external and visible sacraments and with the external bonds of one profession of faith, worship and government (nos. 18 and 68ff.).

The members of the Mystical Body of Christ are those who live in the unity of faith, sacraments and government (no. 21). Even sinners are members of the Church as long as they keep these three bonds (no. 22). Pagans, heretics, schismatics and those excommunicated are not members (nos. 21, 100–102), "even if they may be inclined toward the Mystical Body of the Redeemer by a kind of unconscious desire and hope" (no. 101).

A beautiful idea closely linked with the Mystical Body is that the Holy Spirit is the soul or animating principle of the Church. The notion was developed by the Fathers of the Church by reflecting on the full meaning of certain statements of the New Testament. Thus, St. Paul teaches: "For in one Spirit we were all baptized into one body . . . and we were all given to drink of one Spirit" (1 Cor 12:13); "Preserve the unity of the Spirit in the bond of peace: one body and one Spirit . . . one Lord, one faith, one Baptism" (Eph 4:4f.). On this point St. Augustine preached the following: "The Holy Spirit is for the body of Christ, what the soul is for the body of man. The Holy Spirit does in the whole Church, what the soul does in all the members of the body."

The intimate nature of the Church is essentially spiritual or mystical because she depends on the mystery of divine grace. She is also a union of men which is produced by the Holy Spirit through Christ the Lord. Therefore the Church is essentially the Mystical Body of Christ. She is a *body* because she is a community of men who have the same purpose and share in the same divine life.

She is a *mystical* body because her purpose and life are supernatural, that is, they belong to the mysterious realm of divine grace. In conclusion, she is the *Body of Christ* because she derives her purpose and life from him under the efficacious movement of the Holy Spirit.

5

A HIERARCHICAL CHURCH

Since the Church is the community of the faithful of the whole world, it follows necessarily that she is an external or visible society. This truth is also indicated by St. Paul's affirmation that the Church is the *body* of Christ, that is, a visible organism.

The Catholic Church has been present in history since the time of the Apostles as a visible, hierarchically organized society. She claims, and has officially pronounced on many occasions, that Jesus Christ himself willed and established a hierarchical Church, giving her, through Peter and the Apostles, the offices of bishop, priest and deacon. And since the Church was established for the salvation of men of all time and nations until the end of the world, Jesus also willed that the Apostles have *successors* in each age. According to the official teaching of the Church, those successors in our time are the pope, bishops, priests and deacons who rule, teach and sanctify in the Church.

"Hierarchical" means that there are certain "sacred powers" in the Church which have been handed down in a direct line from Jesus Christ, through his Apostles, to the Church of our time. It also means that each bishop receives his sacred power directly from another bishop. In other words, it is not a democratic affair in which the community possesses the power and then confers it on the man of its choice who then assumes the power of bishop.

The hierarchical powers of the Church include the power to teach, the power to rule and the power to sanctify, all authoritatively in the name of Jesus Christ. These powers correspond to Jesus' threefold office of prophet, king and priest. The Church teaches that Jesus conferred these three offices, with their corresponding powers, on his Apostles and their legitimate successors.

In the course of her long history, there have been many heretics and dissenters who have denied, in one way or another, the hierarchical constitution of the Church. Some have said that Jesus had no intention of establishing a visible Church with bishops, priests and sacred authority; for them, the Church is an internal, invisible reality of the heart that arises from the preaching of the Gospel and faith in Jesus.

Others rejected the special priesthood and the hierarchy, and acknowledged only the general priesthood of all the faithful. Against them the Council of Trent solemnly declared: "If anyone says that in the Catholic Church there is no divinely instituted hierarchy consisting of bishops, priests, and ministers: let him be anathema" (*Denzinger* 966).

In the late eighteenth century the Gallicans said that Christ conferred his power on the totality of the faithful, and that they in turn bestow it on bishops and priests. Pope Pius VI rejected that position as heretical (see *Denzinger* 1502). It is, then, the official teaching of the Church that Christ gave spiritual power to the Apostles immediately. She teaches that the Mystical Body of Christ possesses both an external, juridical dimension (= legal organization) and an inner, mystical or spiritual dimension (= divine grace). In the same way, in Christ, the head of the Church, there is both the visible human nature and the invisible divine nature; also in the sacraments we find outward signs and inward grace.

In the New Testament we read that Jesus bestowed his threefold office of Redeemer on his Apostles: "As the Father has sent me, so am I sending you" (Jn 20:21). He commanded them to proclaim the Gospel throughout the whole world and for this conferred on them his authority (Mt 28:19; Mk 16:15; Lk 10:16). He gave them extensive spiritual powers, such as binding and loosing (Mt 18:18), baptizing (Mt 28:19), forgiving sins (Jn 20:23) and celebrating the Eucharist (Lk 22:19).

According to St. Paul, the Apostles thought of themselves as representatives of Christ: "Through him we received grace and our apostolic mission to preach the obedience of faith to all pagan nations in honor of his name" (Rom 1:5). Again: "People must think of us as Christ's servants, stewards entrusted with the mysteries of God" (1 Cor 4:1). Faithful to the Lord's command, the Apostles preached the Good News throughout the known world; they also made laws for the Christians (Acts 15:28f.), imposed sanctions (1 Cor 4:21), and passed on Church power to others by the imposition of hands (Acts 6:6; 1 Tim 4:14; Titus 1:5).

So the Apostles demanded submission and order in

all things related to faith and the sacraments. It should be clear, then, from the teaching and actions of the Apostles, that the Church is a hierarchical body, with Christ as her head.

6

BISHOPS ARE SUCCESSORS OF THE APOSTLES

In the last essay mention was made of the fact that the bishops throughout the world are the successors of the Apostles. Now I would like to elaborate on that point and bring out more clearly that the powers bestowed by Jesus on the Apostles have been, by the divine will, transmitted to and conferred on the bishops of the Catholic Church.

The Son of God came into this world in order to redeem all mankind from the power of Satan, sin and death. He accomplished this by his life, passion, death and resurrection. But the fruits of the Redemption must be applied to each individual. For that purpose he established his Church on Peter, the Rock, and on the other Apostles. At his command they went out into the whole known world at the time, preached the Gospel, converted pagans, baptized them and established local churches in many places.

Since they could not be everywhere at one time, they

needed helpers and co-workers. Thus they appointed bishops, presbyters or elders, and deacons to teach, sanctify and govern the various churches. This is clearly brought out by St. Paul when he appoints Timothy and Titus to oversee their local churches (see Titus 2:1; I Tim 5:19–21; Titus 1:5).

It is clear, therefore, from the mission of Jesus and from the practice of the Apostles, that Our Lord intended his Church to be perpetual—to endure until the end of time. When the Apostles realized that Jesus would not come again during their lifetime (all but John died as martyrs), in order to perpetuate their mission they appointed bishops as their successors in the threefold office of teaching, leading and sanctifying the Church.

The divine origin of the episcopate is implied in Jesus' solemn promise of assistance, given to the Apostles shortly before his Ascension into heaven: "Go, therefore, make disciples of all the nations; baptize them. . . . And know that I am with you always; yes, to the end of time" (Mt 28:20). That promise presupposes that the apostolic office is perpetuated in the legitimate successors of the Apostles.

According to the Council of Trent, "the bishops who succeeded in the place of the Apostles belong by excellence to the hierarchical order, and are appointed by the Holy Spirit to rule over the Church of God" (*Denzinger* 960). With regard to the perpetual office of bishops in the Church, Vatican Council I said: "Just as he sent the Apostles, whom he had chosen for himself out of the world, as he himself was sent by the Father (see Jn 20:21), so also he wished shepherds and teachers to be in his Church, until the consummation of the world" (*Denzinger* 1821).

The Second Vatican Council repeated and developed the previous teaching of the Church on the office of bishop. "This sacred Synod teaches that *by divine institution* bishops have succeeded in the place of the Apostles, as shepherds of the Church" (Constitution on the Church, no. 20). A little further on in the same document the Council Fathers said: "Just as, by the Lord's will, St. Peter and the other Apostles make up one apostolic college, so in an equal manner the Roman Pontiff, Peter's successor, and *the bishops, successors of the Apostles* are joined together" (no. 22).

In addition to the testimony of the New Testament about the office of bishop, which is found in Acts, Titus, 1 and 2 Timothy, and Revelation 2 and 3, there are other early Christian records. Thus St. Clement, the third pope after St. Peter, writing to the Church in Corinth (Greece) about the year 97 A.D., said: "Our Apostles through the Lord Jesus Christ knew that disputes would arise about the episcopal office. For this reason, as they had received exact knowledge of this in advance, they appointed the above named (bishops), and subsequently gave directions that when these should fall asleep, other tried men should take over their duties" (*Corinthians* 44, 1–2).

The great St. Ignatius of Antioch, who was devoured by lions in Rome in the year 107 A.D., mentions the leading role of bishops a number of times in his letters to various churches. Thus, writing to the Church at Smyrna in Asia, he said: "Nobody is supposed to do anything which concerns the Church without the Bishop. Only that Eucharist is regarded as valid and legal that is consummated under the Bishop or by one authorized by him. There, where Jesus is, the Catholic Church is. It is not permitted to baptize without the Bishop, or to hold the agape. But whatever he finds good, that is also pleasing to God, so that everything that is done is certain and lawful. . . . He that honors the Bishop is honored by God; he that does anything without the Bishop, serves the devil" (*Smyrn.* 8, 1–2).

Jesus, therefore, willed that his Apostles have successors for all time. Those successors are now present in the Church and we call them "bishops".

7

THE PRIMACY OF ST. PETER

The next point we will consider is that of the *primacy* of St. Peter, that is, his special prerogatives in relationship to the other Apostles and his special place in the Church of Jesus Christ. With the infallibility bestowed on her by the Lord, the Church clearly teaches that Jesus appointed Peter to be the first of all the Apostles and to be the visible head of the whole Church; he also immediately and personally gave Peter a true primacy of jurisdiction over the Church.

The word "primacy" comes from the Latin word *primus* which means "first". So primacy means first in rank. With regard to St. Peter and his successors, the popes of Rome, over the centuries there has been much debate about the nature of this primacy. There is such a thing as a *primacy of honor* which means that the one who has it deserves special marks of distinction at public gatherings; but it does not imply any authority over others. Many Protestants are ready to grant such a primacy to the pope. The Roman Church, however, claims much more.

A *primacy of jurisdiction* consists in the possession of full and supreme legislative, executive and juridical power. Since the earliest times, the Catholic Church has claimed a primacy of jurisdiction for St. Peter and for his lawful successors, the popes of Rome.

There are many powerful opponents of this teaching. The Greek Orthodox deny it; the medieval heretics, Wycliffe and Hus, denied it; almost all Protestants deny it. The Gallicans (and, now, certain American theologians) oppose it by saying that Christ bestowed his spiritual power on the whole Church. According to this view the Church, by a democratic procedure, appointed Peter as its servant and spokesman. For the Modernists, Christ did not confer any primacy on Peter or on the Church. It was, they say, a development or invention of post-apostolic times to meet the needs of the Church.

What does the Catholic Church say about the primacy of Peter? In 1870 the First Vatican Council promulgated the following official definition: "If anyone says that the blessed Apostle Peter was not constituted by Christ the Lord as the Prince of all the Apostles and the visible head of the whole Church militant, or that he received immediately and directly from Jesus Christ our Lord only a primacy of honor and not a true and proper primacy of jurisdiction: let him be anathema" (*Denzinger* 1823).

The invisible head of the Church, his Mystical Body, is the risen Christ. Peter is the visible head or ruler of the Church, representing or taking the place of Christ on earth. As such he is the Vicar of Christ.

The Church's teaching and constant tradition about the primacy of jurisdiction of Peter (and his successors) is firmly rooted in the testimony of the New Testament. From their first encounter Jesus singled out Peter for a special distinction. He changed his name from Simon to Peter or Rock (Jn 1:42). The name Peter (Cephas or Rock) indicates his office as the foundation of unity and stability. In the lists of the Apostles in the Gospels Peter is always named first. He was closely associated with the Lord in the Transfiguration and the Agony in the Garden. The Lord paid the temple tax for himself and for Peter (Mt 17:27) and ordered him to strengthen the brethren (Lk 22:32).

Jesus promised the primacy to Peter at Caesarea Philippi (Mt 16:17–19): "I now say to you: You are Peter and on this rock I will build my Church. And the gates of the underworld can never hold out against it. I will give you the keys of the kingdom of heaven: whatever you bind on earth will be bound in heaven; whatever you loose on earth will be loosed in heaven."

In these words addressed solely to Peter, Jesus is promising to confer on him supreme power in the Church. As the rock he is the principle of unity and stability, like the foundation of a house; as the holder of the keys, he has the power to admit others to the kingdom of God; the power to bind and loose is the power to interpret and enforce the law.

After his Resurrection Jesus conferred the primacy on Peter: "Feed my lambs. . . . Feed my sheep" (Jn 21:15–17). In ancient and biblical language, a shepherd is one who has authority over his sheep; in its application to human beings, "to feed" means to rule.

After the Lord's Ascension into heaven Peter immediately began to exercise his primacy or leadership of the Church. He conducted the election of Matthias to replace the traitor Judas (Acts 1:15ff.). He preached the first Christian sermon on Pentecost and converted three thousand people (Acts 2). He admitted the first pagan converts into the Church (Acts 10 and 11). Later St. Paul went up to Jerusalem "to see Peter" (Gal 1:18).

The sense of tradition is perhaps best summarized in the common expressions: "Vicar of Christ" and "Prince of the Apostles". St. Ambrose said it very succinctly: "Where Peter is, there is the Church."

8

THE PRIMACY OF THE POPE

We have seen that Our Lord conferred on St. Peter the primacy of jurisdiction in the Church. The next question to consider is whether or not Jesus wanted that primacy to be a perpetual institution in his Church and, if so, where it was to be located.

It is the solemn teaching of the Catholic Church that, according to the will of Christ, Peter must have successors in his primacy over the whole Church and for all time. The Church also teaches as a doctrine of faith that the bishop of Rome is the successor of Peter in the primacy. Let us now consider the major arguments in support of these two points.

Vatican Council I declared in 1870: "If anyone says that it is not according to the institution of Christ our Lord himself, that is, by divine law, that St. Peter has perpetual successors in the primacy over the whole Church; or if anyone says that the Roman Pontiff is not the successor of St. Peter in the same primacy: let him be anathema" (*Denzinger* 1825).

It is true that Jesus did not explicitly mention successors in the primacy when he promised it to Peter in Matthew 16 and then conferred it on him in John 21, but it is clearly implied within the nature and purpose of the primacy. That purpose is to preserve for all time the unity and solidarity of the Church. Since the Church is to perdure until the end of the world and since Peter, being mortal like the rest of mankind, would live only a certain number of years, the obvious intention of Jesus is that the office of Peter should be handed on to someone else. The Church, after all, is founded on the rock of St. Peter (Mt 16:17–19) and cannot stand without the Petrine foundation.

From the above we see that Peter has and must continue to have successors in the primacy. The Church is spread throughout the world. There are thousands of bishops and dioceses. Which one, from among all of them, is the successor of St. Peter? The constant tradition of the Church, going back even to the first century, is that the *bishops of Rome* are the successors of Peter in the primacy.

We are dealing here with both a historical question and a matter of faith. We know that Peter went to Rome and that he suffered a martyr's death there on the Vatican hill—on the exact spot where today is located St. Peter's Basilica. Peter mentioned Rome once at the end of his

First Letter (5:13): "Your sister in Babylon, who is with you among the chosen, sends you greetings." Christians of the time referred to Rome as "Babylon"; so Peter says that he is writing to them from Rome. Also, many early Christian writers mention that Peter was in Rome: St. Clement of Rome (97 A.D.), St. Ignatius of Antioch (107 A.D.) and St. Irenaeus of Lyons (about 180 A.D.).

In this connection it is important to note that no other place but Rome has ever claimed to be the burial site of St. Peter.

The doctrine was defined by the Council of Florence in the fifteenth century: "We define that the holy Apostolic See and the Roman Pontiff have primacy over the whole world, and that the same Roman Pontiff is the successor of St. Peter, the Prince of the Apostles, and the true Vicar of Christ, the head of the whole Church, the father and teacher of all Christians; and that to him, in the person of St. Peter, was given by our Lord Jesus Christ the full power of feeding, ruling and governing the whole Church" (*Denzinger* 694).

Like other Church teachings, the doctrine of the primacy of the Roman bishops developed over a period of many years. It took time, reflection and guidance by the Holy Spirit for the Church to grasp explicitly what was there implicitly from the beginning. In 97 A.D. St. Clement of Rome sent a fatherly letter to the troubled Church in Corinth urging peace and unity. In 107 A.D. St. Ignatius of Antioch wrote about the preeminence of "the Church founded by the two famous Apostles Peter and Paul at Rome". Pope St. Anicetus (154–165) and Pope St. Victor I (189–198) dealt with the Orientals about setting the date for the annual celebration of Easter.

Pope St. Stephen I in the third century rebuked St.

Cyprian of Carthage on the disputed point about the re-baptism of heretics. Stephen said that he possessed "the succession of Peter, on which the foundations of the Church are erected".

At the Council of Chalcedon in 451 the Fathers accepted the now-famous dogmatic letter of Pope St. Leo I with the cry: "Peter has spoken through Leo!"

Scholastic theologians, following St. Thomas Aquinas, base the primacy of the pope on the need for unity in the Church. For the unity of the Faith, they argue, it is necessary that one person be at the head of the whole Church. Guided by the Holy Spirit, he can resolve the disputes about the meaning of the Faith.

9

THE POPE IS JUDGED BY NO ONE

We have been considering the primacy of Peter and his successors, the popes of Rome. We have seen that primacy means "first in rank" and that the Church believes that the pope possesses a *primacy of jurisdiction* over all the faithful throughout the world. In theological language the word "jurisdiction" means spiritual power over others, that is, the right to direct them in the way of salvation and to bind them in conscience. Now I would ask you to reflect on the nature or meaning of papal primacy.

Over the centuries there have been many attempts on the part of kings, bishops and theologians to limit, both in theory and in practice, the primacy and power of the pope. Various forms of "episcopalism" have exaggerated the rights of local bishops to the detriment of the power of the pope.

The theory of "conciliarism" denies the supreme authority of the pope and declares that he is subject to the authority of an ecumenical council.

Various democratic theories, sometimes called "Caesaropapism", claim that Christ conferred his divine power immediately on the Church, the people of God, and they in turn bestow it on the pope through their representatives, either bishops or the king (that is, the secular power—whatever form it may take at a given time in history).

A clear answer to these theories from the Church is crucial for her unity and continuity. Peter is the Rock of stability on which Jesus built his Church. If there were doubt about the source of divine authority in the Church, it would soon splinter into many locally autonomous groups with no central head. In fact, that is what happened to the Protestants once they separated themselves from the Chair of St. Peter.

Church teaching on this point developed over the centuries. As in many other areas of Church life and doctrine, the belief and practice of the Church preceded the theological explanation. Our Lord promised the primacy to Peter (Mt 16:17–19) and after his resurrection conferred it on him (Jn 21:15–17), as we have seen. He was the leader of the Apostles and preached the first Christian sermon on that first Pentecost (Acts 1 and 2).

The first bishops of Rome, successors of St. Peter,

were generally conceded a special place in the hierarchy of the Church. They either convened or approved the first Councils. Council after Council expressed, in one way or another, the primacy of the pope. Clear statements of the primacy of jurisdiction of the pope were made by the Second Council of Lyons (1274), the Council of Florence (1439) and Vatican I (1870). So the dogmatic teaching of the Catholic Church on this matter is that the pope possesses full and supreme power of jurisdiction over the whole Church, not merely in matters of faith and morals, but also in Church discipline and in the government of the Church. The same doctrine was reaffirmed by Vatican II.

The pope has full episcopal power over the whole Church in matters of faith and morals and in the government of the Church. His power is *ordinary*, that is, it comes with his office and therefore comes directly from Christ our Lord; he exercises it in his own right and not as the delegate of a Council or some other group. His power is also *immediate* in the sense that it reaches every bishop, priest and lay person. Thus, the pope can deal directly with any of the faithful without going through the local bishop, if he so wishes.

The pope's power is also *supreme*, that is, there is no jurisdiction in the Church equal to or superior to that of the Holy Father. The power of the pope exceeds that of each individual bishop and of all the other bishops together. This means that all the bishops in the world as a group (apart from the pope) are not equal to or superior to the pope.

Because of his supreme power, the pope has the right of direct contact with all of the bishops and all of the faithful. Therefore the Church rejects the efforts of various governments, such as the Chinese communists, to restrict or prohibit contact between the pope and the local churches.

As the supreme lawgiver in the Church, the pope is not legally bound by past ecclesiastical laws; for a good reason he can change them. He is bound only by the divine law. Thus, Pius XII changed the rules for fasting and abstinence and Pope Paul VI changed many liturgical norms, for example, by allowing Mass to be celebrated in the vernacular languages.

According to an ancient saying, "the First See is judged by no one". The reason is that there is no higher spiritual judge on earth than the pope. He has the right to decide all Church disputes. For the same reason, there is no right of appeal from a decision of the Holy Father to a higher court. No such court exists, not even a General Council. These points were all clearly spelled out by the First Vatican Council in 1870.

10

WHEN IS THE POPE INFALLIBLE?

The pope is the supreme Pastor or Shepherd over the whole Church. As we have seen, in virtue of the promises made to Peter and his successors the pope is the supreme ruler and teacher of the Church. We call his teaching authority, which he has from Christ himself, his *Magisterium* (the word is derived from the Latin *magister*, which means "teacher"). One aspect of the papal Magisterium that has been much discussed and disputed in recent years is its *infallibility*. So now let us consider what the Church teaches about the infallibility of the pope.

First of all, infallibility is the quality of not being able to err or to lead others into error; more specifically, it means immunity from error or freedom from error in teaching the universal Church in matters of faith or morals. It is the official, dogmatic teaching of the Church that the Holy Father is infallible when he teaches authoritatively and definitively, as head of the entire Church, in matters of faith and morals. Clear examples of this are the definition by Pope Pius IX in 1854 of the Immaculate Conception of Mary, and the definition by Pope Pius XII in 1950 of Mary's glorious Assumption into heaven, body and soul.

The teaching primacy of the Pope was proclaimed by such Councils as Lyons II (1274) and Florence (1439). It was defined in its most explicit form by the First Vatican Council in 1870: "The Roman Pontiff, when he speaks *ex cathedra*, that is, when, acting in the office of shepherd and teacher of all Christians, he defines, by virtue of his supreme apostolic authority, doctrine concerning faith or morals to be held by the universal Church, possesses through the divine assistance promised to him in the person of St. Peter, the infallibility with which the divine Redeemer willed his Church to be endowed in defining doctrine concerning faith or morals; and such definitions of the Roman Pontiff are therefore irreformable because of their nature, but not because of the agreement of the Church" (*Denzinger* 1839).

In order to understand this dogma of the Roman Catholic Church properly, the following points should be noted:

1) The bearer of the infallibility is every lawful pope as successor of St. Peter, the Prince of Apostles. But the pope alone is infallible, not others to whom he delegates a part of his teaching authority, for example, the Roman congregations.

2) The object of his infallibility is his teaching of faith and morals. This refers especially to revealed doctrine such as the Holy Trinity. But it also includes any nonrevealed teaching that is in any way connected with revelation.

3) The condition of the infallibility is that the pope speaks *ex cathedra*, that is, as teacher of all the faithful with the full weight of his apostolic authority. If he speaks merely as a private theologian, or as the head of his own diocese of Rome, he is not infallible. He must also have the intention of deciding *definitively* for all the faithful a teaching of faith or morals. This intention must be made clear by the formulation of the doctrine or from the circumstances.

4) The source of the pope's infallibility is the supernatural assistance of the Holy Spirit, who protects the supreme teacher of the Church from error and therefore from leading the faithful into error.

Consequently, the *ex cathedra* definitions of the pope are unchangeable "of themselves", that is, not because others in the Church (such as theologians) first instructed the pope or subsequently agree to what he says.

The New Testament does not say explicitly that Peter and his successors are infallible, but it most certainly implies it. Thus, Christ made Peter the rock foundation of his Church, that is, the source of her unity and stability (Mt 16:18). The unity of the Church, however, is not possible without purity of faith, so Peter is the supreme and infallible teacher of the Faith. Christ also gave Peter the power of binding and loosing, that is, the authority to declare and explain revelation.

Jesus prayed that Peter should be strengthened in his faith and that he should strengthen the brethren: "I have prayed for you, Simon, that your faith may not fail, and once you have recovered, you in your turn must strengthen your brothers" (Lk 22:32). Dangers to the Faith exist at all times, so in order to fulfill this task properly, in matters of faith and morals the pope must be infallible.

The teaching primacy of the pope from the earliest times was expressed in the practice of condemning heretical opinions. St. Thomas Aquinas argued that there must be one faith in the whole Church (cf. 1 Cor 1:10). But unity of faith could not be preserved if the pope could not definitively decide questions of faith.

11

WHAT IS A BISHOP?

In the past few chapters we have been reflecting on the primacy of the Holy Father, his magisterium and his infallibility. The Church is surely a hierarchical community with the pope at its head, as the successor of St. Peter and the Vicar of Christ on earth. But he does not rule the Church alone. He is joined and assisted in directing the Church by the bishops throughout the world who are in communion with him. Let us now for a few moments consider the nature and role of the Catholic bishop.

We might ask ourselves: What is a bishop? The answer is that he is a leader or pastor of a diocese, that is, a certain portion of the people of God, clearly delineated by territorial boundaries. Thus, in the United States we have almost 200 dioceses, designated for the most part as segments of a particular state, such as Virginia which is divided into the two dioceses of Richmond and Arlington. Some few states, such as Idaho, have only one diocese.

Another question that might occur to you is: Where do bishops come from? Who instituted the office of bishop in the Church? As you probably know, most Protestants do not admit the office of bishop in the Church. The Orthodox churches do have bishops as an essential element in their structure.

The Roman Catholic Church teaches that the office of bishop exists by divine right, that is, it was instituted by Christ and his will in the matter was communicated to the Apostles, either directly or by the inspiration of the Holy Spirit. Thus, the Church says that, by the will of Christ, bishops are successors of the Apostles who sanctify, teach and rule a local church. They have this authority only in communion with the See of Peter and in subordination to the pope.

The divine institution of the episcopacy is not taught explicitly by the New Testament, but it is affirmed implicitly and practically. We see this from the fact that Jesus built his Church on Peter and the Apostles. He sent them out "to all nations" to teach and baptize until the end of time (see Mt 28:18–20). This means that he wanted them to have successors for all succeeding ages; that is what the bishops are—successors of the Apostles.

The Apostles were Shepherds and Guardians of the Church, and that is what the bishops are today.

This is no novel doctrine, since it can be traced as explicit teaching of the first Fathers of the Church, beginning with St. Ignatius of Antioch who was martyred for the Faith in 107 A.D. The Council of Trent taught that the bishops "succeeded in the place of the Apostles" and were "placed by the Holy Spirit to govern the Church of God" (*Denzinger* 960). Trent also made the following declaration of faith: "If anyone says that in the Catholic Church there is no divinely instituted hierarchy consisting of bishops, priests, and ministers: let him be anathema" (*Denzinger* 966).

Vatican I in 1870 also taught that Christ "wished shepherds and teachers to be in his Church until the consummation of the world" (*Denzinger* 1821; see also 1828). More recently, Vatican II taught explicitly that the episcopacy is a divine institution: "This sacred Synod teaches that *by divine institution* bishops have succeeded to the place of the Apostles as shepherds of the Church" (Constitution on the Church, no. 20).

It is important to note that local ordinaries, that is, bishops of dioceses, possess by divine right the ordinary power of government over their dioceses. The power is "ordinary" because it is directly connected with the office of bishop—the two go together like "love and marriage". The diocesan bishop exercises his power of government in his own name. Thus, the bishop is not a delegate or representative of the pope; he is an independent pastor of the flock entrusted to him, even though he remains subordinate to the pope in some matters, especially with regard to the unity of the Church in matters of faith and morals.

It is the faith of the Church that the Apostles were divinely instructed to pass on their pastoral office to the bishops. So the bishops are the successors of the Apostles in the sense that all the bishops are successors of the College of Apostles. The Bishop of Rome is the only one who can trace his lineage back to one particular Apostle—St. Peter.

The power of the local bishop is limited to the territory committed to him; it is also limited by the papal power which is superior to it. Tradition and canon law spell out certain important matters that are reserved exclusively to the pope. Finally, bishops' conferences are human creations, not divine. They were created by Pope Paul VI after Vatican II to help in implementing the decrees of the Council.

12

SOME NOTES ON COLLEGIALITY

Since the Second Vatican Council there has been much discussion about the "episcopal college" and the activity of the bishops and the pope under the rubric of "collegiality". After explaining what a bishop is in the Catholic Church, it might be helpful to clear up a few points about *collegiality*.

The word "college" here causes some problems because it is not used in the usual American sense as "an institution of higher learning". That is just one meaning of the word. Fundamentally it refers to a society of colleagues or companions; it is a moral bond that binds together a group of people in some common purpose. It can refer to a group of equals, such as a school faculty, or to unequals. When used with reference to the apostolic college or the episcopal college it means all the bishops of the Roman Catholic Church united under the pope as an episcopal community. Here, it should be obvious, it does not refer to strict equals, since the pope has a special dignity and power by reason of being the successor of St. Peter and the Vicar of Christ on earth—titles that do not apply to any other bishop.

For many centuries theologians held that membership in the episcopal college was a mere consequence of being appointed a bishop by the Roman Pontiff. Vatican II teaches us that the episcopacy is by its very nature collegial. What the Council means is that when a priest is consecrated a bishop, provided that he is in hierarchical communion with the Roman Pontiff, by that very fact he becomes a member of the apostolic or episcopal college.

By his membership in the college of bishops the new bishop participates in the sacred powers of sanctifying, teaching and governing, but in the exercise of these powers he is subject to the directives of the Holy Father. He also acquires directly from God the basic ability to govern a diocese with the normal and ordinary authority of a bishop, if and when the pope appoints him to such an office.

The above doctrine was solemnly affirmed by the Second Vatican Council. It is now considered Catholic doctrine, but it is not a defined dogma of the Church. If you want to read what the Council said about collegiality you will find it in Dogmatic Constitution on the Church (nos. 21–23).

The word "college" as applied to the bishops is not found in the Bible, but the biblical *foundation* for the doctrine of collegiality is briefly indicated by Vatican II in Jesus' words in Matthew 18:18, by which all the Apostles (and their successors) received from him a general power of binding and loosing similar to the power given to Peter; it is also suggested by Matthew 28:16–20 where Jesus commissioned all of them to go into the whole world to preach and baptize.

The doctrine of collegiality was barely mentioned by the Fathers of the Church and was not developed by the older theologians. It is an understanding of the nature of the Church that came to full consciousness in the twentieth century, especially in the decades immediately preceding Vatican II.

The Council notes that there is a certain *proportion* between the apostolic college and the episcopal college. This means that the relationship between the pope and the bishops today is something like the relation that existed between Peter and the other Apostles. Accordingly, the episcopal college succeeds the apostolic college in full and supreme power over the whole Church. The power of the college, however, cannot be exercised without the consent of the head, the Roman Pontiff.

The pope is a member of the college; in fact, he is the most important member. As a member of this group the pope always retains his primacy of jurisdiction over every member of the Church. He can act either with the college or outside of it—he always remains perfectly free in this regard.

It follows then that the college of bishops is not the only supreme power in the Church. Thus, the pope can act alone as head of the college or he can act together with the college. On the other hand, the college of bishops can never act without the pope, since without the head there is no collegial body and no collegial action. A practical consequence of this doctrine is that for an ecumenical council like Vatican II to be valid it must be convoked and presided over by the pope and its final decrees must be personally approved by him.

Because of its supreme power in the Church, the episcopal college enjoys infallibility in its Magisterium. What we said previously about the infallibility of the pope also applies proportionately to the infallibility of the episcopal college. This is especially true when they gather together in an ecumenical council to consider urgent questions of faith and morals.

13

CHRIST IS THE HEAD OF THE CHURCH

In our essays on the Church up to this time we have been concentrating on various aspects of the visible or external constitution of the Church of Jesus Christ. Now we will move on to consider the internal constitution or make-up of the unique ark of salvation.

We have already seen that Christ personally founded

the Church. In 1943 Pope Pius XII said in his important letter on the Mystical Body: "The divine Redeemer began to build the Mystical Body of his Church when he was preaching and giving his commandments; he completed it when he hung in glory on the Cross; he manifested and promulgated it by the visible mission of the Paraclete, the Holy Spirit, upon his disciples" (no. 26).

During the time of his public life Jesus laid the foundations of the Church by selecting and training the Apostles, by appointing Peter to be their head, and by committing to them the revelation from the Father. On the Cross, Jesus finished the construction of his Church. The Old Covenant ceased with the tearing of the temple curtain and the New Covenant, sealed with the blood of Christ, came into being. The flowing out of blood and water from the pierced side of Jesus is a symbol of the birth and emergence of the Church. Water and blood signify the two chief Sacraments of the Church, Baptism and the Eucharist. Many of the Fathers of the Church pointed out that just as Eve, the mother of the living, proceeded from the side of the sleeping Adam, so also the Church, the second Eve and the mother of those living by grace, proceeded from the side of the second Adam, sleeping on the Cross.

Christ not only founded the Church. It is also a doctrine of Catholic faith that he is and remains the *Head of the Church*. The imagery used here is that of a body with head and members. In the natural order the human body is a unity of head and members. Each member has its own functions and dignity, but there is a certain preeminence to the head because it directs, guides and profoundly influences all the other members. Thus, in 1302 Pope Boniface VIII said that "the Church represents one single Mystical Body whose head is Christ" (*Denzinger* 468). Using the same imagery the Council of Trent declared: "Christ Jesus continually infuses strength into the justified as the head to the limbs and the vine to the grapes" (*Denzinger* 809).

Speaking of the Church as the body of Christ and Jesus himself as her head has a solid foundation in the New Testament. Listen to what St. Paul said: "Now the Church is his body, he is its head" (Col 1:18), and again: "If we live by the truth and in love, we shall grow in all ways into Christ, who is the head by whom the whole body is fitted and joined together . . ." (Eph 4:15–16).

Just as the head is the most important member of the human body, so also the God-Man Jesus Christ enjoys a unique preeminence within humanity. By reason of the Hypostatic Union, which we explained previously, he is both God and man. He is, as God, the only-begotten Son of the Father (Col 1:15), as man, the first-born of the dead (Col 1:18), as God-Man, the sole mediator between God and man. As the head of a body guides the other members, so Christ directs the Church by pouring out his Spirit into the hearts of men. St. John says in his Gospel: "From his fulness we have, all of us, received— yes, grace in return for grace" (1:16), and "Without me you can do nothing" (15:5).

We should never forget Our Lord's promise which is recorded for us at the end of St. Matthew's Gospel, "And know that I am with you always; yes, to the end of time" (28:20). The relationship between Christ and the Church is so intimate that the two form one single Mystical Person. We find a certain identity between Christ and Christians expressed in the following words of Jesus: "I was hungry and you gave me to eat; I was thirsty and you gave me to drink" (Mt 25:35). The same truth is expressed when the heavenly Jesus says to Saul, "Saul, Saul, why are you persecuting me?" (Acts 9:4).

The union between Christ and his Church is so close that St. Augustine says: "Christ [i.e., the Church] preaches Christ, the body preaches its head and the head protects his body." The reason for the union of Christ with his Church that results in one mystical person is the fact that Christ, by his divine power, operates through the Apostles and their successors and also informs all the faithful with his grace.

St. Paul teaches that "Christ is the head of the Church, he is the Redeemer of his body" (Eph 5:23). This means that he does more than make vicarious atonement for us; he also frees us from sin by applying his redeeming and sanctifying grace to all of us who believe and walk in the way of salvation.

14

THE SOUL OF THE CHURCH

We have seen that Jesus is the head of the Church, which is his Mystical Body. The Church is the living community of the faithful throughout the world. Being compared to a human body, it has a visible, physical aspect, namely, all those who belong to it through faith in Jesus Christ and Baptism. But there is more to the

Church than visible members who go to church on Sunday and partake of the Sacraments.

Living members of the Church must possess the grace of God and be animated by the Holy Spirit. That which gives life to the body is called the "soul"; it is the principle of life in all living things. In a similar way, the Holy Spirit gives spiritual life to all the members of Jesus' Mystical Body. It is for this reason that, since the time of St. Augustine in the fifth century, the Holy Spirit has often been called "the soul of the Church".

Recent popes have stated explicitly that the Holy Spirit, whom Jesus pours out on the Church and gives to us especially in the sacraments, is the soul of the Church. Just as there is no life in the human body without the soul, so also there is no supernatural, spiritual life in those Christians who are separated from Christ by mortal sin. Thus, in 1897 Pope Leo XIII said: "Let it suffice to state that, as Christ is the head of the Church, so is the Holy Spirit her soul" (*Divinum Illud*, no. 6). In his 1943 encyclical letter on the Mystical Body of Christ, Pius XII repeated and confirmed what Leo had said about the Holy Spirit being the soul of the Church (no. 57). He stressed that all life and growth of the Mystical Body proceed from the indwelling of the Holy Spirit.

The New Testament does not say explicitly that the Holy Spirit is the soul of the Church. This is a metaphor that was possible only after the Fathers of the Church had taken over the Greek idea that man is composed of two basic principles—body and soul. The idea, however, is surely implied in many passages of the New Testament. Thus, St. Paul writes: "There is one Body, one Spirit, just as you were all called into one and the same hope when you were called" (Eph 4:4; see also 1 Cor 12:13).

The same teaching is affirmed in the many passages that speak of the internal, hidden activity of the Holy Spirit in the Church: The Holy Spirit remains with the disciples of Jesus for all time (Jn 14:16); he lives in them as in a temple (1 Cor 3:16; 6:19); he teaches them and reminds them of all that Jesus said to them (Jn 14:26); he effects the forgiveness of sins (Jn 20:22ff.), rebirth (Jn 3:5) and spiritual renewal (Titus 3:5).

The Fathers of the Church bear witness to the intimate relationship between the Holy Spirit and the Church. St. Irenaeus expressed this idea beautifully at the end of the second century: "Where the Church is, there is also the Spirit of God; and where the Spirit of God is, there is the Church and all grace."

St. Augustine compared the activity of the soul in the body to that of the Holy Spirit in the Church: "What the soul is for the body of man, that the Holy Spirit is for the body of Christ, that is, the Church. The Holy Spirit operates in the whole Church that which the soul operates in the members of the one body."

Just as the soul has a different effect in the various members of the body, so also does the Holy Spirit. Through one he works miracles, through others he proclaims the Gospel; in one he preserves marital chastity, in another perseverance in a time of severe temptation.

St. Thomas Aquinas followed Augustine in this line of thought, but he also made use of another metaphor. Thomas spoke of the Holy Spirit as the "heart" of the Church because of the ancient idea that the heart is the central organ out of which all life proceeds to the other members and organs. Leaving aside metaphors, Aquinas says that the Holy Spirit unites, quickens, teaches, sanctifies and dwells in the Church. The metaphor "soul" seems to sum up all these activities.

Since the Holy Spirit is the soul of the Church and so gives it life, it follows that those who culpably remain outside the body of the Church cannot share in the Holy Spirit and in the life of grace communicated by him. We infer, however, from the universal salvific will of God (see 1 Tim 2:4) that those who have never heard of Christ or those who are caught up in invincible error about the true Church of Christ can receive the grace of the Holy Spirit outside the body of the Church. Such persons must cooperate with the graces given to them by God and they must have at least an implicit desire to belong to the Church of Jesus Christ. If they cooperate they will save their souls, but their spiritual state is precarious and greatly inferior to that of the Christian faithful who belong to the Church and are strengthened by the sacraments.

15

THE EVERLASTING CHURCH

Having considered the divine origin of the Church and her basic constitution, we will now take up some reflections on the properties or essential characteristics of the Church of Jesus Christ. By a "property" is meant a quality which derives from the very nature of the Church and is found only in her.

The first property or characteristic of the Church that we will consider is her *indefectibility*. The documents of the Church say clearly that she is indefectible, that is, she is and will remain until the end of the world the only institution of eternal salvation because she was established by the God-Man Jesus Christ for this purpose. Moreover, his presence in his Church through the promise of the Holy Spirit, plus his promise of divine assistance, guarantee that the Church will survive until the second coming of the Lord.

By saying that the Church is "indefectible" we are asserting that she is imperishable, that she will continue in existence until the end of time. We are also asserting the essential immutability of her teaching and structure. Indefectibility, however, does not include accidental changes in such things as fasting regulations, canon law and liturgical language. Thus, since the Second Vatican Council we have witnessed many rather dramatic changes in these and other areas, but there has been no essential change in the nature of the Church and her teaching.

The indefectibility of the Church, or the fact that she is unique, imperishable and unchangeable in her essential structure, has often been denied in the course of history, either explicitly or implicitly. Spiritualists and illuminists since the days of the early Church have promised a new age of the Holy Spirit in which a more perfect church of the Spirit would replace the "earthy" Church of popes, bishops and priests. The Protestant Reformers of the sixteenth century claimed that the Church of Christ had been distorted and corrupted by the papacy, and that they would restore it to its pristine simplicity. Modernists and process theologians of all stripes claim that the Church is constantly evolving into something new and essentially different from what it was in the past.

In 1870 Vatican I declared that the Church was founded on the rock of Peter and "will remain firm until the end of the world" (*Denzinger* 1824). In the first draft of the

Constitution on the Church, which was not voted on but which reflects the thinking of leading theologians of the nineteenth century, we read the following from Vatican I: "We declare, moreover, that, whether one considers its existence or its constitution, the Church of Christ is an everlasting and indefectible society, and that, after it, no more complete nor more perfect economy of salvation is to be hoped for in this world. For, to the very end of the world the pilgrims of this earth are to be saved through Christ. Consequently, his Church, the only society of salvation, will last until the end of the world ever unchangeable and unchanged in its constitution."

That same teaching was repeated twenty-six years later by Pope Leo XIII in his famous encyclical on the Church, *Satis Cognitum*: "It is the duty of the Church to carry to all men of all ages the salvation won by Jesus Christ and all the blessings that flow from it. It is therefore necessary, in accordance with the will of its founder, that it should be the only Church in the whole world for all time" (*Denzinger* 1955).

The indefectibility of the Church is a basic teaching of the Bible and is connected with the idea of the Church as the new people of God. The latter idea was elaborated in Vatican II. In the New Testament the Church is likened to a house built on rock that is able to withstand both storm and tempest (Mt 16:18; 7:24–27). The reason for the perpetuity of the Church is that the risen Christ will be with his Apostles and their successors until the end of the world (Mt 28:20). Thus, their faith will never fail and the Holy Spirit has been conferred on them to lead them to all truth (Jn 14:16, 26).

The basic reason, therefore, for the indefectibility of the Church resides in her essential relationship to the risen Christ, and with the Holy Spirit who is her "soul", as we have seen. In opposition to the "spiritualists" who promise a new and more perfect Church in the future, St. Thomas Aquinas teaches that we are not to expect a Church more richly endowed with the grace of the Holy Spirit than the Church bequeathed to us by the Apostles and their successors (*Summa Theologica* I–II, 106, 4).

16

THE HOUSE OF TRUTH

A second property or characteristic of the Church worth considering is her *infallibility*. We have already seen that the pope is infallible when he speaks *ex cathedra* on a matter of faith or morals. "Infallibility" means the impossibility of falling into error.

The Church as a whole throughout the world, in the teaching of her bishops and the assent of the faithful, is also infallible in doctrines concerning faith and morals. Thus, Vatican Council I taught the infallibility of the Church when it declared: "The Roman Pontiff when he speaks *ex cathedra* . . . possesses through the divine assistance promised to him in the person of St. Peter the infallibility with which the divine Redeemer willed his Church to be endowed in defining doctrine concerning faith or morals" (*Denzinger* 1839).

The Church cannot err in matters of faith and morals,

that is, she is infallible because Christ promised the Apostles and their successors, the bishops, the perpetual assistance of the Holy Spirit. Consider the following words of the Lord: "I shall ask the Father and he will give you another Advocate, the Spirit of truth" (Jn 14:16); "And know that I am with you always; yes, to the end of time" (Mt 28:20). The constant assistance of Jesus and the Holy Spirit in the course of history guarantees the absolute truth and integrity of the Catholic faith taught by the Apostles and their successors.

In their battle against false teaching the ancient Fathers stressed that the Church built on the Apostles always preserved the faith received from Christ pure and untainted with error. St. Irenaeus (d. 202) said that the faith of the Church is always the same because she possesses the Holy Spirit: "Where the Church is, there is also the Spirit of God, and where the Spirit of God is, there is the Church and all grace; but the Spirit is truth." He also made the beautiful statement that the Church is *the house of truth* because there is no false teaching in it.

Just as in the case of papal infallibility, the primary object of the infallibility of the Church is the formally revealed truth concerning faith and morals. This teaching was defined as an article of faith by Vatican I (*Denzinger* 1839). What this means in the concrete is that the Church is the final arbiter of the meaning of revelation contained in the Holy Bible and in tradition. In performing this function the Church not only spells out positively what is to be believed, for example, in the various *Creeds* of the Church and in the proclamations of the various ecumenical councils, but she also refutes and rejects errors that are contrary to and destructive of Catholic faith (for example, materialism, pantheism, atheism).

The secondary object of the infallibility of the Church is truths of Christian teaching on faith and morals which are not formally revealed, but which are closely connected with revelation. The reason for this is that the Church could not adequately protect and transmit the whole revelation if she were not able to pronounce on crucial matters closely related to the truths of faith. In this category are certain historical facts, such as the historical existence of Jesus and the Apostles, the presence and martyrdom of Peter in Rome; certain natural truths whose denial would undermine Christian faith, such as the freedom of man's will and the immortality of the soul. Other matters such as the canonization of the saints are also included here. For the Church is infallible when she declares that someone like Elizabeth Ann Seton is a saint in heaven and may be the object of general veneration.

The possessors of the infallibility of the Church are the Holy Father (when he speaks *ex cathedra*) and the whole body of Catholic bishops throughout the world when they teach in union with the pope on matters of faith and morals. We have already considered the infallibility of the pope.

The whole body of bishops is also infallible when they, either assembled in a general council or scattered throughout the world, propose a teaching of faith or morals as one to be held by all the faithful. As successors of the Apostles they are the pastors and teachers of the faithful (see Lk 10:16). The bishops exercise their infallible teaching power in an extraordinary manner when, in conjunction with the pope, they gather together in an ecumenical council, as they did at Vatican Council II, 1962–1965. They also exercise their infallible teaching authority in an ordinary manner when, scattered in their dioceses and in moral unity with the pope, they unanimously promulgate the same teachings on faith and morals.

They did exactly that for centuries with regard to the Assumption of Mary until the doctrine was defined by Pope Pius XII. They are doing it now on the immorality of abortion, active homosexuality and artificial contraception.

17

THE VISIBLE CHURCH

Having reflected on the indefectibility and infallibility of the Church, we will now examine briefly a third property or characteristic of the true Church of Jesus Christ, namely, the fact that she is an external and visible society. For it is a point of Catholic teaching that the Church Jesus founded on Peter and the Apostles is not only a spiritual reality, but is also visible or perceptible to the senses.

The visibility of the Church has often been denied in the course of Church history. Apparently the human factor and human weaknesses found in bishops, priests and ordinary lay Catholics in the Church are too much for those with a more "spiritual" view. One way to eliminate the defects and limitations in the human factor is to deny that the Church is a visible society. Thus, John

Calvin said that the Church consists only of those who are predestined to heaven—a group that is known only to God. Most Protestants have denied that Jesus established a hierarchical Church, that is, that the pope and the bishops have authority from God to teach, sanctify and rule. That denial led inevitably to the doctrine of the invisible Church.

They do not deny, of course, that Christians come together to pray and sing and read the Bible. But for most of them Church organization from top to bottom is a mere human creation that is not really necessary in order to attain salvation. All that is needed, in their view, is some kind of Christian faith—and that comes from reading the Bible and perhaps hearing the Word of God preached, either in some church or on television. But they deny the divine origin of the Magisterium and the seven sacraments.

The Council of Trent in 1563 declared that there is in the Church a "visible sacrifice of the Eucharist" and "a new, visible, and external priesthood" (*Denzinger* 957). The First Vatican Council in 1870 taught that Christ appointed Peter to be the "visible foundation" of the unity of the Church (*Denzinger* 1821). We have already considered these points in detail in the essays on the hierarchy of the Church and on the primacy of Peter and his successors.

Vatican I also pointed out that certain characteristics of the Church are aids to belief: "The Church itself, because of its marvelous propagation, its exalted sanctity, and its inexhaustible fruitfulness in all that is good, because of its catholic unity and its unshaken stability, is a great and perpetual motive of credibility and an irrefutable proof of its own divine mission" (*Denzinger* 1794).

Pope Leo XIII in his important encyclical letter on the Church, *Satis Cognitum* (1896), clearly taught the visibility of the Church: "If we consider the chief end of his Church and the proximate efficient causes of salvation, it is undoubtedly *spiritual*; but in regard to those who constitute it, and to the things which lead to these spiritual gifts, it is external and necessarily visible" (no. 3). There is a triple bond that unites the members of the Church to each other and makes them recognizable as *Catholics*: profession of the same faith throughout the world, use of the same seven sacraments, and subordination to the same papal authority.

It is also helpful to recall from the Gospels that Jesus, in his parables and discourses, compares his Church to an earthly kingdom, a flock, a building, a vine, a city set on a mountain top. St. Paul compares the Church to the human body.

In this connection it is important to remember that our Savior, Jesus Christ, is both God and Man. This means that in him there is a marvelous unity of both the invisible and the visible, the divine and the human, the spiritual and the material. God became man in the Incarnation; the invisible divinity became visible in some sense in Jesus of Nazareth. Thus, Jesus said to Philip: "To have seen me is to have seen the Father, so how can you say, 'Let us see the Father'?" (Jn 14:9). Since the Church is the Body of Christ and the continuation of his presence on earth, the ultimate theological reason for her visibility is found in the Incarnation of the second Person of the Blessed Trinity.

The Church also has her invisible dimensions—truth, grace, the Holy Spirit. The divine, mystical and invisible side of the Church is an object of faith, while the social and visible aspects are perceptible to the senses. The true Church of Jesus Christ, therefore, is a divinely established, two-dimensional reality that is both visible and invisible.

18

THE FOUR MARKS OF THE CHURCH

In addition to the three characteristics of the Church we have considered in previous chapters, there are also the four properties or "marks" of the Church which we profess in the Creed at Mass each Sunday: "We believe in one holy, catholic and apostolic Church." These four qualities flow from the very nature of the Church founded by Jesus Christ and in their fullness they belong exclusively to her.

When we speak of unity, sanctity, catholicity and apostolicity as the "four marks" of the Church we refer to them as the visible signs of the true Church of Christ, that is, the means of knowing for sure which is the true Church of Christ among those which claim this title. The point we want to make is that these four "marks" are found only in the Catholic Church.

When we say that the Catholic Church is "one" we are not only affirming that it is the only true Church of Christ, and therefore that all the other Christian bodies are defective in some way; we are also saying that the Church is undivided in itself, that it has internal and external unity. Internal unity is achieved through the possession of the Spirit that Jesus poured out on his Church on Pentecost and continues to pour out on those who believe and receive the sacraments. External unity is attained through the unity of doctrine, worship and government—all of which the Catholic Church has.

Fundamentally, "holiness" means the infinite fullness of the divine being, power and goodness. Human persons and things are said to be "holy" to the extent that they are attached to God. The Church is holy in her origin because she was founded by the God-Man and is animated by the Holy Spirit. She is holy in her purpose which is the glory of God and the salvation of men. The means she uses to attain her goal are holy: the Word of God contained in the Bible, the sacraments, the Holy Sacrifice of the Mass, her religious communities and her sacramentals. The Church is also holy in her fruits or results, that is, she is known from the holiness of those men and women who, filled with the faith of the Church, make full use of the means of grace and holiness put at their disposal by the Church. These are the "saints" of the Church, both canonized and uncanonized.

Catholic means "universal". The Church is Catholic both externally and internally. *Externally* the Church is a unified body that authentically derives from Jesus Christ and is both in intention and in actuality spread throughout the world. *Internally* the Church of Christ is endowed with all the supernatural means (Gospel, grace, sacraments) necessary to effect the eternal salvation of all people at all times in every land.

The Church is catholic in the sense that she was destined by Christ for all men of all times and places. Seen in this light the Church can be said to be qualitatively universal. But that would not be convincing if the Church were not also in some sense quantitatively or actually universal. St. Paul even in his day (about 58 A.D.) could speak of the Faith as being known throughout the whole world. With the mass media that is more true today than ever before.

The apostolicity of the Church means that she is essentially identical everywhere and since the time of St. Peter with the Church of the Apostles. Apostolicity is manifested in three ways: 1) by the Church's apostolic origin, that is, she was founded by Christ on the Apostles and through them; 2) by her apostolic doctrine, that is, the identity of her faith with that preached by the Apostles; 3) by her apostolic succession, that is, the uninterrupted chain of legitimate bishops who link the Church of the Apostles with the Church of today.

Apostolicity roots the Church in historical events that have occurred in a certain place at a definite time. She alone claims to possess, in the person of the pope in Rome, the power of the keys that Jesus Christ conferred on St. Peter and his successors for all time. Historically, she has always acted in this confidence.

The four marks or notes of unity, sanctity, catholicity and apostolicity are not just hidden characteristics; they are also external, recognizable signs of the true Church of Christ. Thus, Pope Pius IX declared: "The true Church of Christ, by virtue of Divine authority, is constituted and is knowable by the four characteristics, which we confess in the Creed as an object of the Faith" (*Denzinger-Schönmetzer* 2888).

19

WHO ARE MEMBERS OF THE CHURCH?

A little earlier in this book, when I explained that the Catholic Church is the Mystical Body of Christ, I defined the Church as "a supernatural union of men in Christ, which is based on the vital influence of the Holy Spirit and on the external bonds of the same faith, sacraments and government".

We should recall that Pope Pius XII, in his 1943 encyclical letter *The Mystical Body of Christ*, taught the identity between the Catholic Church and the Mystical Body: "In order to define and describe this true Church, which is the holy, Catholic, apostolic, Roman Church, nothing can be found more noble, more excellent, more divine, than that pronouncement, by which it is called 'the Mystical Body of Christ' " (no. 13).

Vatican II repeated the same doctrine: "The society equipped with hierarchical offices and the Mystical Body of Christ . . . are not to be considered as two things, but they form one complex reality, which combines the human and the divine elements" (Constitution on the Church, no. 8).

I raise the point about the equivalence between the Church and the Mystical Body of Christ because I want to say a few things about the very difficult question of who belongs to the Church. This problem is often approached under the aspect of membership. From this point of view, the question is often asked: Who are the *members* of the Church?

Some theologians have maintained that a person can be a member of the Mystical Body of Christ and remain outside the Catholic Church, that is, not be a member of the Church. That idea was explicitly rejected by Pope Pius XII.

According to the documents of the Second Vatican Council, there seems to be a difference between *membership in the Church in the true and strict sense*, and various ways of being *linked or related to* the true Church of Christ.

According to the long-standing tradition and teaching of the Church, in order to be truly and strictly a member of the Church and of the Mystical Body, one must receive Baptism and keep the resulting union of faith, government and worship, which can be broken by heresy, schism or excommunication. It is the constant and explicit teaching of the Magisterium that Baptism is the door of the Church and the means by which a person becomes a member of the Church or the Mystical Body.

In order to keep membership in the Church one must maintain the unbroken union of faith, government and worship. These are the necessary consequences of Baptism. Pope Pius IX explicitly said that non-Catholic religious groups are not members of the Church founded by Christ (Apostolic Letter *Iam Vos Omnes*, 1868, *Denzinger* 2997f.).

To this point Pius XII said: "Only those must be considered as members of the Church, who have received the bath of regeneration, who profess the true faith, and have not miserably withdrawn from the union of the Body

144

nor have been separated from it by the legitimate authority on account of very serious offenses" (*The Mystical Body of Christ*, no. 21, *Denzinger* 3802). Vatican II states: "Those are *fully incorporated* into the society of the Church, who . . . are joined to Christ in the Church's visible structure, that is, through the bonds of the profession of faith, of the sacraments, and of the ecclesiastical government and communion" (Constitution on the Church, no. 14).

By the words "fully incorporated" the Council seems to imply that there is also some kind of imperfect incorporation into the Church that applies to those who are not full members. This will be developed in more detail in the next chapter.

From the above we can conclude that the following types of persons are certainly not members of the Church in the true and strict sense: all non-baptized persons, formal and public heretics and schismatics, and those who have been solemnly excommunicated as persons to be avoided by Catholics.

It should be noted here, however, that all other Catholic sinners—no matter how evil they might be— certainly remain members of the Church. The reason for this is that they still have the faith; they still recognize the authority of the Church and are free to participate in her worship. (They show this when they go to confession and have their sins absolved.)

Those who remain in mortal sin lack sanctifying grace and so are cut off from the fullness of the divine life. As such they are like dead members of the body. But the Holy Spirit can still influence them and bring them to conversion. This is a type of spiritual resurrection through which the dead members of the Church are brought back to life spiritually.

20

"OUTSIDE OF THE CHURCH THERE IS NO SALVATION"

Having pondered the difficult question about who are the members of the Church, we will now take up the thorny matter of the necessity of the Church for eternal salvation, or the obligation to belong to the Church. It is a solemn teaching of the Catholic faith that membership in the Church is necessary for all men in order to be saved.

The proposition: "Outside of the Church there is no salvation" can be traced all the way back to the third century in the writings of Origen and St. Cyprian. Since that time it has been repeated many times in official documents of councils and popes. Thus, the Fourth Lateran Council in 1215 declared: "There is but one universal Church of the faithful outside which no one at all is saved" (*Denzinger* 430). The same doctrine was proclaimed by the Council of Florence (1438–45), Popes Boniface VIII and Pius IX, and by the Holy Office in 1949 in the famous case of Fr. Leonard Feeney, S.J.

Opposing contemporary religious indifferentism, Pius IX stated the Catholic teaching clearly: "By Faith it is to be firmly held that outside the Apostolic Roman Church none can achieve salvation. This is the only ark of salvation. He who does not enter into it, will perish in the flood. Nevertheless equally certain it is to be held that those who suffer from invincible ignorance of the true religion are not for this reason guilty in the eyes of the Lord" (*Denzinger* 1647).

The Church is a necessary means of salvation. The Lord does more than politely suggest that men and women should belong to the Church he founded on St. Peter, the Rock. In order to reach eternal salvation one must belong to the Church. For Jesus told his Apostles before his Ascension into heaven: "Go out to the whole world; proclaim the Good News to all creation. He who believes and is baptized will be saved; he who does not believe will be condemned" (Mk 16:15–16).

We must be very careful, however, to understand "Outside of the Church there is no salvation" the way the Catholic Church understands it. It certainly does not mean that only those are saved who are physically baptized in the Catholic Church and remain in it until their death. This is suggested by Pius IX when he speaks of those who remain "outside" the Church because of their "invincible ignorance" and are therefore not guilty in the eyes of the Lord. Those are invincibly ignorant of the necessity of the Church who have never heard the gospel or, having heard it, do not see that it logically requires their membership in the Holy Roman Catholic Church.

For those who are truly invincibly ignorant, actual membership in the Church can be replaced by a desire or longing for the Church. We find this "desire" *explicitly* present in catechumens who are seeking baptism. But it is also *implicitly* present in all those who are faithfully trying to carry out the will of God for them to the best of their ability. In this way even those who are in fact outside the Catholic Church can achieve eternal salvation.

The maxim: "Outside of the Church there is no salvation" must be reconciled with the revealed truth that God desires the salvation of all men (see 1 Tim 2:4). Accordingly, the recent Magisterium has softened the apparent rigor of the maxim by declaring that one can be saved outside the Church by reason of his subjective disposition and good faith, and also of his unconscious desire and connection with the Church. This position was expressed by Pius IX, by Pius XII in his encyclical letter on the Mystical Body, and by the Holy Office in the Leonard Feeney case.

The full sense of the maxim, therefore, implies the following: 1) since the Church is the Mystical Body of Christ, all the means of salvation are found only in the Church, and so only in the Church are men and women regularly and commonly saved (see Vatican II, Ecumenism, no. 3). 2) All means of salvation *belong* to the Catholic Church, even those that are found accidentally outside the social structure of the Church, such as, for example, Holy Scripture, Baptism, Eucharist (see Vatican II, Constitution on the Church, no. 8). 3) Therefore, all those who are supernaturally helped by God and all those who are saved outside the Catholic Church belong in one way or another to her and they are connected with her at least by an implicit desire (see Vatican II, Constitution on the Church, no. 15; Holy Office re Fr. Leonard Feeney, *Denzinger* 3870).

By admitting that non-Catholics in good faith, in virtue of their connection with or desire for the true Church, can be and are saved, the Church has not fallen into religious indifferentism. Her understanding has developed, as shown in the writings of Pope Pius XII and in the documents of Vatican II, with regard to the influence of God's grace on all mankind.

21

THE COMMUNION OF SAINTS

The Catholic Church is often called "the communion of saints". We are all familiar with this expression because it appears at the end of the Apostles' Creed, which we learned in our childhood and which we say at the beginning of the Rosary: "I believe in the Holy Spirit, the Holy Catholic Church, *the communion of saints*. . . ." Let us reflect now for a few moments on the meaning of this expression because it contains, at least implicitly, many of the essential elements of the Catholic faith.

When the Church is referred to as "the communion of saints", what is meant is the community of all the faithful in Christ—those on earth, those in purgatory and those in heaven. The community embraces all those redeemed and sanctified by the grace of Jesus Christ. *Church* in this sense transcends the earthly limits of time and space and reaches into the non-temporal life with God.

The communion of saints is a vital fellowship between all the redeemed, on earth and in the next life, that is based on the common possession of the divine life of grace that comes to us through the risen Christ. Awareness of this revealed reality helps us overcome the narcissistic individualism that is so common in our modern culture.

The communion of saints also involves a mutual communication and exchange of supernatural goods (prayers, merits) between the faithful living on earth (Church militant) and those who died in peace with God, and are either in purgatory (Church suffering) or in heaven (Church triumphant). Since all are united together in a common supernatural life that comes from Jesus Christ through his Spirit, all are able to share that life with one another and so can help one another.

The expression "communion of saints" first appeared in the fifth century and seems to have been included in the Apostles' Creed about that time. From earliest times it carried a double meaning, since the Latin *communio sanctorum* can mean both "common possession of sacred realities", and "fellowship of the saints", that is, of all redeemed persons.

The idea behind the phrase "communion of saints" is surely based on Holy Scripture. Jesus said that those who believe in him should be joined together in a unity modeled on his own unity with the Father. Thus, we read in John 17:21, "May they all be one. Father, may they be one in us, as you are in me and I am in you." He also said that he is the vine and we are the branches; the branches live in virtue of the life drawn from the vine (see Jn 15:1–8). The same idea is contained in St. Paul's treatment of Christ as the head of the body which is the Church, while we are the members that suffer together and rejoice together (see 1 Cor 12:25–27).

Coming down to more recent times, Pope Pius XII in his letter on the Mystical Body of Christ had this to say about our mutual sharing in sacred realities: "There can be no good and virtuous deed performed by individual members of the Mystical Body of Christ which does not, through the Communion of Saints, redound also to the welfare of all." It is clear, therefore, that there is a spiritual commonwealth among all the members of the Mystical Body. It embraces all the graces acquired by Jesus Christ and all the good works of the faithful which are performed with the help of his grace.

It is a basic principle of Catholic theology that the norm of praying is the norm for believing (*lex orandi lex credendi*). Among Catholics, faith in the communion of saints from the very beginning found practical expression in the intercessory prayer which was offered in the liturgy for the living and the dead. St. Paul and many of the Fathers of the Church exhort the faithful to pray for themselves and for others.

We see this tradition reflected in the Canon of the Mass, Eucharistic Prayer III, where we invoke Mary and the other saints "on whose constant intercession we rely for help." It also comes into play in the "Prayer of the Faithful" which is now an integral part of the Mass between the Liturgy of the Word and the Liturgy of the Eucharist.

You will find an extended treatment of the Church's belief in the communion of saints in the Vatican II Constitution on the Church, numbers 49–51. There the Council explains that we members of the Church can help one another in a horizontal way because we all share in the divine life of Jesus Christ and his Spirit which is communicated to us through faith and the sacraments, especially the Holy Eucharist.

22

MASTERPIECES OF GOD'S GRACE

The practice of Our Lord and of SS. Peter and Paul with
regard to praying for members of the Church on earth,
the early veneration of the Christian martyrs, and the
constant tradition of the Church of invoking the intercession of the saints in heaven, are living examples to us.
We should pray for one another. We should also venerate
the saints in heaven and invoke their intercession.

The pious practice of veneration of the saints was a
trademark of Catholics in the early Church and perdured
up until the time of the Reformation. Along with the
rejection of purgatory, the Protestant Reformers also
rejected the ancient tradition of invoking the intercession
of the saints. This applied equally to devotion to the
Blessed Virgin Mary. They maintained that, since Jesus
Christ is the only mediator between God and man, it is
not only useless to pray to the saints but also an offense
against the majesty of Christ.

In order to state clearly for all time the Catholic
position on the saints, the Council of Trent declared: "It
is a good and useful thing to invoke the saints humbly
and to have recourse to their prayers and their efficacious
help to obtain favors from God through his Son Jesus

Christ our Lord who alone is our redeemer and savior" (*Denzinger* 984).

The Bible does not explicitly refer to the veneration and invocation of saints, but it does assert the principle out of which Church teaching and practice developed. There are clear examples of veneration of angels in the Old Testament (see Dan 8:17; Tob 12:16). The basis for the veneration of angels is found in their personal dignity which is rooted in their immediate vision of God (see Mt 18:10). Like the angels, the saints are in immediate union with God (1 Cor 13:12; 1 Jn 3:2). Therefore we should venerate them just as we do the angels.

Since, according to Revelation 5:8 and 8:3, the angels and saints lay the prayers of the holy on earth at the feet of God and support them with their own intercession, it is very reasonable that we should invoke their help.

The Christian martyrs were the first saints to be venerated by members of the Church. St. Augustine defended the practice against the accusation of those who said it amounted to the adoration of men. As justification for this veneration he mentioned imitation of their example, sharing in their merits, and the grace we receive from God because of their intercession.

The Reformers' objection that the veneration of the saints takes away from the mediatorship of Christ is not convincing, since the faithful know that the intercession of the saints is inferior to and subordinated to the one mediatorship of Christ because the power of their prayers depends solely on his redemptive merits. When we venerate the saints, therefore, we are really glorifying Christ whose grace was triumphant in them.

The saints are masterpieces of God's grace. When we honor them we are honoring their Creator, their Sanctifier and their Redeemer.

What about the veneration of relics of the saints? According to Catholic tradition it is a good and holy practice. Confirming this, the Council of Trent declared: "The sacred bodies of the holy martyrs and of other saints living with Christ . . . should be venerated by the faithful" (*Denzinger* 985). The reason for the veneration of relics is found in the fact that their bodies were temples of the Holy Spirit and that through them God bestows many benefits on the faithful. Many cures, both physical and spiritual, have been effected by relics. Thus, in the Acts of the Apostles we read about St. Paul that "handkerchiefs or aprons which had touched him were taken to the sick, and they were cured of their illnesses, and the evil spirits came out of them" (19:12). It is important to remember that veneration of relics is a relative veneration, that is, it refers really to the person of the saint who is in immediate union with God.

What about venerating images of the saints (pictures, statues, etc.)? The iconoclasts of the eighth century were opposed to it, as were the Reformers of the sixteenth century. The practice of venerating images of the saints developed strongly in the Greek Church during the fifth to seventh centuries. There is a long tradition to support it. The Council of Nicaea in 787 A.D. declared that it is permissible to set up "holy images" of Christ, Mary, angels and saints, and to show them a certain reverence. This is not the adoration due to God alone, but veneration and respect. The Council of Trent repeated the same points.

It is inspiring to find beautiful representations of Jesus, Mary, angels and saints in our churches and homes. The Church encourages their use so that we will strive to be more like the saints.

23

PRAYERS FOR THE
POOR SOULS IN PURGATORY

One of the most consoling aspects of the Church's teaching on the communion of saints is that there is an abiding sense of community among all the faithful in Christ—those on earth, those in purgatory and those in heaven. This means, among other things, that the living faithful on earth can come to the assistance of the poor souls in purgatory by offering up for them prayers, alms, sufferings and especially the Holy Sacrifice of the Mass.

Since Protestants do not believe in purgatory and since they seem to assume that Christians who die go directly to heaven, in their funerals they do not pray for the deceased. Rather, they pray for the surviving members of the dead person's family and for his or her friends.

The Catholic practice in the time of mourning is very different. Catholics pray fervently "for the repose of the soul" of the departed loved one. They offer up to God rosaries and various kinds of prayers. They have Masses said. This is an ancient Catholic practice that can be traced back to at least the second century; it is based on the Church's faith in the communion of saints and the capacity for mutual assistance between the members of the Mystical Body, whether still on earth or already in the life beyond the grave.

In late second century Judaism we find the conviction that those who had died with some sin on their soul could be helped by prayer and sacrifices of atonement. Thus, we read in 2 Macc 12:41–45 that Judas Maccabeus had prayers and sacrifices offered to God for his fallen soldiers: "This is why he had this atonement sacrifice offered for the dead, so that they might be released from their sin" (verse 45). Christians then took over from Judaism belief in the power of prayers of intercession for the dead.

Ancient Christian tomb inscriptions from the second and third centuries frequently contain an appeal for prayers for the dead.

After more than a thousand years of Catholic devotion, the Second Council of Lyons in 1274 finally officially codified Catholic doctrine in the matter: "If those who are truly penitent die in charity before they have done sufficient penance for their sins of omission or commission, their souls are cleansed after death in purgatorial or cleansing punishments. . . . The suffrages of the faithful on earth can be of great help in relieving these punishments, as for instance, the Sacrifice of the Mass, prayers, almsgiving and other religious deeds which, in the manner of the Church, the faithful are accustomed to offer for others of the faithful" (*Denzinger* 464). The same doctrine was confirmed by the Council of Florence in the fifteenth century and by Vatican II (Constitution on the Church, no. 51).

In Church terminology prayers for the poor souls in purgatory are often called "suffrages"—a word derived from the Latin *suffragium* which means "supplication". The way suffrages work is that the satisfactory value of prayers and good works is offered to God in substitution for the temporal punishments for sins, which the poor souls still have to render. God accepts the offerings and because of them remits all or a portion of the temporal punishments due to sins—depending on the spiritual value of the work offered and on the subjective disposition (informed by charity) of the one making the offering. All of this is made possible by the unity of the Mystical Body of Christ which is brought into being by grace and charity.

Another consequence of the communion of saints is that those in heaven can help the poor souls in purgatory by their prayers. The saints can no longer gain merits before God as we can, but they are able to petition God by their prayers that he have mercy on the poor souls.

Since the poor souls are members of the Mystical Body and are assured of their eternal salvation, the question has been raised about whether or not they can intercede for other suffering souls and for the faithful here on earth. Even though famous theologians of the past have been divided on the point, there is a very old custom among Catholics of invoking the help of the poor souls in purgatory. The Church does not encourage the practice, but she has also never condemned it. This means that one may, in good conscience, not only pray for but also to the poor souls.

What about suffrages for the damned in hell? Can we help them in any way by praying for them or offering Masses for them? It has been the common opinion among theologians that prayers for the damned cannot help them. They do not belong to the Mystical Body and they cannot repent. St. Thomas Aquinas, following Pope St. Gregory the Great, teaches that suffrages for the damned are of no avail to them and that it is not the intention of the Church to pray for them (see *Summa Theologica*, Supplement 71, 5).

24

CHURCH AND WORLD

For over a century, in fact since the end of Vatican Council I in 1870, popes, theologians and Catholic intellectuals have been very interested in the nature and purpose of the Church. To a large extent Vatican II was a council about the Church. All sixteen documents deal with one or another aspect of the Church; two of the most important documents are the Dogmatic Constitution on the Church and the Pastoral Constitution on the Church in the Modern World.

In this section we have been considering the Catholic doctrine about the nature and purpose of the one Church founded by Jesus Christ. We saw that the Church is the faithful of the whole world, united into a universal community of the same faith, worship and government. We saw that the Church is a perfect society with her own spiritual, supernatural end; she is also fully equipped with all the spiritual means necessary for the attainment of that end.

In this final essay on the Church I would like to point out that the Mystical Body of Christ, because it is a society of men and women with a visible and social structure, lives and acts in a wider world. Her activity, therefore, reaches beyond the purely interior and spiritual dimension of Christian faith into the external environment of the world at large. So the activity of the Church is both human and social, and religious and supernatural.

The Church's activity in the modern world can be aptly referred to as Christian humanism. This means that the Church is concerned about man's whole welfare—both in this temporal world and in the eternal world to come.

Since she is a perfect society with her own divinely-given purpose, the Church claims the inherent right of acquiring, owning and administering temporal goods, freely and independently from the civil authority. She also has the right of obliging the faithful to support the divine worship, the ministers of the Church and other Church activities. The Church also claims a special right of deciding in mixed or overlapping matters which concern both Church and State, especially with regard to marriage and education. The norms for these points are found in the Code of Canon Law.

The Church also has a mission in the social order. She has the right and duty from Christ himself to proclaim her true and divinely revealed doctrine to all mankind and to apply that doctrine to contemporary problems and so give moral guidance. She does this both by correcting errors in current philosophical, ethical, economic and political doctrines, and by positively teaching the principles that are the basis for a philosophy or economics or social order that is authentically Christian.

The above is important and essential to the mission of the Church, but we must never forget that it is secondary. The primary activity of the Church in the world is religious and supernatural. In order to come into being and to expand on earth, the Church must be missionary; she must send preachers of the gospel to pagan countries, to make converts and to establish new Christian communities. She has a solemn command from the Lord Jesus to do this (see Mt 28:19). How the gospel should be spread today was explained by Vatican II in its Decree on the Church's Missionary Activity and also by Pope Paul VI in his encyclical letter on evangelization (1975).

Since Vatican II the Church has become involved in ecumenical activity with regard to the non-Catholic Christian world. Previous to the Council, ecumenism was mainly a Protestant phenomenon. During the Council the Bishops came to the realization that division among Christians is a scandal to the world and that positive steps should be taken to bring about the unity of Christians. To this end the Council, while stressing the oneness of Christ's Church, recommended dialogue with the other churches; it also said that charity and truthfulness should characterize our dealings with each other. Good will is to be presumed on both sides. Because of the seriousness of the split and the importance of unity, all are urged to pray for Christian unity. At present we do not see how it can be attained so we put our trust in the Lord and beg him to bring it about.

The Church of Jesus Christ is the only ark of salvation. Her purpose is to assist us to attain eternal life in heaven, with the Father, the Son and the Holy Spirit. She is also called the Mystical Body, kingdom of God, People of God, the Spouse of Christ and the New Jerusalem. These names point to her spiritual and supernatural purpose and in their own way relate the "pilgrim Church" to that heavenly Jerusalem that will be established forever when Christ comes in his glory at the end of the world.

PART III

THE SACRAMENTS

I

A SACRAMENT IS A SACRED SIGN

There is much more to the Christian belief in the sacraments than a brief definition of what we mean by a
sacrament and a list of the seven acts of faith that fulfill
the definition. The whole life of the Church takes place
in and through the sacraments of the New Covenant.
Without the sacraments there would be no Church, no
Christian community, no direct, certain contact with the
healing and sanctifying power of almighty God.

In the following essays I will attempt to explain the
Church's teaching on the sacraments in a way that will
be readily intelligible to the busy lay Catholic. For those
who studied their faith carefully in high school or college
it is intended to be a helpful refresher. For those who
do not know much about the sacraments and perhaps
sometimes wonder why the Church lays such stress
on them, the essays will offer a basic instruction or
catechesis in the faith of the Church as it pertains to the
grace-filled acts of Christ in human history, namely, the
seven sacraments.

Let us begin, then, with an explanation of what we mean by the word "sacrament". It is very important at the outset to stress that a sacrament is a *sign* or *symbol* of something else. It is an outward sign of the inner, mysterious activity of Jesus Christ in sanctifying and saving men and women. Thus, the washing with water, along with the words "I baptize you in the name of the Father and of the Son and of the Holy Spirit", is an external sign of an interior, spiritual transformation that is effected by the plan and power of God.

The English word "sacrament" is borrowed from the Latin word *sacramentum*, which literally means "a sacred or holy thing", coming from the verb *sacrare*. In Roman profane literature the loyalty oath taken by a soldier, which required an invocation of the pagan gods, and oaths in general were called *sacramenta*. In Roman law, when two parties disputed over a sum of money, it was placed in a temple until the conflict was resolved. The word *sacramentum* was used in legal language to refer to that money.

The Greek word for sacrament is *mustyrion* (English = mystery). The original Greek word means something hidden or secret. In the Old Testament it is used to refer to the secrets of God. St. Paul used the word in speaking about the "mystery" of our redemption in Jesus Christ (see Eph 1:9; Col 1:26ff.). It has the further meaning of a sign or symbol of some divine reality; for example, Paul speaks of marriage as a symbol of the mysterious bond between Christ and his Church in Ephesians 5:32. When St. Jerome in the fourth century translated the Greek New Testament into Latin, in the version known as the Vulgate, he chose the Latin word *sacramentum* as the proper and exact rendition of the Greek word *mustyrion*.

In agreement with the usage of Scripture, the Fathers of the Church applied the word *sacramentum* to the Christian religion as a whole, to the individual doctrines, and also to the various liturgical acts such as Baptism and the Eucharist. It was not until the twelfth century that the Catholic theologians succeeded in formulating the definition of a sacrament—the definition that most Catholics now living were taught from childhood or learned at their first instructions. Once the Church attained a clear notion of the nature of a sacrament, she was able to look at her history and practice and there she found that there are only *seven* official acts of the Church that fulfilled that definition. Of course the Church had always administered the seven sacraments, but there were also other acts of the Church related to the sanctification of the faithful. A clear distinction between those instituted by Christ and those instituted by the Church was not made until the definition was attained in the twelfth century. Thus, before the twelfth century there was much speculation on how many "holy acts" of the Church there might be. One theologian went so far as to list eighteen of them, including such things as reading Scripture, fasting, taking vows and going on a pilgrimage.

In the early fifth century St. Augustine made a significant theological breakthrough when he saw that a sacrament is a "sacred sign". He also described a sacrament as "a sign pertaining to divine things" and "a visible sign of invisible grace".

Two outstanding theologians in the early scholastic period, Hugh of St. Victor (d. 1141) and Peter Lombard (d. 1160), perfected the incomplete definition of St. Augustine by adding the notion that a sacrament is not just a sign but also a "cause of grace" in the soul of the believer. When that point had been reached it was not long before the theologians saw that the notion is verified in seven, and only seven, saving acts of the Church.

2

WHAT CONSTITUTES A SACRAMENT?

We began our treatment of the sacraments by pointing out that a sacrament is a "sign" of some kind. A sign is one thing that leads us to the knowledge of another thing. For example, road signs tell us how to get to our destination; in the order of nature, smoke is a sign of fire. Likewise, a sacrament is an outward sign instituted by Christ to give sanctifying grace.

There are three basic elements that constitute a sacrament of the Church:

1) An external, sensibly perceptible sign of sanctifying grace. This is illustrated by Baptism, since the person being baptized must be touched by flowing water, either by pouring or by immersion.

2) A sign that causes grace. The sacraments signify sanctifying grace, the divine life of the soul. The sacraments, however, are totally different from all other signs in this, that they not only signify something else

(namely, divine grace) but they also *give it*, *confer it* or *cause it* in the soul of the recipient.

3) Instituted by Christ. The third basic element in a sacrament is institution by the God-Man, Jesus Christ. This is important because it means that God wills to communicate himself to man in and through certain definite outward signs. Because the sacraments were instituted by Christ, the Church as the People of God or the community of the faithful comes into existence. The Church did not invent the sacraments; rather, she received them from her divine Founder. Jesus, however, was not as precise with regard to all the sacraments as he was with Baptism and the Eucharist. The Church does have something to say about the matter and the words in those sacraments where Jesus left the details to the decision of the Apostles and their successors.

It should be obvious why it is appropriate to refer to the sacraments as "sacred signs". For they are signs of something very holy, namely, sanctifying grace, or, to use other words, of God himself working in those who receive the sacraments with faith. But they are also called "sacred signs" because they not only signify divine grace but also cause grace to be present in the soul.

On this point there is and has been a basic disagreement between Catholics and most Protestants since the time of the Reformation in the sixteenth century. By reason of their doctrine of justification or salvation, the Reformers, Luther and Calvin, looked upon the sacraments as pledges of the divine promise of the forgiveness of sins by means of the awakening and strengthening of fiducial faith. According to them, faith alone justifies. Thus, in their view the sacraments are not means whereby grace is conferred, but means whereby faith is stirred into action. For the Reformers, therefore, the sacraments have only a psychological and symbolic meaning. They did not look upon them as causes of grace.

The Council of Trent in the sixteenth century rejected this teaching of the Protestants. The Council declared: "If anyone says that these sacraments were instituted only for the sake of nourishing the faith: let him be anathema" (cf. *Denzinger-Schönmetzer* 1605).

Some modern liberal theologians, especially among German Protestants, have looked upon the sacraments as mere imitations of the pagan mystery-cults which were widespread among the Greeks and Romans during the time of Christ and the Apostles. According to this view, then, there is nothing original about the Christian sacraments—they are merely adaptations of rites borrowed from others. In both instances they are mere human creations and so do not put man in direct contact with God.

Some Catholics at the beginning of this century, usually called "Modernists", denied that the sacraments were immediately instituted by Christ. They considered them to be man-made symbols of certain religious feelings, but in no sense to be instituted by God or to be causes of divine grace. These views were strongly condemned by Pope St. Pius X in 1907.

According to Catholic belief and practice for almost two thousand years, God comes to us hidden under the humble veils of bread, wine, water, oil and fleeting human words. If you stop to think about it, this is truly amazing! The more we reflect on the wonders involved in the seven sacraments, the more we should praise God for his wisdom and his goodness.

3

THE OUTWARD SIGN

It has been pointed out that a sacrament is an outward sign instituted by Christ to give grace. When we define a sacrament as an "outward sign" we are saying, in effect, that it is something external, visible, perceptible to the senses. If that is so, then there must be some element or some material involved in each of the seven sacraments. And so there is, as we shall see. Accordingly, the sacraments of Christ are not just interior, invisible, spiritual or mental acts of some kind that take place in the inner recesses of the human spirit.

For many centuries the Church has spoken of the sacramental rites as consisting of two parts: matter and form. It is easy to note that holy Scripture makes reference to two elements in five of the sacraments (see Eph 5:26; Jn 3:5; Mt 28:19). The early Fathers speak of these two elements as objects (e.g., water, wine, bread, oil) and the prayers that sanctified them. St. Augustine said that "the word comes to the element and a sacrament results." During the twelfth and thirteenth centuries, a time of systematization in theology and of growing influence from the thought of Aristotle, the terms "element" and "word" were replaced with "matter" and "form".

The latter terminology was officially adopted by the Church in the fifteenth century. Thus, the Council of Florence in 1439 said: "All these sacraments are brought to completion by three components; by the things as matter, by the words as form, and by the person of the minister effecting the sacrament with the intention of doing what the Church does." Further, the Council of Trent in 1551 declared: "Moreover, this sacrament [Penance] is recognized as differing from Baptism in many ways. For besides the fact that the matter and form making up the essence of the sacrament are very different . . ." (*Denzinger-Schönmetzer* 1671).

When speaking of the sacraments, then, the term "matter" refers to the sensible objects used, while the term "form" refers to the words or formulae. This is evident in Baptism. For during the rite, water is poured over the head of the one receiving the sacrament while the priest says: "I baptize you in the name of the Father and of the Son and of the Holy Spirit." Thus, in every sacramental action, the meaning of the sensible objects used (matter) is determined by the words (form). Together the two elements compose the one sacramental sign. In the life of the Church, by the will of Christ, there are only seven such sacramental signs, each being distinct and different from the others.

Scholastic theology, especially as developed by St. Thomas Aquinas in the thirteenth century, has profoundly influenced the teaching of the Church with regard to the sacraments. The Scholastics developed the notions of matter and form as applied to the sacraments. They also went further and distinguished between the outward sacramental sign, the inner conferral of sanctifying grace and, in three sacraments (Baptism, Confirmation and Orders), the permanent "mark" on the soul which they referred to as the "character" of the sacrament.

Unfortunately, from the seventeenth to the twentieth centuries, Catholic moral theology tended to function quite independently of dogmatic or doctrinal theology. One result of this separation was that a certain "minimalism" set in with regard to the popular understanding of the sacraments. By that I mean, there was much emphasis on the minimal requirements with regard to matter and form in order to be sure about the *validity* of the sacraments. In this approach, validity tended to overshadow the full meaning of the sacraments as participation in the death, resurrection and glorification of the Lord Jesus.

Much of the theological work in this century before the Second Vatican Council was directed to reviving the full meaning and richness of the sacraments. The Council, in its Constitution on the Sacred Liturgy (1963), directed that the rites of the seven sacraments should be reformed so that the full meaning might be brought out to all the participants. That work is now happily ended. However, it will take many years for the Catholic people to absorb the changes and to come to a deeper appreciation of the full meaning of the renewed rites.

4

THE SACRAMENTS CONTAIN
AND CAUSE GRACE

In the past few essays I stressed the fact that the sacraments are signs. Now I would like to concentrate on the teaching of the Church that the sacraments, in a very mysterious way, contain the grace which they signify and actually bestow it on those who do not place any obstacles in the way.

The Reformers looked upon the sacraments as having only a psychological efficacy, that is, according to them, the sacraments are symbolic rites that stir up a subjective faith in the one who receives them. Thus, in their view, it is this subjective faith, or "fiducial faith" (which is an internal, mental conviction of being saved by Jesus Christ) that causes grace in the soul and thereby effects justification and sanctification. The Council of Trent in the sixteenth century rejected that view of the Protestants and taught that the sacraments have an objective efficacy, that is, an efficacy independent of the personal, subjective disposition of the recipient or the minister.

Let us listen to the Council of Trent: "If anyone says that the sacraments of the New Law do not contain the grace which they signify or that they do not confer that grace upon those who do not place an obstacle to its reception . . . let him be anathema." And again: "If anyone says that, as far as God's part is concerned, grace is not given through these sacraments always and to everybody, even if they receive the sacraments correctly, but only sometimes and to some people: let him be anathema" (*Denzinger* 1606, 1607).

It follows from the teaching of Trent that the sacraments confer grace immediately. However, it is also true that, in the adult recipient, faith is a necessary pre-condition. But the whole point to the Catholic teaching is that it is not faith that causes grace, but the sacraments.

In another place the Council of Trent defined that the sacrament of Baptism is an instrumental cause of grace (*Denzinger* 1529). An "instrumental cause" is one that truly influences the effect, but receives its full power from a higher agent. For example, tools are instruments. A carpenter uses a saw to cut wood. Depending on the kind of saw used, the result will be different. The carpenter does the same sawing with the saw, but the saw also contributes something to the effect. There is something similar in the activity of the sacraments. According to the will of God, as manifested to us through his only Son, Jesus Christ, he wishes to communicate his grace to us through or by means of the sacraments. Thus the sacraments are true causes, albeit instrumental ones.

Thus, in a very true sense Trent said that "the sacraments contain grace". This does not mean that they contain grace in the same way that a carton contains milk. Rather, it means that they can be and are used by God to communicate his grace to sinful men.

The Fathers ascribe the sanctification of the soul immediately to the sacramental sign, particularly stressing the power of the water in Baptism to bring about inner sanctity. As a matter of fact, the practice of infant baptism, which goes back to early Christianity, is a definite proof that the efficacy of Baptism was regarded as being independent of the personal activity of the person baptized.

In order to designate the objective efficacy of the sacraments, the scholastic theologians said that they work "ex opere operato", that is, "by the power of the completed sacramental rite". Trent accepted this terminology and incorporated it into official Catholic teaching (cf. *Denzinger* 1608). The expression is used in contradistinction to the subjective dispositions of the recipient. The formula "ex opere operato" says, negatively, that the sacramental grace is not conferred by reason of the subjective activity of the recipient, and positively, that grace is caused by the validly operated sacramental sign, provided that no obstacle (such as disbelief) is placed in its way.

Opponents of Catholicism have often ridiculed this notion, accusing us, falsely, of believing that the sacraments work automatically without any cooperation on our part. Thus they make the "ex opere operato" out to be something like a spiritual machine, or like a Coke machine: drop in a coin and out pops a beverage. Nothing could be further from the truth. Catholics do not attribute any "magic" to the sacraments.

The Church teaches that subjective preparation for the sacraments in the adult recipient is absolutely necessary. The special point, however, in this part of Catholic doctrine is that the subjective disposition of the recipient is not the cause of grace; rather, as I said above, it is a necessary pre-condition. Moreover, the measure of the grace effected "ex opere operato" also depends on the intensity of the subjective disposition. Trent said that in the reception of the sacraments we receive grace according to the measure given by the Holy Spirit and "according to each one's own disposition and co-operation" (*Denzinger* 1529).

5

SACRAMENTAL GRACE

The purpose of the seven sacraments is to produce sanctifying grace or divine life in the person who receives them worthily. Baptism and Penance are called "the sacraments of the dead" because the former confers grace for the first time, while the latter restores sanctifying grace which has been lost through deliberate mortal sin. Thus, in both cases the soul is "dead" spiritually before the fruitful reception of the sacrament. The other five sacraments are often referred to as "the sacraments of the living", because they increase the sanctifying grace which is present in the soul—a soul which is already "alive" spiritually due to the reception of Baptism and perseverance in the love of God.

It is a dogma of the Catholic faith that all the sacraments of the New Covenant confer sanctifying grace on the receivers. For the Council of Trent teaches: "All true justification [i.e., sanctifying grace] either begins through the sacraments, or once begun, increases through them, or when lost is regained through them" (*Denzinger* 1600). As we have seen, according to the same Council the sacraments are infallibly effective in producing divine grace in the soul so long as the recipient is properly disposed.

The teaching of Trent and of other councils as well is based upon the testimony of Holy Scripture and the constant tradition of the Church. A number of passages point to grace (or the effects of sanctifying grace) as the result of the sacraments. Thus, according to the second letter to Timothy, 1:6, the effect of St. Paul's imposition of hands (i.e., ordination) is "the grace of God". Other passages speak of the effect of the sacraments as "regeneration" (Jn 3:5), "purification" (Eph 5:26), "forgiveness of sins" (Jn 20:23), communication of the "Holy Spirit" (Acts 8:17) and the conferring of "eternal life" (Jn 6:54). The revelation of God made known to us in these and many other passages was systematized by the theologians and incorporated into official Catholic teaching by the Council of Trent. It has been and still remains part of the living teaching of the Church.

In these essays I will try, as much as possible, to stay away from theological opinions that are far removed from what is necessary to understand the essentials of Catholic faith. At times, however, commonly accepted opinions which do contribute to that full understanding will be mentioned. One of them that fits in here concerns the notion of "sacramental grace". Sacramental grace is defined as the grace that is produced by the sacraments. The question that confronts the theologian and the

Catholic well educated in his faith is this: Since the seven sacraments all confer sanctifying grace, do they all confer the *same* sanctifying grace? Or is the grace given by each of the sacraments different?

If, by sanctifying grace, we mean the supernatural life of the soul—the eternal life of God communicated in a most mysterious way to the created soul who loves God, then, since there is only one God and one life of God, there can be only one sanctifying grace. So, in one sense, we can reply to our question by saying that the seven sacraments all confer the same sanctifying grace.

However, there is more to it than that. Clearly, God has instituted *seven* saving acts which we call "sacraments". God does not do anything superfluous. If there were absolutely no difference between the effects of the seven sacraments, then six of them would seem to be superfluous. But there is a difference between the seven sacraments: The seven sacramental signs or rites are very different from each other and each one performs a different function in the Mystical Body of Christ, the Church. We will see this more clearly as we work our way through the seven sacraments.

Suffice it to say for now that human life is multifaceted, complex, constantly changing. We encounter different problems at each stage of our life from the cradle to the grave. There are also different ways of living out our Christian life—in the married state, as a religious, as a priest, as a single person. At all stages of our life we need the help or grace of God—birth, puberty, marriage, old age, death. Thus, the sacraments have been given to us by God to help us share in his life at all the crucial stages in our lives. Accordingly, even though the same sanctifying grace is given in each of the sacraments, there are also extra helps or "side benefits" that accompany each of them. So "sacramental grace" includes both sanctifying grace and the title or claim to those extra helps or graces that go along with the fruitful reception of a sacrament. Thus, those who receive the sacrament of Matrimony not only receive an increase of sanctifying grace at the time of their marriage, but they also receive a certain pledge from God that he will help them to live out their commitment in a Christian way if they remain faithful to him.

6

SACRAMENTAL CHARACTER

We know from the constant tradition of the Church that three of the sacraments—Baptism, Confirmation and Holy Orders—can be validly received only once. Already in the third century Pope St. Stephen declared that apostates and those baptized by heretics, once they had repented and had expressed their desire to return to the Church, were to be reconciled by the "laying on of hands" and were by no means to be re-baptized. In this teaching he claimed to be merely repeating the tradition from the Apostles. Thus it is clear that from the earliest times it was recognized that Baptism could be validly received only once. The same notion was also later applied to Confirmation and Orders.

The Fathers of the Church saw in Scripture a basis for

the belief that Baptism affects the soul permanently and thus cannot be repeated. In support of this view they spoke of the effect of the sacrament as a "seal" or "mark" or "imprint", relying on the words of St. Paul: "Now it is God who is warrant for us and for you in Christ, who has anointed us, who has also stamped us with his seal and given us the Spirit as a pledge in our hearts" (2 Cor 1:21–22; see also Eph 1:13–14 and 4:30).

St. Augustine in the early fifth century was the first to refer to the permanent effect in the soul resulting from Baptism as a "character". He used the word "character" to describe the reality which underlies and helps explain the Church's belief and custom that Baptism, Confirmation and Orders are not to be repeated. Furthermore, the word was officially sanctioned both by popes and Councils in the Middle Ages so that it became a part of the ordinary catechesis of the Church in her teaching on the seven sacraments. Thus, at one time or another, most Catholics have at least heard about the sacramental character. Those who remember the basics of the catechism can tell you that it is "an indelible mark on the soul".

The word "character", which is Greek in origin, originally meant a mark carved or engraved on stone or metal as a sign of ownership. In contemporary culture a brand on cattle as a sign of ownership might be called a "character". Today each company has its own copyrighted "logo", imprinted on each of its products, as an indication of who produced it. It is like the familiar "Made in USA". The word also means a distinctive quality by which one thing is distinguished from all others.

Obviously, however, the human soul, which is spiritual and not material, cannot be marked or "branded" in the same way that material things like cattle can.

So the word "character", when applied to the effects of Baptism on the soul, is necessarily used in a figurative sense. Theologically, then, the sacramental character is an indelible seal or mark on the soul, produced by the sacraments of Baptism, Confirmation and Holy Orders.

There is no doubt about the existence of the sacramental character, since it was defined by the Council of Trent and so is to be held by divine faith: "If anyone shall say that in the three sacraments, namely, Baptism, Confirmation and Orders, there is not imprinted on the soul a sign, that is, a certain indelible mark, on account of which they cannot be repeated: let him be anathema" (*Denzinger* 1609). The character therefore is permanent in this life and, although the Church has never said so definitively, we have no reason to believe the character is lost after death.

For the curious mind, the question naturally arises here: What is the sacramental character for? What is its purpose? St. Thomas Aquinas, following Augustine, says that it is a "consecration", a designation for divine worship. Jesus Christ himself is the unique High Priest. Since all Christian worship flows from Christ's priesthood, the character is a participation in the priesthood of Christ and an assimilation to Christ the High Priest. Thus, it is a spiritual power conferred by Christ to receive or produce something sacred; for instance, the character of Holy Orders gives the recipient of the sacrament the power to consecrate the Eucharist.

St. Thomas sharpened the distinction between sanctifying grace and the character, clarifying the point that one can validly receive a sacrament and so the character, even though one does not receive the grace (for example, being confirmed while in a state of mortal sin). He pointed out that the sacraments have a two-fold effect: to take away sin and to perfect the soul in things pertaining to divine worship in the Christian religion. The character pertains to the latter, since it is "the seal of Christ as man" by which we are set apart for divine worship here on earth.

A sacramental character is a spiritual quality which gives the one who receives it a special position in the service of the Church. The indelible character received in Baptism enables one to receive the other sacraments; in Confirmation, the character enables one to profess the Christian faith before its enemies; in Holy Orders, the character enables one to confect the sacraments and to confer them on others.

7

CHRIST HIMSELF INSTITUTED THE SEVEN SACRAMENTS

We believe that the Church was founded by our Lord and Savior Jesus Christ. The salvific acts of Christ and the Church as the embodiment of the risen Christ are to be found in the seven sacraments. A question that has come up often since the revolt of Luther in the sixteenth century is whether the sacraments were instituted by Christ or whether, in the course of time, they were created by the Church in order to respond to the religious needs of the faithful. Many Protestant scholars since Luther have held that the sacraments were not instituted by Christ but by the Church. Similar ideas were espoused by some Catholic theologians toward the end of the nineteenth century and the beginning of the twentieth century. Those who held and hold such views are called "Modernists" in Church documents, and they were condemned on more than one occasion by Pope St. Pius X.

It is a dogma of the Catholic faith that all the sacraments of the Church were instituted by Jesus Christ. This truth was infallibly defined by the Council of Trent in the following words: "If anyone says that the sacraments of the New Law were not all instituted by Jesus Christ our Lord . . . let him be anathema" (*Denzinger* 1601).

We must remember what sacraments are. They are efficacious, visible signs of invisible grace. Since they produce divine grace in the soul, it follows that only God, the source of all grace—which is just another word for his own divine life—can institute a sacrament as its principal cause.

Although almost all Catholic theologians agree on the fact of Christ's institution of the sacraments, there is some disagreement as to the manner in which he accomplished this. Usually a distinction is made between a mediate and an immediate institution. The first refers to a situation in which Christ would have conferred the power of instituting the sacraments on the Apostles, leaving to them the right to determine the sign or form of the sacraments. Immediate institution means that Christ himself determined the meaning of the sacraments, that he gave at least some general indication of the rites to be used and instructed his Apostles to carry out his will.

Since the twelfth century some theologians (e.g., Hugo of St. Victor, St. Bonaventure) have held the view that Confirmation and the Anointing of the Sick were instituted by the Apostles under the inspiration of the Holy Spirit. However, following St. Albert the Great and St. Thomas Aquinas, most theologians have taught the doctrine of the immediate institution of all the sacraments by Christ.

We know from Holy Scripture the words by which Christ instituted Baptism (Mt 28:19), the Eucharist (Mt 26:26–28; Mk 14:22–24; Lk 22:19–20; 1 Cor 11:24f.), the sacrament of Penance (Mt 16:18f.; Jn 20:22f.) and Holy Orders as the power of the keys and the power of binding and loosing. The other sacraments, according to the testimony of tradition, were in existence in apostolic times. However, the Apostles assumed to themselves no right of institution, but regarded themselves merely as "ministers of Christ and dispensers of the mysteries of God" (1 Cor 4:1).

Accordingly, all the sacraments were immediately instituted by Christ our Lord. It follows from this that their substance or basic meaning is immutably fixed for all time. Thus, the Church does not have the power either to add new sacraments or to abolish one or all of the traditional ones. The Council of Trent teaches that the Church has always had the power to make changes in the administration and accidental rites of the sacraments, provided that she preserves "their substance unimpaired" (*Denzinger* 1728). This accords with the history of the Church during which a number of changes have been made in the administration of the sacraments.

In our own time we have witnessed a revision of the rites of all seven sacraments. For example, the Mass may now be said in the vernacular, face-to-face confession is now allowed, communion under both species is provided in certain circumstances and so forth. In 1947 Pope Pius XII made a number of significant changes in the rite of ordination, but at the same time he insisted that "the Church has no authority over the 'substance of the sacraments', that is, over the elements that Christ our Lord himself, according to the testimony of the sources of divine revelation, determined should be kept in the sacramental sign . . ." (*Denzinger* 3001).

Thus, we can see from the words of Scripture and from the constant practice of the Church that, although Christ instituted all seven sacraments before ascending into heaven, he did not completely specify the matter and form of all the sacraments as clearly and definitely as he did for Baptism and the Eucharist. Hence, Christ gave to his Apostles and to their successors the power to make certain determinations in the matter and form of some of the sacraments.

8

GOD DESIRES THE SALVATION OF ALL

We have seen that our Lord and Savior Jesus Christ instituted seven sacraments for the salvation of mankind. A question that has often arisen in the course of history, and one that is still asked, is this: Are the sacraments necessary for eternal salvation? The same idea may be expressed in other words: Can anyone outside the Church be saved?

The Church replies to this question by saying that the sacraments are indeed necessary for salvation. Since Christ himself instituted them and bound them up with the communication of divine grace, they are necessary to us for the achievement of salvation, even if not all are necessary for each individual. In the ordinary course of events, three of them are so necessary that without their use salvation cannot be attained. Thus, for the individual person, Baptism is necessary to enter the Church. Because of man's weakness, grievous sin remains possible, so Penance is required in order to regain grace that has been lost. For the Church in general, Holy Orders is necessary so that the sacraments will be available to all.

The other sacraments are necessary insofar as salvation cannot be easily gained without them. Thus, Confirmation is the completion of Baptism, and the Sacrament of the Sick in one of its effects completes Penance. Matrimony is the basis of the family which perpetuates the Church in history, while the Eucharist is the end or crown or summit of all the sacraments.

The sixteenth century Reformers denied the necessity of the sacraments for salvation, claiming that "faith alone" (*sola fides*) is sufficient. They attributed symbolic value only to the sacraments—as an aid to faith—and denied that they cause grace in the one who receives them. In response to this serious challenge the Council of Trent replied: "If anyone says that the sacraments of the New Law are not necessary for salvation, but that they are superfluous; and that men can, without the sacraments or the desire of them, obtain the grace of justification by faith alone, although it is true that not all the sacraments are necessary for each individual: let him be anathema" (*Denzinger* 1604). Therefore, the answer of the Church to our opening question is that the sacraments are necessary for salvation.

But what about the hundreds of millions of people who have never heard of Christ, who have never been baptized and so remain outside the Church and away from the sacraments? This is a very difficult theological problem that from time to time has stirred up much controversy in the Church. In the late 1940s there was much agitation over this question in Boston when Fr. Leonard Feeney, Director of St. Benedict's Center in Cambridge, Mass., persisted in his view that outside of the physical confines of the Catholic Church there is no salvation. Feeney based his case on the ancient and certain teaching that "outside the Church there is no salvation" (that is, *extra ecclesiam nulla salus*), but he understood it in a narrow or restricted way that was contrary to tradition.

In 1949 Pope Pius XII condemned the view of Fr. Feeney. Unfortunately, Feeney persisted in his view, refusing to recant, so he was finally excommunicated in 1953. However, twenty years later Fr. Feeney made a profession of Catholic faith and was received back into the Church.

The theological solution to this thorny problem is found in the notion of the "desire" of the sacraments—a phrase that was used by the Council of Trent and was repeated by Pius XII in his response to Fr. Feeney. The basic idea here is that the Church (with her seven sacraments) is the only way to salvation—so those who belong to her and remain faithful are saved while the rest are lost. In Christian art Noah's ark—the only means of surviving the flood—is often used as a symbol of the Church.

It must be recalled that God desires the salvation of all men and that all come to a knowledge of the truth (cf. I Tim 2:1–6). *All* have one Redeemer (I Tim 4:10) and the Word of God enlightens *all* (Jn 1:9). Since, obviously, all men do not yet belong visibly to the Church, it follows that God's grace is operative beyond the limits of the Catholic Church. Christ died for all men and offers all men his grace. We do not know in detail how he accomplishes this, but we are certain that God loves all men just as he makes his sun shine on the good and the evil.

So those who are not baptized into the Church, those who do not know about Christ and the Church are objects of God's grace. The point is that all grace is the grace of Christ and is given through the Church. Grace is also ordered to the Church and the sacraments. So those who follow God's will in their own state of life to the best of their ability can be said to have at least an *implicit desire* for the sacraments and the Church. Accordingly, even though they are "outside" the visible confines of the Church, by reason of the faith and love they have they are related to the Church in some way and so can attain to eternal salvation. In this sense, then, it remains true that outside of the Church and the sacraments there is no eternal salvation.

9

WHO CAN ADMINISTER
THE SACRAMENTS?

Our Lord instituted the seven sacraments and committed them to the care of the Apostles and their successors. When considering the sacraments it is important to note that the primary minister or the principal agent is Jesus Christ himself. It is Jesus, sending the Holy Spirit into our hearts, who sanctifies us in and through the sacraments. Obviously, as created material symbols they have no power to convey divine and eternal life to men independently of the power and will of God.

Jesus made this point very clear in his public life. He sent out his Apostles, armed with his power, to cure the sick and to drive out devils. After his resurrection and just before he gave his Apostles power to forgive sins, he said to them, "As the Father sent me, so am I sending you" (Jn 20:21; see also 17:18). St. Paul says that the human minister is only the servant and representative of Christ: "People must think of us as Christ's servants, stewards entrusted with the mysteries of God" (1 Cor 4:1).

A question naturally arises here about who can validly

administer the sacraments. Since the human minister acts as the representative of Christ (he is an "ambassador for Christ", 2 Cor 5:20), he requires for this purpose a special delegation of power by the Church of Christ. Thus, a special episcopal or priestly power, conferred by the sacrament of Holy Orders, is necessary for the valid administration of the sacraments, except for Baptism and Matrimony. In the latter the partners administer the sacrament to each other, while the priest or deacon witnesses it for the Church. In the former, since Baptism is necessary for eternal salvation, anyone can administer it in a case of necessity—laymen, women, children, and even non-believers, provided that they use the correct matter and form and at least have the intention of doing what the Church does.

In response to those who say that anyone can administer the sacraments, the Council of Trent explicitly rejected the opinion that "all Christians have the power to preach the word and to administer all the sacraments" (*Denzinger* 1610).

Beginning with the Donatists in the early fourth century in North Africa, over the centuries there have been various heretics with a "spiritualizing" tendency, such as the Waldenses, Wycliffians and Hussites, who have maintained that the validity of the sacraments depends on the faith and/or state of grace of the minister. In practice, this means that if the priest who administers Baptism, the Eucharist, Penance and so forth is in the state of mortal sin, then the sacraments are invalid. The Church has always reacted very strongly against such views, branding them as heretical. Thus Trent said very clearly: "If anyone says that a minister in a state of mortal sin, though he observes all the essentials that belong to effecting and conferring the sacrament, does not effect or confer the sacrament: let him be anathema" (*Denzinger* 1612).

Doubts about this point first arose in the third century in North Africa. There were severe persecutions at the time. Some bishops and priests, out of weakness, apostatized but still continued to administer the sacraments. Others fell into heresy and did the same. St. Cyprian of Carthage thought that the Baptism of heretics was invalid. Accordingly, he held that when they asked to be received into the Catholic Church they should be re-baptized. The matter went to Pope St. Stephen I who ruled in 256 that such people were not to be re-baptized but to be absolved from their sins, since the original Baptism was valid.

The error of the Donatists, who demanded not only orthodoxy but also the state of sanctifying grace in the minister for the valid administration of the sacraments, was rejected by St. Augustine. He argued that, since the primary minister of the sacraments is Christ himself who gives to the sacraments their objective efficacy, the validity and efficacy of the sacraments do not depend on the subjective condition of the minister, provided that he confers the sacramental sign with the intention of doing what the Church does. This follows from the instrumental relationship of the human minister to Christ the primary minister.

Of course, the minister is bound in conscience to administer the sacraments in a state of grace. In fact, to do otherwise is to commit a sin of sacrilege. However, a further reason why the valid administration of the sacraments is independent of the worthiness of the minister is to provide certainty and peace of conscience for the faithful. For if the validity of the sacraments was dependent on the faith and state of grace of the minister, the faithful who receive the sacraments would never know for certain whether or not they had really received them. For the faith and holiness of the minister are inner, subjective matters that cannot be discerned just by looking at a priest. Since Christ is the primary minister, he guarantees that all the sacraments, duly administered, are infallibly effective, even if the human minister is unworthy.

10

WHO CAN RECEIVE A SACRAMENT?

Since a sacrament is a visible sign that communicates divine grace through the senses, only a living human person, that is, a being composed of body and soul, is an appropriate subject for the reception of the sacraments. Thus, it should be obvious that animals cannot receive the sacraments. The same applies to dead human beings. I mention the dead in this context because in the course of history there have been groups who have believed in baptizing the dead and even giving them Holy Communion. Both of these practices have been forbidden by the Church.

Any living human person, therefore, is an apt subject for the reception of a sacrament, provided that he or she is properly disposed. The proper dispositions include faith, repentance of one's sins and the desire or intention to receive the sacrament in question. Thus, a baptism conferred in jest is invalid. Also, there must be freedom in the reception of the sacraments. There have been times in the history of the Church when overzealous political leaders have forced others to be baptized under threat of punishment or death. Pope Innocent III in the year 1201 declared that forced Baptism is invalid.

There is one exception to the requirement of a free intention on the part of the recipient of a sacrament and that is the case of infant baptism. Since there is no doubt that the valid reception of the sacraments requires faith, repentance of sin and a right intention, there has been and still is much speculation among theologians with regard to the whys and wherefores of infant baptism. The fact is that it has been practiced since the earliest days of the Church. At some point, of course, the child must make its own act of faith and personally ratify its baptism. But there is no doubt about the validity of infant baptism. The same Pope Innocent III declared: "Original sin, which is contracted without consent, is by the power of the sacrament, remitted without consent."

In general, with regard to the reception of the sacraments please note the following: There is an important distinction between the *valid* and the *worthy* reception of any sacrament. Many Catholics are unclear in their minds about this teaching of the Church. To receive a sacrament validly means that it has really been received. A sacrament is invalidly received when there is some major defect. This can happen, for example, when someone is baptized who does not have faith, when a person goes to confession and is not at all sorry for his sins, when a person who is already married attempts a second marriage; if a bishop should attempt to ordain a woman to the priesthood such a procedure would be invalid. Thus, when the sacraments are conferred invalidly they often *appear* externally to be valid, but in reality the sacrament and the grace of the sacrament are not conferred.

A more complex theological notion surrounds the idea of the *unworthy* reception of a sacrament. The main point is this: It is possible to receive a sacrament validly but unworthily. This means that a sacrament of the living is received, for example, Confirmation, Holy Orders or Matrimony, but the grace of the sacrament is not received because the one who receives the sacrament is in the state of mortal sin. Take the example of someone who is married in the Catholic Church before a priest but is in the state of mortal sin at the time of the wedding. Is the marriage valid? It is most certainly valid, provided that all the other requirements were in order, but the party who does such a thing does not receive the grace of the sacrament until he or she makes a good confession and receives absolution. The same situation can happen in the reception of the other sacraments, such as Confirmation and Holy Orders. It is also possible to receive the sacrament of Baptism validly but unworthily. This could happen if someone received the sacrament with faith but with no sorrow or repentance of his sins. In all of these cases, when the person in question is truly sorry for his sins and he repents and goes to confession, not only does he receive the grace of the sacrament of Penance, but he also receives the grace of the sacrament which was received validly but unworthily.

The reason for the revival of these sacraments is both the mercy of God who knows our weakness and the impossibility of repeating these sacraments.

BAPTISM INTO THE BODY OF CHRIST

After having given some of the general theological and pastoral principles that relate to the seven sacraments of the Church, I now propose to treat each of the sacraments in detail. Accordingly, the first sacrament to consider is Baptism, since it is by Baptism that a person becomes a member of the Church and thereby participates in the divine life of Jesus Christ.

The word "baptism" comes from a Greek word which means "plunge" or "dip". In English "baptize" has come to mean "purify" or "cleanse" and it is usually associated with water in one way or another, since water is our principal purifying agent.

In Christian thinking and theology, Baptism is defined as the sacrament of spiritual regeneration which is conferred by the application of water while consecrating one to the Most Holy Trinity, Father, Son and Holy Spirit. The Baltimore Catechism defines Baptism as "the sacrament that gives our souls the new life of sanctifying grace by which we become children of God and heirs of heaven." The key ideas, therefore, are spiritual regeneration, divine adoption and a title to heaven or eternal life. Baptism also means conformity to Christ in his death and resurrection.

There is no doubt that Jesus himself instituted the sacrament of Baptism. While speaking to Nicodemus, he said: "I solemnly assure you, unless a man is born again of water and the Spirit, he cannot enter into the kingdom of God" (Jn 3:5). Before ascending into heaven Jesus commanded his disciples to baptize all nations: "All power in heaven and on earth has been given to me. Go, therefore, and make disciples of all nations, baptizing them in the name of the Father, and of the Son, and of the Holy Spirit, teaching them to observe all that I have commanded you; and behold, I am with you all days, even unto the consummation of the world" (Mt 28:18–20; see also Mk 16:15–16). After the Apostles had received the Holy Spirit they preached the necessity of Baptism. Thus, on the very first Pentecost St. Peter said: "Repent and be baptized every one of you in the name of Jesus Christ for the forgiveness of your sins; and you will receive the gift of the Holy Spirit" (Acts 2:38).

It should be noted that baptism, as a religious rite of purification, existed in Israel and in other parts of the Middle East prior to the time of Christ. The first example that comes to mind is the baptism of St. John the Baptist. The purpose of St. John's baptism was to stir up repentance for sin and to ask God for forgiveness. But his baptism was not a sacrament. There were also other groups that practiced baptism with a religious significance, such as the group of Essenes who lived near the Dead Sea at Qumran where the now famous "Dead Sea

Scrolls" were found in the late 1940s. Since man has a rational soul that naturally seeks God, since he is also a sinner, and since water is man's primary cleansing agent, it is not at all surprising that water was used prior to Christ in various religious rites in the attempt to make man more pleasing to God and thus ward off divine wrath. What Jesus did in instituting the Christian sacrament of Baptism was to take a pre-existing human rite that had no intrinsic spiritual efficacy and to elevate it to a new plane: Jesus gave a new meaning and power to Baptism so that it could now communicate the very life of God to those who worthily receive it.

By Baptism we are made children of God and heirs of heaven. We are made participators in the divine life by means of sanctifying grace which is poured into our very being. It should be remembered, however, that by means of the sacrament of Baptism we are incorporated into the body of Christ which is the Church. We become members of the People of God, the holy community which is animated by the Holy Spirit and whose head is Christ himself. So Baptism is not just something individualistic. For Baptism first incorporates us into the Church; then comes our sanctification. In the past, perhaps, the personal consequences of Baptism were stressed more than the communitarian. Recent biblical and dogmatic studies have brought into Catholic consciousness the importance of the communal dimension of Baptism.

The Fathers of the Church saw many symbols or prefigurements of Christian Baptism in the Old Testament. Some of those symbols are: the hovering of the Spirit of God over the primitive waters, the flood in the time of Noah, circumcision, the march through the Sea and through the Jordan River. A rather explicit prophecy of Baptism is found in Ezekiel 36:25: "I will sprinkle clean water upon you to cleanse you from all your impurities, and from all your idols I will cleanse you."

12

WATER AND WORDS

When we hear the word "baptism" we naturally think of water and the invocation of the Most Holy Trinity. There have been those in the history of the Church who, contrary to the teaching and tradition dating back to the Apostles, have said that Baptism is not necessary for salvation or that any liquid will do in place of natural water. But our Lord said, "Unless a man is born again of water and the Spirit, he cannot enter into the kingdom of God" (Jn 3:5).

What our Lord meant and what the Church has always done is to baptize with plain ordinary water. The Lord's statement therefore is not to be understood in a symbolic or "spiritual" sense. The Council of Trent in the sixteenth century was very clear on this point: "If anyone says that true and natural water is not necessary in Baptism, and therefore interprets metaphorically the words of our Lord Jesus Christ, 'Unless a man is born again of water and the Spirit': let him be anathema" (*Denzinger* 1615).

There are many ways in which God could cleanse man from his sins and communicate to him the divine life. But what we are concerned about is what God actually did, not what he could have done. It is a matter of divine revelation that original sin and all actual sins, if there be any, are remitted by Christian Baptism which requires a flow of real water and a calling upon the name of the Father, the Son and the Holy Spirit.

In the course of history Baptism has been conferred by the application of water in three different ways: by immersing the one being baptized into the water, by pouring water on the forehead or by sprinkling. Some Protestant groups use immersion; the Greek Orthodox Church does too. This seems to have been the most common form of Baptism up until about the thirteenth century. Since that time pouring water over the head of the person being baptized has been the usual form in the Roman Catholic Church.

Of course, pouring water or immersing people in water is, by itself, not sufficient for Baptism. The action of applying water must be accompanied with the words: "N——, I baptize you in the name of the Father, and of the Son, and of the Holy Spirit." The words should coincide as closely as possible with the pouring of the water. This Trinitarian form of Baptism is based on the text in Matthew 28:19. It is also found in the oldest Christian literature.

In the Acts of the Apostles we find a number of statements to the effect that some of the first Christians were baptized "in the name of Jesus Christ" (Acts 22:38) or "in the name of the Lord Jesus Christ" (Acts 8:16; 19:5). St. Paul uses similar expressions in Romans 6:3

and Galatians 3:27. Scholars are not sure about the exact meaning of these expressions. Perhaps some baptisms were performed "in the name of Jesus Christ"; but the expression does not necessarily exclude the trinitarian formula. In any event, if the simple formula was used in the early stages, it soon was replaced with the trinitarian one. For since the first century the tradition of the Church has been to baptize in the name of the Father, Son and Holy Spirit.

It is important to note that Baptism has nothing to do with magic of any kind. The power of the sacraments is the power of God himself, since the principal minister is Jesus Christ, working in and through his human minister. However, there is more to Baptism than using real water and the correct formula. Baptism is a sacrament of faith. This means that the one who asks for Baptism must have faith in Jesus Christ as his Savior (cf. Mk 1:15; Acts 2:38). The primary norm for Baptism is the adult who makes an act of faith in Jesus and asks the Church for Baptism. Infants, it is true, who are incapable of a personal act of faith, are also baptized. This is a very special and difficult theological problem, namely, how and why infants can receive Baptism. I will take up this question in more detail in a later essay in this book. For now suffice it to say that the Church has practiced infant baptism since the first century and has always defended the practice against those who have condemned it. For example, in this country various types of Protestants (some Baptists, Pentecostals) baptize only adults.

As we have seen, the sacraments are signs or symbols that not only point to grace but also confer it. Fresh, clean water is the principal purifying agent in our material world. In the sacrament of Baptism the Lord makes use of ordinary water to cleanse our souls from all sin, to make us children of God and heirs of heaven. It is all so simple and all so profound.

13

BAPTISM HAS CONSEQUENCES

It is possible to become so familiar with certain spiritual realities that we tend to forget their dignity and importance. One such reality is the sacrament of Baptism. In a Christian family and in a Christian culture Baptism can almost be taken for granted if we do not occasionally reflect on what it means and what it accomplishes in those who receive it with faith and sorrow for sin.

St. Paul says that those who are baptized become "a new creature", "a new man". He says this because of the undreamed-of supernatural effects that God produces in the person who worthily receives Baptism. It might be well to recall briefly the main effects of the sacrament.

The first effect of Baptism is the infusion of sanctifying grace—the divine life—into the soul of the one baptized. This is also referred to as the grace of regeneration, for the baptized person is "born again" into a new spiritual life of friendship with God. The source of this new life of grace is God himself who operates through his Church and the minister who confers the sacrament. As a result of the washing with water we become new creatures in the spiritual order; God recognizes us as his adopted children and makes us heirs of eternal life with his only begotten Son, Jesus Christ.

Please note, too, that Baptism produces an intrinsic, real change in the soul of the baptized, contrary to the teaching of Luther who thought that the baptized remain unchanged in themselves but that God ignores their sins because of the merits of Jesus Christ.

A second effect of Baptism is the remission of all sins—both original sin and all personal sins, both mortal and venial. Thus, we read in Acts 2:38: "Do penance, and be baptized every one of you in the name of Jesus Christ for the remission of your sins. And you shall receive the gift of the Holy Spirit." The Council of Trent said that "God hates nothing in the regenerated because there is no condemnation for those truly buried with Christ by means of baptism into death (see Rom 6:4). . . ." The same Council goes on to say that "absolutely nothing delays their entrance into heaven" if they were to die immediately after Baptism or before any sin is committed.

The Church distinguishes between the "guilt" of sin and the "punishment" due to sin, either in hell or in purgatory. It is a dogma of the Church, that is, a divinely revealed truth, that *all* punishment due to sin, both eternal punishment for mortal sins and the temporal punishment in purgatory for forgiven mortal sins and unrepented venial sins, is remitted by the waters of Baptism. In fact, St. Augustine taught that the person who dies immediately after Baptism goes directly to heaven.

Even though the Christian is a "new creature", it is

obvious that certain evils such as concupiscence, suffering and death remain after Baptism. However, for the Christian they no longer have the character of punishment but are rather a means of testing him and assimilating him to Christ who suffered and died for him. In the resurrection these evils will be removed from the just by the power of the sacrament of Baptism.

Along with sanctifying grace God also imparts to the baptized person the infused theological virtues (i.e., faith, hope and charity), the moral virtues (i.e., prudence, justice, temperance and fortitude), and the gifts of the Holy Spirit (i.e., wisdom, understanding, knowledge, counsel, piety, fortitude and fear of the Lord). These virtues and gifts enable the Christian to live a Christian life and to respond to the invitation of God's grace.

14

THE NECESSITY OF BAPTISM

The question I will now treat is the following: Is Baptism necessary for salvation? This is a difficult theological problem because, on the one hand, both Jesus and the Church stress the need for Baptism, and on the other hand, it is obvious that millions of human beings die without Baptism. If we say that Baptism is necessary for salvation, are we not then logically forced to maintain that those who die without Baptism are eternally lost?

Jesus said to Nicodemus who came to him at night: "Unless a man be born again of water and the Holy Spirit he cannot enter into the kingdom of God" (Jn 3:5). The same idea is repeated in Mark 16:16 and Matthew 28:19. In view of these texts, Catholic tradition has strongly stressed the necessity of Baptism for salvation. For example, in the third century Tertullian said that "nobody can be saved without Baptism".

In the sixteenth century some of the Protestant Reformers doubted the necessity of Baptism. In response, the Council of Trent declared: "If anyone says that Baptism is optional, that is, not necessary for salvation: let him be anathema" (*Denzinger-Schönmetzer* 1618). Accordingly, it is a revealed truth of faith that Baptism by water is, since the promulgation of the gospel, necessary for all men without exception for salvation.

However, this truth must be reconciled with another truth—the universal salvific will of God. God does not predestine anyone to evil or to hell. St. Paul makes this clear in his first letter to Timothy 2:4: God "wants all men to be saved and come to know the truth." Therefore, if Baptism is necessary by the will of God and if many persons, through no fault of their own, have no opportunity actually to receive Baptism, then God must supply for this deficiency in some way. Thus, according to a longstanding Catholic tradition, in addition to Baptism by water there are two other modes of Baptism: Baptism of blood and Baptism of desire.

An unbaptized person receives the Baptism of blood when he suffers martyrdom for the Faith of Christ. Such was the case of the Holy Innocents who were put to the sword by King Herod. During the Roman persecutions many died for Christ who had not yet been baptized with water; they were subsequently revered as Christian martyrs. The scriptural basis for this is found in Matthew 10:39: "He who finds his life will lose it, and he who loses his life for my sake, will find it" (see also Mk 8:35; Lk 12:8; Jn 15:13).

Baptism of desire is present when a person loves God above all things and desires to do all that is necessary for his salvation. Baptism of desire, like Baptism of blood, takes away all sin, original and actual, and the eternal punishment due to sin. It does not, however, imprint a character on the soul, nor does it necessarily take away all the temporal punishment due to actual sins.

Obviously, "Baptism of desire" is a very broad concept. Theologians disagree with regard to the extent of its application. It is commonly agreed that the desire for Baptism does not have to be *explicit*. For if it had to be explicit, then the millions of people who have not heard the gospel and have not even had the opportunity either to accept or reject Baptism would automatically be excluded from salvation.

Therefore, it is sufficient that the desire be *implicit*. But what is an implicit desire of Baptism? Today the usual theological understanding of "implicit" is that the person in question responds to the grace of God that is given to him or her. In the concrete, this means that a person loves God and keeps the commandments according to the lights received. The famous German theologian, Fr. Karl Rahner, S.J., in a number of his writings calls such persons "anonymous Christians"—a theory which has been embraced by some Catholics and rejected by others.

In any event, we know that Baptism is necessary for salvation. The idea of Baptism of blood and desire helps explain how people can be saved who, for one reason or another, have not been baptized with water. We know for sure that God is good and that his grace is offered to all men (1 Tim 2:4). This means that God offers to all men the opportunity to save themselves. Those who have been baptized with water are the recipients of a very special grace for which they should be thankful.

15

WHAT HAPPENS TO INFANTS WHO DIE WITHOUT BAPTISM?

It is a revealed truth of faith that Baptism is necessary for salvation, in accordance with the words of Jesus: "Unless a man be born again of water and the Holy Spirit he cannot enter into the kingdom of God" (Jn 3:5). In the previous essay we pointed out the role of Baptism of blood and Baptism of desire for adults who have not received Baptism in water. But what happens to infants—innocent human beings with original sin but no personal, actual sin—who die without Baptism? It would seem that they cannot enter heaven (that is, enjoy the face to face vision of God). On the other hand, it would seem unjust to consign them to hell for all eternity, since they have not personally rejected God by any mortal sin.

Over the centuries many theories have been proposed by saints and theologians in order to clarify the fate of infants who die without Baptism. The most common opinion until now has been that, since Baptism is necessary for salvation, unbaptized infants who die cannot enjoy supernatural happiness. Aware of the necessity of Baptism, St. Augustine seems to have maintained that unbaptized infants go to hell, although some scholars dispute this. By the thirteenth century, however, most theologians had reacted against the rigorism of Augustine. Seeing that there are two aspects to hell, namely, the pain of loss (of the vision of God) and the pain of sense (or positive punishment for sin), men like Anselm, Abelard, Peter Lombard, Thomas Aquinas and Albert the Great said that such infants do indeed suffer the pain of loss but no pain of sense, since they have not personally sinned. From this idea came the notion of Limbo, a word which seems to have been coined by St. Albert the Great (d. 1280). "Limbo" is a Teutonic word which literally means the "hem or border" as of a garment, or "anything joined on". The word was not used by the Fathers and it does not occur in Holy Scripture. Limbo is used by theologians to designate the state and place either of those souls who did not merit hell and its eternal punishments but could not enter heaven before the Redemption (the fathers' Limbo) or of those souls who are eternally excluded from the Beatific Vision because of original sin alone (the children's Limbo).

Instead of postulating Limbo as a state and place off by itself (which it seems to be in the popular imagination), some have suggested that it is a part of hell, that is, a place containing those who do not see God face to face but do enjoy perfect natural happiness.

Up until the twentieth century there were not many theologians who argued for the eternal salvation in heaven for infants who die without Baptism. However, since 1900 there have been a number of Catholic theologians who have proposed ways in which unbaptized infants might be saved. Perhaps the most common theory is that God illumines, in some mysterious way, the minds of infants so that they are enabled to make a free choice for God or to posit an act of perfect love for God. Not satisfied with Limbo as a solution to the problem, these theologians do not see how such a solution does full justice to the doctrine of God's universal salvific will. They respect the necessity of Baptism, but at the same time they deny the existence of Limbo. Thus, they describe the supernatural illumination of the infant's intellect at the moment of death as a form of Baptism of desire. To date, however, the Church has not officially endorsed the theory of illumination; if anything, she has been quite wary of it as lacking any convincing proof either from Scripture or tradition.

This whole matter is still very much an open question with regard to the doctrine of the Church. The Church has never officially endorsed the existence of Limbo, even though it has appeared often in Catholic catechisms.

On the other hand, there are those who want to hold for the eternal salvation of all unbaptized infants who die without Baptism. This solution ignores the necessity of Baptism and was sharply rebuked by Pope Pius XII in 1958.

Accordingly, the common solution still remains: Such infants are in Limbo, a place where they suffer the pain of loss because of original sin but are immune from the pain of sense.

Research and discussion on this whole problem are not closed. There is much room for doctrinal development here. For the present, only Limbo as a solution to the problem seems to preserve intact the doctrine and practice of the Church regarding the absolute necessity of Baptism for eternal salvation. Any solution that ignores this important truth is no solution.

According to our present understanding of revelation, God has not seen fit to tell us how he deals with infants who die without Baptism. But one thing we know for sure: God is infinitely merciful and infinitely just. They are in his hands and he will take care of them.

16

WHO CAN BAPTIZE?

Before his Ascension into heaven Jesus commanded his faithful followers to make disciples of all nations and to "baptize them in the name of the Father, and of the Son, and of the Holy Spirit" (Mt 28:19). This mandate to the disciples raises the question about who can validly administer Baptism.

According to the practice and law of the Church, the ordinary minister of Baptism is the priest, representing his bishop; deacons may also baptize. In case of necessity, however, that is, when there is an imminent danger of death, a layman or laywoman, and even a heretic or a pagan, can validly baptize provided that they use the form of the Church and intend to do what the Catholic Church does in Baptism. Thus, nurses can baptize the dying when a priest is not available.

All that is required is that the one baptizing use the correct formula of the Church, namely: "N——, I baptize you in the name of the Father, and of the Son, and of the Holy Spirit." It is not necessary that the layperson, be he Catholic, Protestant or pagan, have the precise, orthodox understanding of what Baptism is, such as it is taught in the Catholic Church. A bare minimum is required. As long as the one baptizing has the intention of doing what the Church does in such situations, that is sufficient. The reason for the leniency and latitude in this case is the necessity of Baptism for salvation, as we have explained previously. With the many possibilities of sudden injuries and death in our mechanized society, every Catholic should know how to baptize in the case of emergency. This is especially true for nurses who have to work in hospitals where there is no priest and where abortions are performed. When they can do so, they should baptize those dying without the sacrament. This is one of the greatest acts of charity that they can perform for a fellow human being.

An important development in the Church's understanding of Baptism and of the function of the minister occurred in the period of the heresy of Donatism in the third century. The Donatists were heretics; some of them were converted to the Catholic Church. The question arose as to whether or not they should be rebaptized when they were received into the Church. St. Cyprian held that there are no sacraments outside the Church and therefore rebaptism was necessary for them.

Pope St. Stephen I opposed this view on the ground that the efficacy of Baptism comes from the rite (as an act of Christ who works through the sacrament) and not from the minister. If heretics or schismatics, he said, observe the rite, they baptize validly.

The view of Pope St. Stephen I prevailed. In the sixteenth century the Council of Trent stated with regard to the Protestant Reformers that, where the form is respected and the intention of doing what the Church does is present, Baptism by non-Catholics is valid (see *Denzinger-Schönmetzer* 1617). So this is now the official, defined teaching of the Church.

The practice of the Catholic Church in the United States with regard to the rebaptism of Protestants who seek admission to the Church has undergone some changes in recent years. Until 1965 it seems that most Protestants who had been baptized were rebaptized *conditionally* when they came into the Catholic Church. "Conditional Baptism" is a safety measure in cases where one is not sure about the validity of Baptism. When a priest baptizes conditionally he says, "If you are not already baptized, I baptize you. . . ."

Since Vatican II, however, there have been more contacts between the churches and a better understanding of what goes on in the various communities. So the Church is now more ready to admit the validity of Baptism, at least in the mainline Protestant churches, such as the Anglican, Lutheran, Methodist and Presbyterian. Generally now persons coming into the Catholic Church from those groups make a profession of faith and are not rebaptized. However, if there is a well-founded doubt about the validity of the first Baptism, it is still necessary to administer conditional Baptism.

17

WHO CAN BE BAPTIZED?

Jesus commanded his followers to "make disciples of all the nations" (Mt 28:19) and to "baptize them in the name of the Father, and of the Son, and of the Holy Spirit" (Mt 28:19). Since every human being is infected with original sin, that sin must be removed before one can enter into the kingdom of heaven (see Jn 3:5). Accordingly, it is the traditional belief and practice of the Church that every living human person not yet baptized is capable of receiving the sacrament of Baptism. Thus, in danger of death all infants (and fetuses whenever and wherever possible) should be baptized, even without the parents' permission. However, if an infant is not in danger of death, it should not be baptized without the permission of at least one of the parents.

Since the third century various individuals and groups have disputed the validity of infant baptism. On the one hand there is the clear necessity of Baptism (Jn 3:5); on the other hand it seems that faith and repentance are necessary prerequisites for Baptism—personal acts which infants, who do not yet have the use of their intellectual faculties, are not able to make. Nevertheless, in the tradition of the Church it has always been the practice to baptize infants.

The validity of infant baptism cannot be proved with absolute certainty from Scripture, but it is strongly suggested. When St. Paul (1 Cor 1:16) and the Acts of the Apostles (16:15, 33; 18:8) repeatedly speak of the Baptism of a whole household, then the children in the family are included. Another indication is that Christian Baptism replaces circumcision (see Col 2:11) which among the Jews was performed on children.

From the point of view of Catholic doctrine we know from the Council of Trent that the Baptism of infants is both valid and licit. The Fathers at Trent declared: "If anyone says that because infants do not make an act of faith, they are not to be numbered among the faithful after they receive Baptism and, moreover, that they are to be rebaptized when they come to the use of reason; or if anyone says that it is better to omit the Baptism of infants rather than to baptize, merely in the faith of the Church, those who do not believe by an act of their own: let him be anathema" (*Denzinger-Schönmetzer* 1626). Thus, we know with certainty, from the infallible teaching of the Church, that infants can and should be baptized.

The situation of the child or infant is different from that of the adult. Just because the infant cannot personally make an act of faith it does not follow that he/she cannot receive Baptism. The possibility of the Baptism of children flows from the objective efficacy of the sacraments which are the acts of Christ himself, from God's general wish for salvation (1 Tim 2:4) in which infants are also included (Mt 19:14), and from the necessity of Baptism for salvation (Jn 3:5).

According to the teaching of the Church, faith is not absent from the Baptism of infants. In a way that we do not fully understand they are carried by the faith of Christ and the Church and are baptized in that faith. According to St. Thomas Aquinas, the gratuitous character of salvation and its communal nature justify the Baptism of those who cannot yet have personal faith.

For an adult to receive Baptism he must have faith and sorrow for his sins. Scripture explicitly demands faith as a preparation for Baptism (Mk 16:16) and sorrow for sins committed (Acts 2:38). Thus preparation for Baptism among the early Christians consisted mainly in instruction in Christian doctrine and in penitential practices.

An adult should be baptized only when he desires it and has at least a basic understanding of what Baptism is. Oftentimes an implicit desire is all that one can get, especially in the case of an adult who is unconscious and dying. If there is some doubt as to whether the person is already baptized, or whether he has any desire for Baptism, then it should be conferred conditionally.

It follows from the validity of infant baptism that baptized infants are full members of the Church and that, after attaining the use of reason, they are obliged to fulfill the baptismal vows taken on their behalf by their godparents. At this time they will also begin to make acts of faith, hope and love and so let the divine life that is in them show forth to the world.

18

CONFIRMATION—A SECOND
GIFT OF THE SPIRIT

Having treated the main aspects of Baptism, we will now move on to a consideration of the second sacrament of Christian initiation, Confirmation. The word "confirmation" itself means "strengthening". Thus, Confirmation is the sacrament of spiritual strengthening through a special conferral of the Holy Spirit for those who have already received spiritual regeneration in Baptism. Just as, in the order of nature, we distinguish between birth and maturity, so also in the supernatural order there is a difference between spiritual rebirth (Baptism) and spiritual growth or maturity (Confirmation).

The evidence from Scripture that Jesus himself instituted the sacrament of Confirmation is not as clear or convincing as the evidence, say, for his instituting the sacraments of Baptism, Eucharist and Penance. However, there is clear testimony going back to the early third century that the bishops of the Church did impose hands in order to confer the Holy Spirit and that that rite was distinct from Baptism. On the basis of that tradition and on the basis of a few indications in the

Bible, the infallible Church solemnly teaches that Confirmation is one of the seven sacraments instituted by Christ. Thus, the Second Council of Lyons declared in 1274: "The same Roman Church holds and teaches that there are seven sacraments in the Church. . . . Another is the sacrament of Confirmation which bishops confer by the imposition of hands, anointing those who have been reborn" (*Denzinger-Schönmetzer* 860). Likewise, in 1547 the Council of Trent said: "If anyone says that the confirmation of baptized persons is a useless ceremony and not rather a true and proper sacrament . . . let him be anathema" (*Denzinger-Schönmetzer* 1628). So it is a part of our faith, and we know for certain, that Confirmation is a holy sacrament of the Church and that it is conferred (normally by a bishop) by a special anointing and an imposition of hands.

That Christ personally instituted Confirmation can be shown from the Bible in an indirect way only. The prophets of the Old Testament had foretold the outpouring of the Spirit of God over all mankind as a characteristic of the messianic age (cf. Joel 2:28f; Is 44:3–5; Ezek 39:29). Jesus is described in the Gospels as the Spirit-filled prophet who is mighty in word and deed (cf. Lk 4:1). He promised his Apostles (Jn 14:16, 26; Lk 24:49; Acts 1:5) and all the future faithful (Jn 7:38–39) that he would send them the Holy Spirit after his glorification at the right hand of the Father. Thus, on Pentecost he fulfilled his word to the primitive Christian community: "And they were all filled with the Holy Spirit and they began to speak with divers tongues as the Holy Spirit gave them to speak" (Acts 2:4).

A careful study of the Acts of the Apostles shows that

the imparting of the Holy Spirit by the imposition of hands by the Apostles accompanied Baptism. For after converts had been baptized, the Apostles "laid hands on them and they received the Holy Spirit" (Acts 8:14–17; see also 19:1–6). Thus the initiation begun with Baptism was completed with the gift of the Holy Spirit, a gift that was sometimes accompanied by sensible manifestations such as speaking in tongues or prophecy.

According to the testimony of Acts, therefore, the primitive Church was familiar with a new, second gift of the Spirit, distinct from that of Baptism, which was realized by the imposition of the Apostles' hands. This "second gift" was the sacrament of Confirmation. Thus, the Acts of the Apostles informs us about the successive phases of Christian initiation: preaching and conversion, Baptism of water, and imposition of hands that gives the Holy Spirit.

A reference to the two distinct rites can be found in Hebrews 6:1–5. According to Hebrews 6:2 the imposition of hands, which effects the communication of the Holy Spirit, belongs, side by side with Baptism, to the foundations of the Christian religion. This laying on of hands has been considered by Catholic tradition as the beginning of the sacrament of Confirmation. In its own way it perpetuates Pentecost in the Church.

19

THE FRAGRANCE OF CHRIST

Every sacrament consists of a sensible sign which involves things, gestures and words. The words determine the meaning of the actions. Over the centuries there has been some dispute among theologians about the precise nature of the sign of the sacrament of Confirmation.

Two things are involved here: the imposition of hands by the bishop and the anointing with the chrism. Then there is the question about the proper formula of words to be used.

As we have seen, the purpose of Confirmation is to confer the Holy Spirit on the recipient in a special way, to complete what was accomplished in him by the waters of Baptism, to conform him to Christ in such a way that he may be able to radiate Christ to others and to be a clear witness to the faith. Jesus himself is described in the Gospels as a Spirit-filled prophet, for the Holy Spirit descended on him at his Baptism by John (see Mk 1:10) and remained with him (see Jn 1:32). The day before he suffered he promised his Apostles that he would send the Spirit of truth from his Father (Jn 15:26) to stay with them forever (Jn 14:16) and help them to be his witnesses (Jn 15:26). On Pentecost that promise was fulfilled when the Apostles were "filled with" the Holy

Spirit. Suddenly they were transformed from timid disciples into intrepid apostles.

What Confirmation does is perpetuate Pentecost in the Church. In the Acts of the Apostles we read that, after Baptism, the Apostles would lay hands on the new Christians and the Holy Spirit descended upon them. There is no clear indication in the New Testament that the Lord instructed the Apostles to associate anointing with the imposition of hands. However, Church records that go back to the early third century in the East testify to the use of anointing at that time. Although there is some obscurity on the matter, it seems that in the West only the imposition of hands was used until the fourth or fifth century. At that time the rite of anointing, common in the East, was also adopted by the West and soon became the principal rite.

Theologically, there is no difficulty in admitting that since Christ himself did not determine the essential sign of this sacrament, the practice of the Church was able to vary according to time and place. This is in perfect conformity with the general doctrine on the power given to the Apostles and their successors to make precise whatever the Divine Author of the sacraments left undetermined, "their substance being preserved" (Council of Trent, *Denzinger-Schönmetzer* 1728).

From the twelfth century until recently the prescribed form for Confirmation has been: "I sign you with the sign of the cross and confirm you with the chrism of salvation. In the name of the Father and of the Son and of the Holy Spirit."

The Second Vatican Council laid down the following: "The rite of confirmation is to be revised and the intimate connection which this sacrament has with the whole of Christian initiation is to be more clearly set forth" (Liturgy, no. 21). As a result a number of changes have been made in the administration of the sacrament. Confirmation is now preceded by the renewal of baptismal promises and the sacrament is to be conferred during the sacrifice of the Mass, at which Holy Communion is received.

In addition to the above liturgical changes, Pope Paul VI in 1971 also declared that the essence of Confirmation consists in the anointing with chrism (a mixture of olive oil and balsam consecrated by the bishop on Holy Thursday), along with laying on of hands and the pronunciation of a new formula. Here is what the Pope decreed: "In order that the revision of the rite of confirmation may fittingly embrace also the essence of the sacramental rite, by our supreme apostolic authority we decree and lay down that in the Latin Church the following should be observed in the future: The Sacrament of Confirmation is conferred through the anointing with chrism on the forehead, which is done by the laying on of the hand, and through the words, 'Be sealed with the gift of the Holy Spirit' (*Accipe signaculum doni Spiritus Sancti*)."

The rite of imposition of hands and that of the anointing have roots that go back to the most ancient religious traditions of Israel. The imposition of hands is a gesture of blessing. It is apt to signify the Spirit's taking possession of the soul. Anointing with aromatic oil is an ancient rite of consecration for kings, priests and prophets. It symbolizes the presence of the Holy Spirit who empowers the Christian to be a witness for Christ.

219

The sweet smell of the chrism or oil of anointing comes from the balsam and symbolizes "the fragrance of Christ" which the Christian must spread around himself (2 Cor 2:15–16) by his deeds and words. Thus by the sacrament of Confirmation the plenitude of the Spirit who is in Christ is communicated to the Christian.

20

WHY CONFIRMATION?

There is much talk these days, in books, articles and sermons, about "giving witness to Christ". Confirmation, as the sacrament of spiritual strengthening, is the precise aid given to us by Christ to enable us to be bold witnesses for him to those inside the Church and to those outside the Church. For this reason it has been called the sacrament of witness to Christ, the sacrament of martyrdom, the sacrament of Catholic action. Let us take a brief look at what Confirmation accomplishes in the one who receives it worthily.

Like the other sacraments of the living, that is, those which should be received in the state of grace, Confirmation increases the sanctifying grace already present in the soul; it imparts the sacramental grace proper to this sacrament; it confers actual graces and, as with Baptism and Orders, it gives a unique sacramental character which is an indelible mark or quality of the soul.

The sacraments are the divinely instituted "channels" of grace, the divine life of the soul. By Baptism we are regenerated into the life of God. The sacraments of the living increase that life and help to bring it to perfection. So Confirmation helps to bring the Christian to spiritual perfection. Also, along with sanctifying grace are given the infused virtues and gifts of the Holy Spirit. One of the gifts is fortitude which helps the Christian stand up to all obstacles to the practice and profession of his faith. Confirmation strengthens this gift and enables the Christian to remain steadfast in the midst of all adversity, even to the point of giving his life for the faith if that is necessary.

The sacramental grace of Confirmation is the completion or perfection of the grace of Baptism. Of course, through Baptism we become children of God and heirs of heaven because we are the recipients of divine grace; we also possess the Holy Spirit in a beginning way, since the Holy Spirit can never be separated from grace. But Confirmation, as a distinct sacrament of spiritual strengthening, gives us a fuller participation in the Spirit of God. Thus, in the fifteenth century the Council of Florence said: "The effect of this sacrament is that the Holy Spirit is given in it for strength just as he was given to the Apostles on Pentecost, in order that the Christian may courageously confess the name of Christ. And, therefore, the one to be confirmed is anointed on the forehead, where shame shows itself, lest he be ashamed to confess the name of Christ and especially his cross . . ." (*Denzinger-Schönmetzer* 1319).

Actual graces are illuminations of the mind and inspirations of the will, freely given by God, to enable us to lead fully Christian lives. The adult who is confirmed receives these graces from God and also a certain title to them in future need. Actual graces can be either interior or exterior. The interior graces are those that affect the mind and will, in the depths of the heart that only God has access to. Exterior graces are the persons, places and things that divine providence arranges to protect his faithful ones and to help them grow in the life of the Spirit.

Finally, a fourth effect of Confirmation is that it imprints an indelible mark on the soul, called the "sacramental character". Because of this character the sacrament cannot be repeated—just as in the case of Baptism and Orders. The character is a quality of the soul, distinct from that of Baptism, that assimilates the recipient to Christ the Priest, Christ the Teacher and Christ the King. In some sense, then, it empowers the Christian to be associated with Christ in offering sacrifice to the Father, in proclaiming and teaching the Word of God, and in leading the Christian people.

Confirmation is not just an empty ritual. It is a sacrament of power—power to proclaim Christ as God's answer to sin, power to overcome personal weakness and cowardice, power to thwart external threats and obstacles, power to be a witness or martyr for Christ.

We should rejoice in the knowledge that the revised rite of Confirmation brings out more clearly than before the meaning of this imparting of the Holy Spirit to the baptized.

21

THE SACRAMENT OF
CHRISTIAN MATURITY

When we think of Confirmation we usually have an image of the bishop coming to the parish for a special occasion. The conferral of the sacrament is surrounded with exceptional solemnity. And that is as it should be, for the bishop is the ordinary minister of Confirmation. Thus, one of the main reasons for auxiliary bishops in dioceses is to assist the Ordinary in conferring the sacrament of Confirmation.

Bishops are successors of the Apostles. From the very beginning we see the Apostles reserving for themselves the imposition of hands upon the baptized to give them the Holy Spirit (Acts 8:17; 19:6) and the most ancient records show that the administration of Confirmation was reserved to bishops. Accordingly, the "Rite of Confirmation", promulgated by the Sacred Congregation for Divine Worship in 1971, says: "The original minister of confirmation is the bishop. Ordinarily the sacrament is administered by the bishop so that there will be a more evident relationship to the first pouring forth of the Holy Spirit on Pentecost. After the Apostles were filled with the Holy Spirit, they themselves gave the Spirit to the faithful through the laying on of their hands. Thus the reception of the Spirit through the ministry of the bishop shows the close bond which joins the confirmed to the Church and the mandate to be witnesses of Christ among men."

However, by reason of their ordination priests also have the power to confer the sacrament of Confirmation. By Church law the use of this power is restricted to certain very definite cases. Thus, in danger of death, provided a bishop is not easily available, any priest is empowered to confer the sacrament. Pastors also have the right to confer the sacrament in the following cases: when they baptize an adult or a child old enough for catechesis or when they receive a validly baptized adult (e.g., a Protestant) into full communion with the Church. Deacons, since they lack the fullness of Holy Orders, cannot validly confirm.

In the early centuries of the Church, Confirmation was administered soon after Baptism, both for infants and for adults. That infants can validly receive Confirmation is proved by the practice of the Western Church up until the thirteenth century, when it was put off until the child reached the use of reason. Confirmation is still administered to infants in the Eastern Church. Since the sacrament is ordered to the strengthening and perfection of the baptized, it can be administered anytime after Baptism. In the sacrament the Holy Spirit is conferred in a special way—as a help to be strong in the faith and to bear witness to Christ before others. Since the child needs that as well as the adult, there are good reasons for conferring the sacrament on infants. But for some centuries the practice in the West has been to defer the sacrament until the child has reached the use of reason. The current procedure in the United States seems to be to confer the sacrament to those in early adolescence.

Since Confirmation is one of the sacraments of initiation into the Christian life, and since it is so necessary and helpful in overcoming obstacles to the practice of the Faith (God knows that there are many of those in our society), every Catholic should be confirmed. We know that Baptism is necessary for salvation, for St. John says (3:5) that unless a man is born again of water and the Holy Spirit he cannot enter into the kingdom of heaven. The baptized who die in the grace of God will be saved. We know that for certain from the infallible teaching of the Church. Confirmation is not absolutely necessary for eternal salvation, but it is necessary for the perfection of the Christian life. Through neglect or unavoidable circumstances it can happen that some adults have not been confirmed. Postponement of the sacrament is not in itself sinful, provided that it is not done out of contempt.

We are all weak and need whatever spiritual aids we can get. The Lord offers us a special strengthening of the Holy Spirit through the reception of the sacrament of Confirmation, which is often referred to as the "sacrament of Christian maturity".

22

JESUS GAVE THANKS

In the previous essays of this series we have considered the sacraments of Baptism and Confirmation. We will now move on to the treatment of the Eucharist. The three sacraments are often referred to as "the sacraments of initiation" because they initiate the new believer into the full Christian life: Baptism by regeneration, Confirmation by spiritual strengthening, and Eucharist by nourishment on the body and blood of the Lord. Penance and Anointing are sacraments of reconciliation, while Matrimony and Holy Orders pertain to the growth and perpetuation of the Church in history.

The term "Eucharist" is derived from the Greek word which means "thanksgiving". Because Jesus offered a prayer of thanksgiving and blessing when he consecrated the bread and wine at the Last Supper, the word has always been connected with the sacrament of the Lord's Supper. Also, giving thanks before eating bread was a characteristic gesture of the Lord, as we note in the Gospel accounts of the miraculous multiplication of the loaves and in his meeting with the two disciples on the road to Emmaus (Lk 24:30).

"Eucharist" is the special name which was used as

early as St. Ignatius of Antioch (d. 107), Justin Martyr (d. circa 165), and Irenaeus (d. circa 208), although other names also are used: Table of the Lord, Lord's Supper, Blessed Sacrament, agapē (love-feast), breaking of bread, Holy Sacrifice or simply the Liturgy.

The theology of the Eucharist is both profound and far-reaching in its implications for the Catholic. There are three main aspects to be considered: 1) Real Presence, 2) sacrament and 3) sacrifice. In this section we will consider each of these points in some detail and try to make clear what the Church believes and teaches with regard to the Holy Eucharist.

At this point it might help to begin with a definition. Thus, the Eucharist is that sacrament of the New Law in which Christ, under the forms of bread and wine, is really and truly present—Body, Blood, soul and divinity —in order to offer himself in an unbloody manner to the Heavenly Father, and to give himself to the faithful as nourishment for their souls.

The Eucharist was prefigured in the Old Testament in a number of different ways. Some of the prototypes that have been pointed out by Christian writers include: the "tree of life" in the garden of paradise, the sacrifices of Abraham and Melchizedek, the miraculous manna in the desert that nourished the Israelites for many years, the bread of offering in the temple, the various sacrifices of the Old Law, especially that of the Paschal Lamb.

The institution narratives in Matthew, Mark and Luke are full of allusions to the Old Testament. In addition to the ones mentioned above, the notions of exodus, liberation and sacrifice stand out. There is also an es- chatological dimension to the Eucharist inasmuch as the

227

Israelites thought of God's final kingdom in terms of a banquet. With the death and resurrection of Jesus the final age of human history has dawned. Thus, participation in the Eucharist is an anticipation of the joy of heaven and the beginning of it right here and now.

The Eucharist enjoys a certain sublimity or preeminence over the other sacraments because, unlike them, it is not just an instrument of Christ's grace but actually contains him within it—the One who is the very source of all grace. Also, this is seen from the fact that all the other sacraments are ordered to the Eucharist as to their final object. Moreover, the rites of the other sacraments for the most part are followed by the reception of the Eucharist by way of a fitting consummation.

Let me conclude this essay by pointing out that belief in the Mass and the Holy Eucharist is what, more than anything else, distinguishes the Catholic. We Catholics have a treasure here which is infinite—inexhaustible. No effort should be spared to try to understand it better and appreciate it more. For the Eucharist is love, indeed, it is "a sacrament of love in which Christ is eaten, the mind is filled with grace, and a pledge is given to us of future glory."

23

THE CATHOLIC DOCTRINE
OF THE REAL PRESENCE

According to Catholic belief the Holy Eucharist is both a sacrament and a sacrifice. The aspect of the sacrament which I will consider now is what is known as the "Real Presence". By this expression is meant that the true Body and Blood, soul and divinity of Christ are really and substantially present under the Eucharistic species, that is, the appearances of bread and wine which remain on the altar after the Consecration.

"Presence" is one of those basic realities which we all experience and all know, but which is difficult to describe and define. Basically it means "being at hand", "being in front of"; when it is said of persons, often it also has the added meaning of "being for" or "being with", in the sense of accompanying someone.

A moment's reflection will reveal that God is present to us in a number of ways. By his power he is present in all of creation, since he conserves everything in its being. He is present in the souls of the just by his sanctifying grace. He is present in his Church which is the New Israel, the holy people of God. He is present in bishops and priests in a special way by reason of their consecration in Holy Orders. He is present, in a different way, in Holy Scripture and in the proclamation of his holy Word. These are some of the various ways in which God is present to his people.

But when the Church says that the glorified Jesus is really present in the Holy Eucharist, she is talking about a different and very special kind of presence. She means that, by the almighty power of God, a stupendous miracle has taken place, namely, the substance and reality of bread and wine have been changed into the substance and reality of the Body and Blood of the resurrected Jesus Christ who is now seated at the right hand of the Father in heaven. Therefore, since Jesus Christ is God and God is worthy of adoration, it follows that the Lord, truly present under the appearances of bread and wine, is worthy of adoration in the Holy Eucharist. For this reason the Church surrounds the Mass and the Eucharist with various gestures of adoration, such as incense, bows, genuflections, silence, candles, formal liturgical clothing and so forth.

It is not difficult to show from history the unanimity of belief in the Real Presence of Christ in the Eucharist for the first 1500 years of the Church. Occasional doubts about it, such as those of Berengarius of Tours (d. 1088), caused an instant uproar—which attests to the universal acceptance of the Real Presence. This unanimous belief of 1500 years is itself an argument for its truth. For it is impossible that the Holy Spirit could leave the Church in error over a long period of time about one of the central doctrines of Christianity.

Widespread doubts about, and denials of, the Real

Presence appeared in the sixteenth century. The Protestant Reformers were unanimous in rejecting transubstantiation and the sacrificial character of the Eucharist, but they did not agree on the question of the Real Presence. Thus, Luther admitted it but then added that it occurred only during the celebration of Holy Communion. Zwingli, along with many others, simply denied the Real Presence and claimed that the bread and wine are mere symbols of the Body and Blood of Christ. Calvin (later joined by Melanchthon) rejected the substantial or real presence of the Body and Blood of Christ and taught a presence of "power", that is, through the Eucharist a power proceeds from the glorified Body of Christ in heaven and is conferred on the faithful.

Because of the denials and doubts of the Protestant Reformers about the Mass, the Eucharist and the Real Presence, the Council of Trent (1545–1563) took up each of these questions and laid out for all the official, infallible teaching of the Church. Thus, in response to Zwingli, Calvin and their followers, the Council declared: "If anyone denies that the body and blood, together with the soul and divinity, of our Lord Jesus Christ and, therefore, the whole Christ is truly, really, and substantially contained in the sacrament of the most holy Eucharist, but says that Christ is present in the Sacrament only as in a sign or figure, or by his power: let him be anathema" (*Denzinger-Schönmetzer* 1651).

24

MY FLESH IS REAL FOOD
AND MY BLOOD IS REAL DRINK

In the last essay we considered the Church's doctrine and belief in the Real Presence of Our Lord Jesus Christ in the sacrament of the Eucharist. It is worth recalling the words of the Council of Trent on this point: "The holy council teaches and openly and straightforwardly professes that in the blessed sacrament of the Holy Eucharist, after the consecration of the bread and wine, our Lord Jesus Christ, true God and man, is truly, really, and substantially contained under the perceptible species of bread and wine" (*Denzinger-Schönmetzer* 1636).

Over the centuries there have been many attempts to water down the Church's belief. Many have claimed that Jesus did not say at the Last Supper what the evangelists claim he said; others have said that Jesus did not mean his words to be taken *literally* but only symbolically or metaphorically. These attempts at evasion have been so common in the past that one writer in the sixteenth century wrote a book listing *200 different ways* in which the words "This is my body" and "This is my blood" have been interpreted.

In response to these errors the Council of Trent said: "All our predecessors in the true Church of Christ who treated of this most holy sacrament very clearly professed that our Redeemer instituted this wonderful sacrament at the Last Supper, when, after he had blessed bread and wine, he said in plain, unmistakable words, that he was giving them his own Body and his own Blood. These words are recorded by the Evangelists and afterwards repeated by St. Paul (see Mt 26:26ff.; Mk 14:22ff.; Lk 22:19ff.; 1 Cor 11:23ff.). These words have their proper and obvious meaning and were so understood by the Fathers" (*Denzinger-Schönmetzer* 1637).

The Gospels and Paul testify that Jesus said at the Last Supper: "This is my body" over the bread, and "This is my blood" over the wine. The Church has always believed and taught that Jesus meant these words *literally*, not symbolically. In fact, it is demonstrable that unless Christ meant the words literally, the resulting metaphors would be quite confusing and worthless. Symbolism can be ruled out by reflecting that the Last Supper is a sacrifice-meal, inaugurating a new covenant with God— a covenant that the Apostles personally ratify by partaking of the sacrificed victim. But a true (not merely symbolic) victim is necessary both for the sealing of a new covenant by sacrifice and for the sharing in it by others.

The sacrificial dimension of the Last Supper is clear from the accounts of the institution. Jesus put his imminent death before the eyes of his Apostles by showing them his Body and Blood under the separate signs of bread and wine. The bread and wine are themselves rich in symbolism: the bread is broken, the wine is the "blood of the grape" (Gen 49:11), its red color underlying the symbolism. Jesus says his Body will be "given for you" (Lk 22:19); his Blood is "shed for you" (Lk 22:20), or "for the multitude" (Mt 26:28; Mk 14:24).

Jesus said, "Take and eat", "Drink of it". Instead of just pointing to his Blood on Calvary, he took bread and wine and changed them into himself so that we could partake of the sacrifice. Also, the Lord instructed the Apostles and all future Christians to renew his action until the end of time when he said, "Do this in memory of me."

The circumstances of the Last Supper itself give added reason for taking Christ's words literally. It was his last meeting with his Apostles before going to his death; his last words were like his last will and testament. In such situations people speak clearly and openly, not symbolically. If Jesus spoke only symbolically on that occasion, he must have foreseen (as the God-Man) the errors and idolatry into which his words would lead the Apostles and the whole Church.

The Church has always believed in and adored the Real Presence of Christ in the Eucharist. If this were based on a misunderstanding of Jesus at the Last Supper, then Jesus himself would be at fault. Since that is impossible, we must conclude that Jesus is offering us his body and blood under the forms of bread and wine.

The practice of the primitive Church confirms a realistic understanding of Jesus' words. St. Paul said to the Corinthians: "The cup of blessing that we bless, is it not the sharing of the blood of Christ? And the bread that we break, is it not the partaking of the body of the Lord?" (1 Cor 10:16). Paul stresses this idea once again in 1 Cor 11:23–30. Chapter 6 in St. John's Gospel is also worth studying in this regard. There Jesus says, "I am the bread of life" and we find a definite progression of thought from "spiritual" bread to bread and wine as his flesh and blood: "If you do not eat the flesh of the Son of

Man and drink his blood, you have no life in you. . . .
For my flesh is real food and my blood is real drink"
(Jn 6:53–55).

These are the most important scriptural texts used by
the Church in support of her belief in the Real Presence
of Jesus Christ in the Eucharist.

25

WATER INTO WINE, WINE INTO BLOOD

We know that the glorified Christ is really present in the
Holy Eucharist. Since this is something truly remarkable
and since the searching nature of the human mind urges
us to ask more questions, it is not unreasonable to
inquire: *How* does Christ, seated at the right hand of the
Father in heaven, become present in bread and wine?

The Fathers of the first three centuries give witness to
their belief in the Real Presence, but they did not try to
explain how it comes about. Since the fourth century the
Fathers have expressly taught that a marvelous change or
conversion takes place at the Consecration of the Mass.
For example, St. Cyril of Jerusalem says: "Once at Cana
in Galilee by a mere nod he changed water into wine, and
is it now incredible that he changes wine into blood?"

What the Church teaches, and has taught clearly since
the beginning of the thirteenth century, is that the entire
substance of the bread and wine is changed into the

whole substance of the Body and Blood of Christ, while the appearances of bread and wine remain. The name given to this wondrous change is "transubstantiation". The word was first used in the twelfth century and was then adopted by the Fourth Lateran Council in 1215. In this regard, "substance" means the inner reality of a thing, what is fundamental to it, what makes it be what it is. Thus, what makes a dog be a dog, and what makes a tomato be a tomato is called its "substance" or inner reality. The substance underlies the external and perceptible characteristics of shape, color, weight, taste and so forth. It is according to this ordinary meaning of the word that the substance of the bread and wine is understood to be changed into the substance of the Body and Blood of Jesus.

Substance is a reality known by the mind; it is not apprehended by the senses. Hence, we cannot see or touch the substance of a dog or a tomato. What we see and touch are the external characteristics of things— their appearances. Accordingly, the Church teaches that after the substance of the bread and wine have been changed into Our Lord's Body and Blood, only the "appearances" of bread and wine remain, that is, their color, shape, weight, taste and so forth. What were bread and wine now, through the power of almighty God, *really are* the Body and Blood of Christ, even though they still look and taste like bread and wine. The appearances remain but the reality has changed. Therefore, since the appearances of bread and wine remain in the Holy Eucharist, we cannot see Christ with our bodily eyes in this Sacrament, nor do we directly touch him with our tongues and hands. What we touch and taste are the external characteristics of bread and wine.

We do see him, however, with the eyes of faith and we actually receive him as food for our souls, since he is substantially and truly present under the appearances of bread and wine.

The fact of the change of substance of bread and wine into the Body and Blood of Christ and the continuation of the appearances (often called "species") of bread and wine is a matter of faith for Catholics and must be believed, since it has been defined as a dogma of the faith by the Fourth Lateran Council and also the Council of Trent. Thus, Trent declared in 1551: "If anyone says that the substance of bread and wine remains in the holy sacrament of the Eucharist together with the body and blood of our Lord Jesus Christ, and denies that wonderful and extraordinary change of the whole substance of the bread into Christ's body and the whole substance of the wine into his blood while only the species of bread and wine remain, a change which the Catholic Church has most fittingly called transubstantiation: let him be anathema" (*Denzinger-Schönmetzer* 1652).

Summing up the teaching and tradition of the Church in this matter, Pope Paul VI stated in his "Creed of the People of God": "Christ cannot be thus present in this Sacrament except by the change into his Body of the reality itself of the bread and the change into his Blood of the reality itself of the wine, leaving unchanged only the properties of the bread and wine which our senses perceive. This mysterious change is very appropriately called by the Church *transubstantiation*. Every theological explanation which seeks some understanding of this mystery must, in order to be in accord with Catholic faith, maintain that in the reality itself, independently of our mind, the bread and wine have ceased to exist after the Consecration, so that it is the adorable Body and Blood of the Lord Jesus that from then on are really before us under the sacramental species of bread and wine, as the Lord willed it, in order to give himself to us as food and to associate us with the unity of his Mystical Body."

26

A WONDERFUL CHANGE

The Church believes that a miraculous change takes place at the Consecration of the Mass. She believes that the reality of bread and wine is changed into the reality or substance of the glorified Christ, while the species or appearances of bread and wine remain. The Church fittingly calls this wondrous change "transubstantiation". Down through the centuries, and also in our time, there have been and are many false understandings of how Christ is present in the Holy Eucharist.

The teaching of the Council of Trent was directed, in part, against Martin Luther who proposed his theory of "consubstantiation". He claimed that the inner reality or substance of bread and wine remains along with the Body and Blood of Christ. Thus, for him, the effect of the words of Consecration at Mass is to make the substance of Our Lord present by some kind of association with the bread and wine, so that both substances exist together in the bread and wine. According to this theory, therefore, bread and wine are not *changed into* the Body and Blood of Christ; rather, Christ comes to dwell in the bread and wine so that we have two substances existing together. This theory is opposed to the Church's long-standing understanding of what happens at the Consecration. For that reason it was rejected by Trent.

Another explanation, also rejected by Trent, is called "impanation" (from the Latin "panis" which means "bread"). This theory was proposed by a certain Andrew Osiander who died in 1552. According to him, after the Consecration the substances of bread and wine remain and coexist with the substance of Christ; he also claimed that they are taken into hypostatic union with the Body of Christ. The theory is opposed to the Church's teaching; also, it labors under a number of philosophical difficulties that make it impossible.

It is not easy to understand this great miracle of transubstantiation which takes place at every valid Mass. We know of no other change in all of creation like this one. For in other fundamental or substantial changes that we experience, such as nutrition, that is, when we eat food and change it into ourselves, the accidents are radically changed in the process. Thus, digestion radically alters the shape, color, taste, size, etc. of apples, oranges and carrots in the process of converting them into parts of our bodies. Death is a radical and substantial change which leads, sooner or later, to the total disintegration of the formerly unified, active body.

At the Consecration of the Mass, however, by the almighty power of Christ working through his priest, the substance of bread is changed into the Body of Christ, while the appearances or accidents of bread remain. Most theologians hold that the substance of bread is not simply annihilated and the Body and Blood of Christ brought in, or created anew, but rather that the very substance of bread and wine is converted into that of the Body and Blood of Christ. Thus, in transubstantiation the Body of Christ in heaven is not changed in the least. What happens is that the Eucharistic Presences are multiplied by the substance of bread and wine being changed into his substance.

A more recent theory about the Eucharist is called "transignification" or "transfinalization". The theory appeared in Europe about twenty years ago and has been adopted by many American theologians and religious educators. This theory maintains that at Mass the bread and wine merely take on a new meaning: Now they signify or represent the Body and Blood of Christ. The theory is ambiguous in that it allows for two understandings of what happens at the Consecration: 1) it can be understood in the orthodox sense of transubstantiation; 2) but it can also be understood to say that there is no real change of bread and wine into the Body and Blood of Christ—only the *meaning* or *finality* of the bread and wine change. The latter sense is not really new—only the name is new, since Calvin taught the same thing in the sixteenth century and his teaching was also rejected by Trent. Thus, some of those who hold for transignification deny the Real Presence of Christ in the Eucharist—at least they deny his perduring presence in the reserved Hosts kept in the tabernacle after the conclusion of the Mass. Therefore, since the terms "transignification" and "transfinalization" are open to false understanding contrary to the official, traditional teaching of the Church, they should be avoided.

27

PRESENCE OF THE WHOLE CHRIST

We have already considered the Church's teaching about the Real Presence of Our Lord in the Holy Eucharist. The point of this essay will be to consider the manner of Christ's presence in the Sacrament. It is a matter of faith that the Body and Blood of Christ, together with his soul and his divinity and therefore the whole Christ, are present in the Eucharist.

Accordingly, the Body of Christ is present under the form of bread and his Blood is present under the form of wine by the power of the words of Consecration. Does this mean, then, that when we receive Communion under the one form of bread, we receive just his Body and not his Blood? No, it does not. For because of the real connection between the Body and the Blood of Christ, his Blood and his soul are also present with the Body of Christ under the form of bread; the reason for this is that the glorified Jesus is now a living Body (Rom 6:9). Because Jesus' humanity is eternally united to the Word in a wondrous Hypostatic Union, wherever his humanity is, there also is his divinity. Therefore, the divinity is also present under the form of bread. Similarly, under the form of wine along with his Blood, Christ's Body, soul and divinity are also present.

In order to make the Church's teaching that the whole Christ is present under each of the two species of bread and wine perfectly clear, the Council of Trent declared: "If anyone denies that in the venerable sacrament of the Eucharist the whole Christ is contained under each species and under each and every portion of either species when it is divided up: let him be anathema" (*Denzinger-Schönmetzer* 1653). This teaching contains the doctrinal basis for the practice of Communion under one form, that is, receiving the Host alone or the precious Blood alone. Now there are a number of opportunities for the faithful to receive Communion under both forms—a practice which was common in the Church until the thirteenth century. However, Communion under one form was practiced in the early Church—in the Communion of children, of the sick and of those who received at home.

Please note the second part of Trent's definition cited above: "and under each and every portion of either species when it is divided up." What is the Council teaching here? It is responding to a too materialistic concept of Christ's presence in the Eucharist, namely, one should not think that, by dividing up the Host into numerous parts, Christ himself is in any way divided. Before any division takes place Christ is wholly present in every part of the species. Thus, if you take a bottle of water and pour it into four glasses, you have water in each of the glasses; before and after, it is water. In a similar way Christ is present whole and entire in each part of the consecrated bread and wine. According to the Gospel narrative of the institution of the Eucharist all the Apostles drank out of the one chalice. Likewise, in the ancient liturgies of the Church the breaking of the bread for the administration of Communion was done only after the Consecration, and all the communicants drank out of the same consecrated chalice.

After the Consecration we perceive the appearances of bread and wine, but it is the whole Christ who is really and substantially present in a supernatural, unique and mysterious manner. The Lord is there but not with actual extension and measurability. We should not try to imagine his presence as that of a tiny child or as a minuscule Jesus Christ hidden under the appearances of bread and wine.

At the Consecration Christ does not leave heaven and come down to the altar; his condition there is not changed. He simply becomes present in a new way, namely, sacramentally, where he was not before. Thus, the Eucharistic presence of the Lord can be discerned not by the senses of the body, but only by the "eyes of faith".

Let me add here a note about small particles that are detached from the Host. This is a practical point, since we are now permitted to receive Communion in the hand. Many theologians hold that we should think of the Eucharist in terms of *food* to be eaten, and not in scientific terms. According to this view, extremely small particles which may be detached from a consecrated Host, for example, are no longer food. Since the Eucharist is meant to be food, they then conclude that the Lord is not present in such small particles because particles are not food. So one need not venerate such particles as one would the whole Host. This is said in order to help those who might worry about the particles. But small pieces that can be picked up with the fingers should be consumed.

28

HOW LONG IS THE LORD
PRESENT IN THE EUCHARIST?

The result of the Consecration at Mass is that the whole Christ—Body, Blood, soul and divinity—is present on the altar under the appearances of bread and wine. A practical question that has vexed both theologians and the faithful over the centuries is this: How long does the Lord remain present under the species? Does his presence cease as soon as the Mass is over? Or does it remain as long as the visible sign or species remains?

The belief of the ancient Christian Church in the duration of the Real Presence is attested by the custom of bringing the Eucharist to the sick and to prisoners who were absent from the celebration of Mass. The faithful were also allowed to bring the Eucharist to their houses. Likewise, the Mass of the Presanctified, celebrated for centuries on Good Friday, used a Host that was consecrated the day before.

By the year 1536 Martin Luther began to teach that the Body of Christ is present in the Eucharist only while it is being used, that is, during the course of the Communion service from the Consecration to Communion. Hence, he totally rejected the perpetual belief of the Church in the permanence of the presence of Christ in the Eucharist. Accordingly, he repudiated the practice of reserving the Blessed Sacrament in the tabernacle, of the adoration of Christ in Benediction and of eucharistic processions, such as were common in Europe at the time on the feast of Corpus Christi.

The Council of Trent rejected the view of Luther and his followers with this dogmatic definition: "If anyone says that after the Consecration the Body and Blood of our Lord Jesus Christ are not present in the marvelous sacrament of the Eucharist, but are present only in the use of the Sacrament while it is being received, and not before or after, and that the true Body of the Lord does not remain in the consecrated Hosts or particles that are kept or are left over after Communion: let him be anathema" (*Denzinger* 1654).

It follows, then, that the Body of Christ remains as long as the sacramental species remain intact, that is, until they corrupt. When corruption takes place, either with age or with consumption, so that the species are no longer those of bread and wine, the Body of Christ ceases to be present because the signs are gone. Accordingly, we can say with certainty that the Real Presence of Christ in the Eucharist begins with the Consecration and ends only with the corruption of the species.

Since God is the Supreme Being and the Absolute Lord of the universe, since he is our Creator and the Source of all we are and have, to him is due worship in the highest degree. The technical name for the worship due to God and to him alone is "adoration". Jesus Christ is the Word of God (see Jn 1:1ff.), the second Person of the Blessed Trinity, "God from God, light from light". St. Paul puts it well in Philippians 2:9–11: "God raised him high and gave him the name which is above all other names so that all beings in the heavens, on earth and in the underworld, should bend the knee at the name of Jesus and that every tongue should acclaim Jesus Christ as Lord to the glory of God the Father."

The same Lord Jesus humbles himself and makes himself present for us in the Eucharist. Therefore, since he is Lord and since he is really present in the Blessed Sacrament of the altar, the worship of adoration must be given to him in the Eucharist. When we adore Christ in the Eucharist, we are not engaging in "bread worship" or "idolatry", because we are worshipping our divine Lord who is truly present.

In order to make this point perfectly clear and in order to reject the errors of Luther and his followers, the Council of Trent solemnly declared: "If anyone says that Christ, the only-begotten Son of God, is not to be adored in the holy sacrament of the Eucharist with the worship of latria, including the external worship, and that the Sacrament, therefore, is not to be honored with extraordinary festive celebrations nor solemnly carried from place to place in processions according to the praiseworthy universal rite and custom of the holy Church; or that the Sacrament is not to be publicly exposed for the people's adoration, and that those who adore it are idolaters: let him be anathema" (*Denzinger* 1656).

Thus, Our Lord, truly present in the Eucharist, is to be adored. The Eucharist itself should be handled with the utmost reverence and care. In our churches one of the ways in which we show adoration for the Lord is by *genuflecting* when we enter and leave the church, or when we cross in front of the tabernacle. In recent years a certain carelessness in this regard has crept in. We should preserve the practice of genuflecting before the Blessed Sacrament as a concrete way of expressing our adoration of the Lord.

29

THE EUCHARIST: A PLEDGE OF FUTURE GLORY

I have stressed and tried to explain the Church's teaching on the Real Presence of Our Lord in the Holy Eucharist. Let me recall for you that the Eucharist is one of the seven sacraments of the Church and that a sacrament is a visible sign of invisible grace; it is (more technically) an efficacious sign of grace instituted by Christ to confer grace. We find abundant evidence in the Gospels that Jesus instituted the Eucharist at the Last Supper, in the course of which he told his Apostles: "Do this in commemoration of me" (Lk 22:19; 1 Cor 11:24).

The seven sacraments were instituted by Jesus as outward, visible signs (for example, bread, wine, water, oil) that not only signify the invisible grace, which is the life of the soul, but also confer it on those who worthily receive the sacraments with faith. The sacraments are our access to a personal encounter with Christ. They make it possible for us to share in the divine life now in our earthly existence and they are a promise of eternal life in the world to come.

This is true of all the sacraments, but it applies to the Eucharist in a special way, since the Eucharist contains the very Body and Blood of Christ. Theologians normally list three chief effects or fruits of the Eucharist.

The first and principal effect of the worthy reception of the Eucharist is a spiritual, loving union with Christ. Jesus promised this inner communion of soul with himself as a fruit of Holy Communion. In the Eucharistic discourse in St. John's Gospel he says: "He who eats my flesh and drinks my blood lives in me and I live in him" (6:56). The model for this type of intimate union is the unity of the Son with the Father: "As I, who am sent by the living Father, myself draw life from the Father, so whoever eats me will draw life from me" (6:57).

The same idea is brought out by Our Lord in his beautiful image of the vine and the branches—an idea that was used by the Old Testament prophets Isaiah and Jeremiah: "I am the vine, you are the branches. Whoever remains in me, with me in him, bears fruit in plenty; for cut off from me you can do nothing" (Jn 15:5).

From the unity of the faithful with Christ, who is the head of the Mystical Body, there flows the unity of the faithful (as the members of the Mystical Body) with one another. St. Paul pointed out that the faithful are united with one another because they all partake of the same Eucharist: "The fact that there is only one loaf means that, though there are many of us, we form a single body because we all have a share in this one loaf" (1 Cor 10:17). The Fathers of the Church had a great love for symbolism. Since bread is produced from many grains

248

of wheat and wine is made from many grapes, the Fathers saw this as a symbol of the union of the many faithful in the one Mystical Body which is brought about by the worthy reception of Holy Communion.

The second effect of the worthy reception of the Eucharist is that it preserves and increases the supernatural life of the soul. Following St. Thomas Aquinas, the Council of Florence in 1439 taught: "All the effects which material food and drink have on the life of our body—maintaining and increasing life, restoring health and bringing pleasure—all these effects this sacrament (i.e., the Eucharist) has on our spiritual life." Thus, the Eucharist strengthens the power of the will so that it can withstand temptations to sin; it increases the life of grace already present, uniting the person ever more closely with Christ; it purges the soul of venial sins and the temporal punishments due to sin; it gives birth to spiritual joy and peace that enable the Christian to bear witness to Christ and to embrace joyfully the duties and sacrifices of the Christian life.

The third effect of the Eucharist is that it is a pledge of our future glory and our everlasting happiness. Our Lord asserted this truth in the form of a promise: "Whoever eats my flesh and drinks my blood has eternal life, and I will raise him up on the last day" (Jn 6:54). The early Christians saw Jesus' death inseparably joined to his Resurrection and to his Second Coming or Parousia at the end of the world. Partaking in the Eucharist means sharing in the death and Resurrection of Jesus. Thus, St. Paul says that the Eucharist "shows forth the death of the Lord until he comes again" (1 Cor 11:26).

According to the liturgical hymn, "O Sacrum Convivium", the Eucharist is the "sacred banquet, in which

Christ is received, the memory of his Passion is renewed, the mind is filled with grace, and a pledge of future glory is given to us." We approach the Lord's table with faith and love; we return from it with an increase of joy, peace and hope.

30

MINISTERS OF THE EUCHARIST

During the past few years we have witnessed a number of remarkable changes in the administration or distribution of Holy Communion. For centuries only priests, and in rare instances, ordained deacons were permitted to give the Eucharist to the faithful. Now we see brothers and nuns, married men and women, college boys and girls, distributing the Body and Blood of the Lord. From a theological point of view this gives rise to the question: Who is the minister of the Eucharist?

Before answering that question we will first consider briefly the matter of who can validly say Mass. In other words, who has the divine power from God to consecrate bread and wine into the Body and Blood of Christ? Many Protestants in the sixteenth century denied the validity of the Mass and of the Real Presence; hence, this was not a problem for them. However, many of the Reformers taught that all the baptized, that is, all the laity, share in the priesthood of Christ and so share in the power to consecrate. Thus, they rejected the traditional teaching about the essential difference between the ordained priesthood (that is, the Apostles and their successors) and the universal priesthood of the laity.

The Council of Trent rejected both of the above opinions with the following decree: "If anyone says that there is not a visible and external priesthood in the New Testament, or that there is no power of consecrating and offering the body and blood of the Lord, . . . but says that there is only the office and simple ministry of preaching the gospel, or says that those who do not preach are not priests at all: let him be anathema" (*Denzinger-Schönmetzer* 1771). In the same vein, the Fourth Lateran Council taught in the year 1215: "No one can consecrate this Sacrament except a priest who is rightly ordained according to the Church's powers that Jesus Christ gave to the Apostles and to their successors" (*Denzinger-Schönmetzer* 802).

In our own day some Catholic dissidents, principally Hans Küng (in his book *Why Priests?*) and his followers, have denied that only the ordained priest can validly offer Mass; in other words, he asserts that any Christian can confect the Eucharist. Such an opinion is contrary to the tradition of the Church and the teaching of Vatican II: "Though they differ essentially and not only in degree, the common priesthood of the faithful and the ministerial or hierarchical priesthood are none the less ordered one to another; each in its own proper way shares in the one priesthood of Christ. The ministerial priest, by the sacred power that he has, forms and rules the priestly people; in the person of Christ he effects the eucharistic sacrifice and offers it to God in the name of all the people" (Constitution on the Church, no. 10). Therefore, it is the certain, revealed teaching of the Church that the power of Consecration is to be found only in the validly ordained priest.

We know from history that in the very early Church the Eucharist was dispensed by deacons; and in times of persecution the faithful were permitted to take the Eucharist home with them as a means of strengthening themselves in the face of death. Gradually, however, a growing realization of the intimate connection between Communion and the sacrifice of the Mass led to a limiting of the distribution of Communion to the priest. Thus, up until very recently Church law determined that the ordinary minister of the Eucharist was the priest, while deacons could be extraordinary ministers for some weighty reason.

In 1973 in a document entitled *Instruction on Facilitating Sacramental Eucharistic Communion in Particular Circumstances* Pope Paul VI changed the law of the Church with regard to the ministers of the Eucharist. The priest and the deacon are designated the ordinary ministers of the Eucharist. Thus, in normal circumstances they are the ones who should give Holy Communion to the faithful. But there is a growing shortage of priests in most countries; at the same time more and more of the faithful wish to communicate at least once a week. Since the limited number of priests might deprive many of the opportunity to receive Holy Communion, the Pope has judged it appropriate at this time to empower bishops to establish "extraordinary ministers" of the Eucharist. The purpose of this change is to provide for the pastoral necessity of the faithful.

In accordance with that *Instruction* of 1973 many dioceses in the United States now have extraordinary ministers—brothers, nuns, married men and women, boy and girl students—to assist their priests in cases of necessity. They are to handle the Sacred Species with the same reverence and care as their bishops and priests do.

31

RECEPTION OF HOLY COMMUNION

A final point to consider about the Sacrament of the Eucharist is this: Who is qualified to receive it? Since the close of Vatican II in 1965 there has been a dramatic increase in the number of Catholics who receive Holy Communion when they attend Mass. Before the Council at many Sunday Masses only a small proportion of those in attendance would step forward to receive the Body of Christ; now it is by far the majority.

In the early Church it was customary to receive the Lord each time a person attended Mass. For a number of reasons, during the Middle Ages receiving Communion only once or twice a year became the norm. It was Pope Pius X who, in 1905, restored the practice of frequent and regular Communion, not only for adults but also for children.

The Church distinguishes three different types of reception of the Eucharist. 1) There can be a sacramental reception on the part of someone who is in the state of mortal sin. To receive knowingly in mortal sin is sacrilegious, since one would be acting a lie, that is, outwardly accepting Christ's personal signs of unity and love but inwardly rejecting them. Such an act is often referred to as an "unworthy Communion". 2) It is also possible to communicate "spiritually" in what is called "spiritual Communion". This is a desire, coming from a deep faith, to receive sacramental Communion and its fruits when actual reception is illicit or physically impossible. For example, a person in a concentration camp, deprived of the Mass, may earnestly pray and desire to receive the Body and Blood of the Lord. Such a person can receive the grace of the Sacrament without receiving sacramentally. 3) The normal and usual mode of receiving the Sacrament is sacramental-spiritual reception, that is, one receives the Eucharist actually and does so while being in the state of grace. This is sometimes called a "worthy Communion". Those who receive Communion worthily, that is, in the state of sanctifying grace, receive an increase of divine grace by the will of Christ and the intrinsic power of the Sacrament. There is, however, still a matter of "more and less". By that I mean that the greater the faith and desire and personal devotion in the reception of the Lord in the Eucharist, the greater will be the participation of the individual in the fruits and graces of the Sacrament.

For this reason both the Church herself and many spiritual writers urge that Christians properly prepare themselves for the reception of Holy Communion. In order to assure that communicants were properly disposed, from ancient times the Church required fasting from all food and drink from midnight. The purpose of the fast was to help remind Christians that they were to approach the Lord's table with utmost reverence.

Catholics all over the world observed the strict fast from midnight until about 1954, when Pope Pius XII, for pastoral reasons, began gradually to mitigate it. The eucharistic fast, of course, is still in effect, but it has been greatly reduced in its rigor. Now it is required to abstain from food and drink, with the exception of plain water, only for one hour before the reception of Holy Communion. For the sick and the elderly even this requirement has been reduced by Pope Paul VI to fifteen minutes.

Is the sacramental reception of the Eucharist necessary for salvation? It is not necessary for baptized infants, since they are perfectly cleansed by the waters of Baptism. However, for the Christian who has reached the use of reason the Eucharist is a necessary means of salvation. Jesus himself said in John 6:54: "Unless you eat the flesh of the Son of Man and drink his Blood, you shall not have life in you." Those words of Scripture would seem to impose a certain moral obligation on those who know about it and for whom reception of the Sacrament is a real possibility. After the practice of receiving Communion had fallen off drastically in the Middle Ages, the Church in 1215 established a law for all Catholics that is still in force: All those who have reached the use of reason must receive Holy Communion at least once a year during the Easter season; and those who are in mortal sin must first make a good confession and receive absolution from the priest. This is referred to as one's "Easter duty".

It was the great St. Pius X who allowed and recommended daily Communion to all the laity. He set down only two conditions: being in the state of grace and the proper dispositions.

There is a long tradition in the Church of taking time after the reception of the Eucharist to give thanks to God. Thanksgiving after Communion means adoration of Christ within us, dialogue with him and the earnest resolve to try to imitate Christ more closely in our daily deeds and words. Those who receive the Sacrament should make every effort to let Christ shine forth in their lives.

32

THE MEANING OF SACRIFICE

In addition to being a sacrament the Eucharist is also a *sacrifice*. In fact, before it is a sacrament it must first be a sacrifice. Up until a few years ago Catholics, almost without exception, spoke of "the Holy Sacrifice of the Mass". In recent times another terminology has become predominant. Now we hear priests and nuns refer to the Mass as "the liturgy", "the celebration", "the sacred banquet"; or they will use other combinations of these words. There is a true sense in which the Eucharist can be spoken of as "a sacred meal", but as Catholics we should not forget that the Mass is preeminently a sacrifice —a mystical re-presentation of the supreme sacrifice of Jesus on the cross on Calvary.

It is not clear to me why so many bishops and clerics now shy away from referring to the Mass as a "sacrifice". Perhaps it flows from a feeling that the sacrificial dimension of the Mass was overstressed in the pre-Vatican II days, while the fellowship dimension was underplayed. Perhaps it is related to the contemporary abhorrence of anything that is connected with pain, self-denial or self-restraint. Perhaps it derives from a desire to be positive in religion rather than negative and it is felt that emphasis on "sacrifice" is too negative. I really do not know. But I do know that the Mass cannot possibly be understood by Americans or by anyone else if the essential element of sacrifice is omitted from the explanation of it. That the Mass is a true and proper sacrifice should be basic to all teaching on the subject, whether in catechetical instructions or in Sunday sermons.

The word "sacrifice" is derived from the two Latin words *sacrum* and *facere*, meaning "to make holy". In its root meaning it is an act of offering something precious to God; the gift is thereby set apart from all things profane, and is therefore "holy". In English, "sacrifice" can have either a religious or a nonreligious meaning. In the broadest sense, sacrifice is understood as the surrender of some good for the sake of something better. Thus we say that parents make many sacrifices in order to educate their children. In baseball a hitter will make a sacrifice bunt in order to advance his teammate to another base.

Sacrifice also has a religious meaning. In general, this means every interior act of self-surrender to God, and every exterior manifestation of the inner sacrificial disposition, for example, in prayer, alms-giving and self-denial. In the liturgical and ecclesiastical sense, a sacrifice is an external religious act in which a material gift is offered to God by an ordained minister for the fourfold purpose of adoration, thanksgiving, petition and expiation.

A true sacrifice must comprise the following elements: 1) a visible (often precious) gift; 2) a sacrificing priest who is authorized to appear before God as the representative of the community; 3) the purpose of the sacrifice, which primarily consists in the recognition of the absolute sovereignty of God through adoration, thanksgiving, petitions, and secondarily in reconciliation with God through atonement; 4) an act of sacrifice which visibly represents the invisible, inner sacrificial disposition.

The key point in all of this is that, in a religious sacrifice—especially as found in ancient Judaism and in Christianity—a man or a whole community takes something very valuable and removes it from its own dominion (often by destroying it, as in a holocaust). The purpose is to make visibly manifest to all that the man or the community submits itself to the sovereignty or will of God.

Most of the great world religions have had and still do have sacrifices of one kind or another. Religions that are more philosophical or "heady" usually do not practice any external sacrifices.

Those who are familiar with the Old Testament will recognize the above description as applying to many of the sacrifices prescribed for the ancient Israelites; one need only recall the many sacrifices offered in the temple at Jerusalem each year, all during Jesus' life and until the destruction of the temple by the Romans in 70 A.D.

The New Testament is quite explicit in describing Jesus' death on the cross in sacrificial terms. St. Paul is very clear on this point in his letters; the Letter to the Hebrews presents this notion in its most developed form. Since the Mass is essentially related to the sacrifice of the cross as a mystical re-presentation of it, it follows that the Mass is also a sacrifice.

33

THE MASS IS A TRUE SACRIFICE

The point I want to make here is that the Mass, now often called the "liturgy" or the "liturgical celebration", is a true *sacrifice*. Of late there has been so much emphasis on the "meal" or "banquet" dimension of the Mass that, unfortunately, many Catholics—both young and old— seem to have little or no understanding of the sacrificial nature of the Mass.

It should be recalled that the Church solemnly defined at the Council of Trent in 1562 that the Mass is a sacrifice. The Council declared: "If anyone says that in the Mass a true and proper sacrifice is not offered to God or that the sacrificial offering consists merely in the fact that Christ is given to us to eat: let him be anathema." Most of the Protestant Reformers had denied that the Mass is a true sacrifice so this canon was directed against them. The Reformers seem to have misunderstood the Catholic teaching that the sacrifice of the Mass is identical with the sacrifice of Christ on the cross. They seem to have held, erroneously, that the Mass according to Catholic teaching is an independent sacrifice side by side with the sacrifice of Christ on the cross.

It would be most revealing, I think, to ask all the parishioners at a Sunday Mass to write down their definition of the Mass. Those who studied the *Baltimore Catechism* might recall this definition: "The Mass is the sacrifice of the New Law in which Christ, through the ministry of the priest, offers himself to God in an unbloody manner under the appearances of bread and wine" (*Baltimore Catechism* No. 3, question 357). In the previous essay I went into the nature of sacrifice and defined it as "an external religious act in which a material gift is offered to God by an ordained minister for the fourfold purpose of adoration, thanksgiving, petition and expiation".

There are a number of texts in both the Old Testament and the New Testament which indicate that the Mass is a sacrifice. Since the end of the first century Christian writers have pointed to the offering by Melchizedek of bread and wine in Genesis 14 as a type or foreshadowing of the Mass. Another text which seems to point to the Mass, and was so interpreted by many Fathers of the Church, is Malachi 1:11: "From farthest east to farthest west my name is honored among the nations and everywhere a sacrifice of incense is offered to my name, and a pure offering too."

The clearest texts pointing to the sacrificial nature of the Eucharist, however, are in the New Testament. The very words of institution, found in Matthew 26, Mark 14, Luke 22 and 1 Corinthians 11, attest the sacrificial character of the Eucharist. Jesus designates his Body a sacrificial body, and his Blood sacrificial blood, when he says: "This is my Body which shall be *given up for you*" and "This is my Blood which shall be *shed for you*." The expressions "given up for you" and "shed for you" are biblical sacrificial terms which express the offering of a true and proper sacrifice.

Another indication of the sacrificial character of the Eucharist is the fact that Christ made his Body and Blood present under separate forms of bread and wine and thus in the form of a sacrifice. For the separate forms symbolically represent the real separation of the Body and Blood of Christ which was made in the sacrifice of the cross. Jesus also refers to his Blood as "the Blood of the covenant". In so doing he is echoing Exodus 24 which recounts that Moses sealed the Old Covenant of God with Israel by offering a bloody sacrifice. Thus, according to biblical thinking, "the blood of the covenant" is synonymous with the blood of sacrifice.

Let me mention just in passing that many of the early Fathers of the Church, beginning with Pope St. Clement I about 101 A. D., speak of the Eucharist as a sacrifice.

The traditional Mass of the Catholic Church clearly brought out that it was a sacrifice. The same idea is carried over into the New Order of the Mass in English, especially in the first Eucharistic Prayer which is, for the most part, the English translation of the traditional Latin Mass. There the Church prays, right after the Consecration: ". . . we offer to you, God of glory and majesty, this holy and perfect *sacrifice*: the bread of life and the cup of eternal salvation. Look with favor on these offerings and accept them as once you accepted the gifts of your servant Abel, the *sacrifice* of Abraham, our Father in faith, and the bread and wine offered by your priest Melchizedek. Almighty God, we pray that your angel may take *this sacrifice* to your altar in heaven. . . ."

34

THE MASS AND THE CROSS

We have seen that, according to the teaching of the Church, the New Testament and the tradition and practice of the Church, the Mass is a true and proper sacrifice. It is also an article of Catholic teaching that the Mass is the same sacrifice as that of Jesus on the cross on Calvary almost two thousand years ago. It is obvious to any observer that a Mass in a parish church is not exactly the same as the bloody death of Jesus outside the city walls of Jerusalem. So it is both the same and not the same, but under different aspects. Thus, in order to understand the Mass as the Catholic Church understands it, it is necessary to grasp clearly the relationship between the sacrifice of the Mass and the sacrifice of the cross.

Jesus' death on the cross was the perfect, absolute sacrifice that was wholly pleasing to the Father. The sacrifices of the Old Law pointed towards it, and the millions of Masses offered since that time refer back to it. Thus the theologians often speak of the Mass as a "relative sacrifice", since it depends on and commemorates Jesus' offering of himself on Calvary "once and for all". In this vein the Council of Trent said of the Mass in 1562: "This sacrifice was to re-present the bloody sacrifice which he accomplished on the cross once and for all. It was to perpetuate his memory until the end of the world. Its salutary strength was to be applied for the remission of the sins that we daily commit."

On the basis of Trent's explanation, the relationship of the sacrifice of the Mass to the sacrifice of the cross may be more closely defined as a *making-present* (re-presentation), a *memorial* and an *application*.

The Mass is the re-presentation of the sacrifice of the cross insofar as the Body and Blood of Christ are made present under the separate species of bread and wine, thus symbolically or sacramentally representing the historical separation of the Body and Blood of Christ on the cross. Also, the Mass is certainly a memorial or commemoration of the sacrifice of the cross, but it is more than just that: it is also a true and proper sacrifice itself, as the Council of Trent stresses more than once. Finally, the Mass is the means whereby the infinite fruits of Jesus' sacrifice on the cross are actually applied to each human person—all desperately in need of salvation as the result of original sin.

Many Protestants, falsely understanding Catholic teaching on the Mass, have rejected it because it seemed to them somehow to detract from Jesus' supreme sacrifice on Calvary or even to replace it. Such a view is a distortion of Catholic belief. Christ's death on the cross was the one sacrifice that redeemed all mankind; through his sacrificial death he merited the gift of eternal salvation for all those who believe in him and keep the commandments.

According to Catholic belief the Mass is a *re-presentation* of Jesus' sacrificial death on Calvary. The Mass is the same sacrifice as that of the cross because in the Mass the victim is the same and the principal priest is the same, namely, Jesus Christ. This idea was perhaps best expressed by the Council of Trent: "In the divine sacrifice that is offered in the Mass, the same Christ who offered himself once in a bloody manner on the altar of the cross is present and is offered in an unbloody manner. . . . For it is one and the same victim: he who now makes the offering through the ministry of priests and he who then offered himself on the cross; the only difference is in the manner of the offering."

From the above official teaching of the Church we can see that both in the Mass and on the cross the sacrificial gift and the principal priest are the same: Jesus Christ. The difference is to be found in the manner in which the sacrifice is offered. On the cross Jesus physically shed his blood and was physically slain, while in the Mass there is no physical shedding of blood nor physical death, since Christ can now die no more. On the cross Christ gained merit and satisfied for us, while in the Mass he applies to us the merits and satisfaction of his death on the cross.

In comparing the Mass with the cross we find that the victim and the priest are the same, but the mode of offering is different. On the cross Jesus offered himself in a bloody manner; in the Mass he offers himself in an unbloody manner. Also, in the Mass he offers himself through the ministry of the priest who depends on him.

If the above description of the Mass is true, and we have it on the authority of the infallible Church of Christ that it is true, then we are confronted with something very mysterious. But Catholics believe that the Mass is mysterious, that a profound miracle takes place at each and every valid Mass. For in the Mass Jesus' sacrificial death, which occurred almost two thousand years ago, by the power of God and through the ministry of the priest is made present, is commemorated and is applied to the faithful.

35

WHERE IS THE SACRIFICE?

We have explored the Church's teaching that the Mass is a true sacrifice and that, by the power of God, in a miraculous way it is a re-presentation of Jesus' sacrifice on the cross almost two thousand years ago. In the present essay, briefly and simply, I would like to explain at what precise point in the Mass the sacrifice takes place.

We are all familiar with the basic parts of the Mass: 1) Introductory Rite; 2) Liturgy of the Word; 3) Liturgy of the Eucharist; 4) Communion Rite; and 5) Concluding Rite. Since we know that the Mass is a sacrifice—a sacramental or mystical re-presentation of the sacrifice of Jesus on Calvary—one might very well ask: Which part of the Mass contains the sacrificial action?

The Introductory Rite and the Liturgy of the Word perform the function of preparation for the main action, so it is obvious that the sacrifice does not occur there. The Concluding Rite is a dismissal after the main action, so it can safely be set aside. That leaves the Liturgy of the Eucharist and the Communion Rite.

The Liturgy of the Eucharist is composed of the Offertory, the Consecration and the prayers that follow the Consecration. In the Offertory the priest offers gifts of bread and wine which have not yet been changed into the Body and Blood of Christ. But the true sacrificial gift to the Father is not the bread and wine but the Body and Blood of Christ. This means then that the offering of bread and wine serves only as a preparation for the sacrifice.

Likewise, the reception of Holy Communion by the priest and the people cannot be considered the essential sacrificial action, because the sacrificial meal does not pertain to the essence of a sacrifice. There can be a true sacrifice without sacrificial food, as we find, for example, in the sacrifice of Jesus on the cross. Moreover, participation in sacrificial food presupposes that the sacrifice has already been offered. This idea is bolstered by the solemn statement of the Council of Trent: "If anyone says that in the Mass . . . the sacrificial offering consists merely in the fact that Christ is given to us to eat: let him be anathema." It follows, therefore, that the essential sacrificial action of the Mass does not take place in the Communion Rite.

Where then does the sacrifice take place? It occurs in the Consecration where, in imitation of Jesus' actions at the Last Supper, the bread and wine are changed into the Body and Blood of Christ by the ordained priest who functions in the name of Christ. Thus, it is the common opinion of theologians that the essential sacrificial action consists in the transubstantiation alone. The double Consecration represents in a sacramental manner the real historical separation of the Body and Blood of Christ which took place in the sacrifice of the cross on Calvary. The word "sacramental" indicates that the Mass is a symbolic ritual which contains what it signifies. This means that the Eucharist, in virtue of its divine institution by Christ, is not just a memorial of Calvary; nor is it a repetition of the sacrifice of the cross. Rather, the Consecration miraculously renders Jesus' sacrifice on the cross present in a sacramental or mystical way.

We should not forget that at the Last Supper Jesus commanded his disciples to do what he did: "Do this as a memorial of me" (Lk 22:19). And St. Paul clearly related the Mass to the cross when he said: "Until the Lord comes, therefore, every time you eat this bread and drink this cup, you are proclaiming his death" (1 Cor 11:26).

The Council of Trent, in its infallible teaching on the Mass, links together the Mass and Calvary by stressing that the victim and the principal priest are the same in both events, namely, Jesus Christ. The difference between them lies solely in the manner of the offering (bloody and unbloody).

A true sacrifice requires an inward act of oblation and an outward sacrificial act. Since Jesus himself instituted the priesthood of the New Law at the Last Supper, his act of oblation to the Father is made present in the Mass by the intention and words of the priest. The outward sacrificial act is performed in the mystical separation of the Body and Blood of Christ which takes place through the double Consecration of the bread and wine.

36

POWER OF THE MASS

The Mass is the most perfect sacrifice possible because it is the same sacrifice that Jesus offered to his Father on the cross; the victim and priest, as we have noted, are the same; only the manner of offering is different.

Now I would like to consider the various purposes for which the Mass is offered, a point not yet considered. The purpose of the Mass is not exactly the same as the purpose of the historical sacrifice on Calvary. Jesus died once for the redemption of the world; he cannot die again. The Mass, therefore, is not a new redemption of the world. Christ instituted the Holy Eucharist at the Last Supper and gave it to his Church so that, as the central act of worship of the Church, it might be sacramentally repeated and made present for all men of all succeeding ages. Thus, every day the Church is visibly associated with Jesus' sacrifice on the cross and so is able to reap the fruits of that redemptive act.

According to the official teaching of the Council of Trent in 1562, the sacrifice of the Mass is a sacrifice of praise, thanksgiving, expiation and petition. These are the four basic purposes of the Mass, or intentions for which it can be offered by the faithful. Let me explain briefly each of these notions.

Since the Mass is the sacrificial offering of Christ and the Church, it is primarily an act of praise or adoration of God. Because of the infinite value of the sacrificial gift (Christ) and the infinite dignity of the primary priest (Christ), the Mass is the most perfect sacrifice of praise (= adoration) and thanksgiving that is possible to offer to almighty God. And as such it can be offered to God alone.

It should be noted that when the Church celebrates Mass in commemoration of the saints, she does not offer the sacrifice to the saints but to God alone. Masses in honor of this or that saint are offered to God with the intention of thanking him for the grace and goodness he has shown to the saints and of appealing to those saints for their intercession in heaven. This is one concrete way of living out the truth of the communion of saints—the Church militant, the Church suffering and the Church triumphant. The custom of celebrating Mass at the tombs of the martyrs on the anniversary of their martyrdom can be traced back to the second century.

As a sacrifice of expiation the Mass effects both the remission of sins and the punishment due to sins. As a sacrifice of petition it moves God to confer both natural and supernatural gifts. With regard to atonement and forgiveness of sins through the Mass, here is what Trent says: "The holy council teaches that this sacrifice is truly propitiatory, so that if we draw near to God with an upright heart and true faith, with fear and reverence, with sorrow and repentance, through the Mass we may obtain mercy and find grace to help in time of need. For by this oblation the Lord is appeased, he grants grace and the gift of repentance, and he pardons wrongdoings and sins, even grave ones."

Further, the Council of Trent stresses the fact that the Sacrifice of the Mass can and should be offered not only for the living but also for the dead, that is, for the suffering souls in purgatory.

The Mass is the re-presentation of the sacrifice of Jesus on the cross; it is also the sacrifice of the Church, since it was to his disciples that Jesus said, "Do this in memory of me." Thus, every Mass is a Mass of the Church and, in the strict sense, there is no such thing as a "private Mass". At times a priest may have to offer Mass without a congregation being present, but he does so in the name of the whole Church.

Since the Mass is an act of Christ and the Mystical Body, it infallibly attains its effects of adoration, thanksgiving, expiation and petition. For the act of Christ is of infinite value and the act of the Church is always acceptable to God because it is Christ himself, working through his Spirit, who works in the Church. As an act of the celebrating priest and the individual Christians who assist at the Mass, the acceptance and effectiveness of each Mass depend on the intensity of the personal devotion with which it is offered.

What Christ prays for in each Mass is infallibly granted by the Father. However, with regard to the petitions of the priest and the faithful at a given Mass, the results always remain uncertain. The reason is that the necessary conditions or dispositions for granting the petitions, either on the part of the one offering or on the part of the person for whom the Mass is offered, may not always be present.

37

EACH MASS BENEFITS ALL

The Catholic faithful are accustomed to offering many Masses for the same intention, let us say for the repose of the soul of some loved one. Since the Mass is the re-presentation of the sacrifice of Jesus on Calvary and since that sacrifice has infinite value, the question can arise about the value of each Mass and what the results or fruits of each Mass are.

Because of the dignity of the sacrificial gift (Jesus) and of the principal offering priest (Jesus), each Mass has infinite value with regard to the adoration and thanksgiving it gives to God. But what about the value of each Mass when it comes to expiation for sins committed and to begging God for favors, both spiritual and material? According to the common teaching of theologians, the propitiatory and impetratory value of each Mass is finite because these actions refer to human beings who, as creatures, are capable of receiving only finite acts or graces from God. This explains the ancient practice of the Church of offering the Mass frequently for the same intention. If God granted unlimited grace and favors to each person for whom a Mass is offered, then it would not make any sense to offer more than one Mass for each intention.

As an act of intercession the Mass is the occasion for God to bestow spiritual and material blessings on those who offer it and on those for whom it is offered, since one of the purposes of the Mass is to apply the fruits of the cross to men. Also, the Mass effects the remission of temporal punishment due to sin and serves as satisfaction for sin. Through the prayers of the faithful the Mass is also very effective in bringing about the remission of the punishment due to sin for the poor souls in purgatory. The Church therefore encourages Catholics to offer Masses for the repose of the souls of the departed.

Since the Mass applies the fruits of Calvary to men and since those fruits are infinite, what limits them in their application to each individual? The main limiting factor is the *intensity of devotion* with which each person offers the Mass; the amount received depends on the devotion of those who offer and on the disposition of those for whom the Mass is offered. It is like taking a drink from a fountain: the supply is inexhaustible and each person drinks what he can. The importance of personal holiness in the offering of Mass is borne out by the fact that the faithful often seek to have saintly priests say Mass for them and feel specially privileged when they know that cloistered sisters, such as the Carmelites, are praying for them. In these cases they recognize the principle involved: Greater devotion produces greater benefits.

By the fruits of the Mass are understood the effects which it produces in its own right; these are mainly satisfaction for sin and petitions for spiritual and material blessings. Since the fourteenth century theologians have distinguished a threefold fruit of the Mass.

First, there is the general fruit of the Mass. This fruit accrues to the benefit of the whole Church—to the living faithful and to the poor souls in purgatory, since every sacrifice of the Mass is a sacrifice for the Church. Thus, in some way we all benefit from each Mass that is offered.

Secondly, there is the special fruit of the Mass which accrues to the benefit of those persons for whom the Mass is offered in particular, whether they are living or dead. With this in mind, priests normally offer each Mass for a "special" or "first" intention, for example, for the repose of the soul of Aunt Mary. It is also customary for priests to add a number of "second" intentions. When a stipend is offered for a Mass to be celebrated for a particular intention, the priest must offer that Mass as a first intention. The practice of offering Mass for definite persons can be traced back to the third century.

Thirdly, it is commonly held by theologians that there is a personal fruit of the Mass which the Lord grants to the celebrating priest and to all the faithful who are actually present at each Mass. However, Catholics should be alert to the fact that the Mass does not work mechanically like a Coke machine: insert a coin and out pops a can of soda! To receive the fruits of the Mass there must be certain moral dispositions and the amount received depends on the quality of these dispositions.

The decision to attend Mass frequently should be motivated by the desire to enter into the sacrificial offering of Christ—both on the cross and in the Mass. This should also be the basic motive for attendance on Sundays and Holy Days of Obligation when the Church requires the faithful to assist at Mass.

38

A LIFE PRESERVER ON
THE SHIP OF SALVATION

After having treated the basic questions with regard to the Eucharist, we will now move on to the consideration of the Sacrament of Penance. Penance is often referred to as "the Sacrament of Reconciliation" or "the Rite of Reconciliation", although the official name is still "the Sacrament of Penance". To be reconciled with God, to return to his love and friendship after having been separated from him by mortal sin is the effect of this sacrament when it is received devoutly and with true sorrow for sin.

If men and women did not commit sin there would be no need for anything like a rite of Penance. In fact, if there were no sin at all in the world, either original or personal, there would be no need for any of the sacraments.

And what is sin? By "sin" we mean an offense against God, a violation of his divine will, an insult to God. As a result of the sin of Adam, the whole human race fell into the hands of Satan, sin and evil. The only one capable of rescuing man was God himself. In order to redeem man and merit for him eternal salvation, God sent his only-begotten Son, Jesus Christ our Lord, into this world to suffer, die and rise again for us.

The abundant grace and merits of Jesus are applied to each person by the cleansing water of Baptism. Through Baptism, as we have seen, we are actually made holy and pleasing to God—adopted children of God and heirs of eternal life. If we could remain spiritually all our lives what we were at the moment of our Baptism, only growing in grace and the love of God, at our death we would go directly to heaven.

Unfortunately, there is the ugly matter of sin. Though perfectly cleansed at Baptism, our will remains weakened as a result of original sin; we are subject to all kinds of temptations—from the world, the flesh and the devil. Thus, we know both from revelation and from our own personal experiences that we can be unfaithful to the grace of God, that we can reject the friendship of God, that we can sin.

What characterizes Catholic wisdom and teaching about man is that these two truths must both be maintained at the same time: 1) man is good; and 2) man is weak and can fall into the most sordid sins.

All heresies and secular ideologies tend to emphasize either truth, to the exclusion of the other. Thus, the current fad is to stress man's goodness to such an extent that his sinfulness is either denied outright or simply neglected. Moral evil, which proceeds from man's wicked will, is reduced to sociological, psychological or economic factors. In America sin, in the real Christian sense, is out of fashion. The attitude is so common that it prompted one of our best known psychologists, Dr. Karl Menninger, to write a book about it some years ago with the catchy title, *What Ever Happened to Sin?*

There are also those, usually pessimists of one brand or another, who stress man's sinfulness and wickedness to such an extent that his goodness is overshadowed. Certain fundamentalist sects are prone to this error, as also are some of the Eastern religions. It was G. K. Chesterton who remarked that heresy is the exaltation of one truth at the expense of other truths. The Catholic view of man retains both basic truths: man is good but he is prone to sin.

In his mercy Christ our Lord, in addition to the Sacrament of Baptism which cleanses us of all sin and makes us friends of God, instituted another sacrament—Penance—so that those who, through weakness, fall into mortal sin might have a way to escape from their sin and return home to the grace and love of God. Penance is like a life preserver on the Ship of Salvation that is thrown to those who have fallen overboard into the sea of sin. If we were all perfect there would be no need for Penance, but as a matter of fact we are all sinners.

What is Penance? It is the sacrament instituted by Christ by which sins committed after Baptism are forgiven through the absolution of the priest. Penance is also understood as a moral virtue which inclines the will inwardly to turn away from sin and to want to make amends to God. In its external manifestations it leads to the confession of one's sins to a priest and to the performance of various kinds of penitential works, such as prayer, fasting, donations to the poor and the patient bearing of all life's trials.

39

THE KEYS OF THE KINGDOM

We have seen that Penance is "the sacrament instituted by Christ by which sins committed after Baptism are forgiven through the absolution of the priest". That the Church has the power from Christ to forgive sins is not just a pious opinion. For it is a part of divine revelation and the official teaching of the Church that the Church has received from Christ the power of forgiving sins committed after Baptism.

In the course of history it has often been denied by various sects that the Church can forgive sins, in other words, that Penance is a sacrament. Thus, the Protestant Reformers in the sixteenth century denied it; for them, sins were forgiven only through Baptism. In the early centuries of the Church there were many rigorists, such as the Novatians and the Montanists, who held that the Church did not have the power to forgive mortal sins, or at least could not forgive certain very serious sins such as idolatry, adultery and murder. Some of the "spiritualizing" sects in the Middle Ages, such as the followers of Wycliff and Huss, rejected the whole ecclesiastical hierarchy and therefore the sacramental power of bishops and priests.

Catholics have always believed and taught that Jesus gave the Apostles and their successors the spiritual power of forgiving sins. Certainly, he himself exercised an active ministry of the forgiving of sins. When he began to preach he insisted on repentance: "The time has come and the kingdom of God is close at hand. Repent, and believe the Good News" (Mk 1:15). On another occasion he said, "Unless you repent you will all perish in the same manner" (Lk 13:3). On the first Pentecost Peter, the Prince of the Apostles, also recommends penance to sinners who are preparing themselves for Baptism: "Repent and be baptized every one of you" (Acts 2:38).

Two important passages in Scripture bear witness to the fact that Jesus conferred the power to forgive sins on his Apostles. In Matthew 16:19 Jesus promises Peter that he will give him power over the kingdom of heaven: "I will give you the keys of the kingdom of heaven: whatever you bind on earth shall be considered bound in heaven; whatever you loose on earth shall be considered loosed in heaven." The one who has the keys is the one who controls a house; he it is who decides who shall enter or not enter. Since it is precisely sin which hinders one from entering the kingdom of God, the power to forgive sins is included in the power of the keys. Also, in the language of the time, "binding and loosing" designated a real judicial power to include someone or exclude him from the community. This same power of binding and loosing was promised to all the Apostles in Matthew 18:18.

What Jesus promised while living on the earth, he actually conferred on the Apostles after his Resurrection from the dead. On that very day he appeared to them and said: " 'Peace be with you. As the Father sent me, so am I sending you.' After saying this he breathed on them and said: 'Receive the Holy Spirit. For those whose sins you forgive, they are forgiven; for those whose sins you retain, they are retained' " (Jn 20:21–23). With this action and these words Jesus invested his Apostles with the power to forgive sins. This power is twofold: it may be exercised by forgiving sins or, for good reason, by refusing to forgive sins. The effect is real in the order of grace, in the sense that before God the sins are either forgiven or not forgiven.

With regard to John 20:21–23 the Council of Trent said: "The universal agreement of the Fathers has always understood that by such a striking action and by such clear words the power of remitting and of retaining sins, and of reconciling the faithful who have fallen after baptism was communicated to the Apostles *and to their legitimate successors*" (emphasis added).

It should be noted that the power to forgive sins was not conferred on the Apostles as a personal gift or charism, but was transferred through them to the Church as a permanent institution. The same power has been transmitted to their successors (bishops and priests), in the same way as they are empowered to preach, to baptize and to celebrate the Eucharist. The reason for this is the perduring fact of sin which makes the continuance of this power necessary for all times.

40

A TRIBUNAL OF MERCY

Is there such a thing as an "unforgiveable sin"? In the past there have been those, as we have seen, who said that the Church did not have the power to forgive the mortal sins of idolatry, adultery and murder. In our own day we sometimes run into people who, indulging in a form of despair, say that their sins are so great and so heinous that God cannot forgive them.

What does the Church say about this? The practice and teaching of the Catholic Church have always insisted that her power to forgive sins extends to all sin without exception. The Council of Trent summed up this tradition when it said that Christ instituted the sacrament of Penance "to reconcile the faithful with God himself as often as they fall into sin after Baptism". Also, the key texts in the Bible do not put any restrictions on this power, for example, Matthew 16:19; 18:18; John 20:23. These texts all stress the notion "whatever you loose on earth. . . ."

The only limitation on the power of the Church to forgive sins resides in the heart of the sinner himself. The one who truly repents and confesses his sins will always receive absolution and forgiveness. But the Church cannot forgive the obdurate sinner who refuses to be sorry for his sins. This is the "sin against the Holy Spirit" which the Lord says cannot be forgiven. "And so I tell you, every one of men's sins and blasphemies will be forgiven, but blasphemy against the Spirit will not be forgiven" (Mt 12:31; see also Mk 3:28ff.; Lk 12:10; Heb 6:4–6). Before the hardened sinner can be forgiven he or she must turn away from sin and turn toward God.

One area of Catholic doctrine that seriously divides Catholics from Protestants is the belief that by the absolution of the priest sins are truly and immediately forgiven. Basically and briefly, the Protestant notion is that sins are forgiven by faith and Baptism; thus, sins committed after Baptism are said to be forgiven by a renewal of faith and a return to the faith of Baptism. For the most part, therefore, they simply deny that there is a sacrament of Penance. They maintain that "the sacramental absolution of the priest is not a judicial act, but is the mere ministry of pronouncing and declaring that the sins of the person confessing are remitted, provided only that he believes himself absolved" (Trent). The Catholic Church rejects this "declaration theory" and insists that the power of absolution, which is conferred on all priests at ordination, is a real power by which sins committed against God are directly forgiven. Thus the absolution of the priest, given the necessary dispositions in the penitent, *causes* the sins to be forgiven, because it is God himself operating in and through the priest, according to the words of Jesus: "Whose sins you shall forgive, they are forgiven."

The sacrament of Penance is something like a judicial process and the priest performs the function of a judge.

For the power of the keys was given to St. Peter and the power of forgiving sins was given to the Apostles and their successors, as we have shown. The Council of Trent defined that the sacramental absolution of the priest is "a judicial act". Trent also declared: "For our Lord Jesus Christ . . . left priests to be his vicars (see Mt 16:19; 18:18; Jn 20:23), *as rulers and judges* to whose authority Christians are to submit all mortal sins that they have fallen into."

There are a number of similarities between the sacrament of Penance and a judicial process. The latter requires three basic elements: 1) judicial power, 2) knowledge of the facts of the case, 3) a judicial sentence.

All three are present in the sacrament. As we have seen, Jesus transferred the power to forgive sins to the Apostles and to their legitimate successors. In order to exercise his power in a non-arbitrary manner, the priest must know what the penitent has done and what his subjective state of soul is. Once the latter is attained, the priest, in his capacity as God's representative, pronounces a judicial sentence either to forgive or not to forgive the sins. Then in the name of Christ he pronounces the judgment of the Savior's mercy: "I absolve you from your sins, in the name of the Father, and of the Son, and of the Holy Spirit." It should be noted that the imposition of a penance on the sinner, such as saying some prayers or doing some good work, is an exercise of judicial power. However, the sacrament of Penance is a tribunal of mercy in which judgment is not punitive or vindictive, but healing and redemptive. After this "judgment" most sinners feel a great sense of relief and peace. It is as if a heavy burden has been lifted from their shoulders.

41

SORROW FOR SIN

A sacrament is a visible, efficacious sign of divine grace. Like the other sacraments, the sacrament of Penance requires certain exterior or outward actions. It is not just an interior act of the mind or the will, since it is also an action of the Church and the Church is a visible society instituted by Christ to bring all men to eternal life.

As we know from our study of the catechism, the sacrament of Penance requires three acts of the sinner: contrition, confession and satisfaction. In addition, the penitent must receive the absolution of the priest. In this and the following essays I will go into each of these aspects of the sacrament. Let us now consider briefly what is meant by "contrition".

If you have offended someone and then want to be reconciled with him or her, the best and easiest way is to repudiate your own past behavior and to tell the person offended that you are sorry for what you have done. True sorrow and the expression of it to the other person usually produce a quick restoration of former friendship and love.

Our relationship to God is something similar to our dealings with other human persons. By "sin" we mean an insult, an offense against Almighty God. As children of

Adam, we are all sinners even after our reception of Baptism. This means that we still need God's forgiveness. The first step that we must take in order to be forgiven by God is to be sorry for our sins. In order to be forgiven by God we must have true contrition for our sins. And what does the Church mean by "contrition"? Contrition is defined as sincere sorrow for having offended God, and hatred for the sins we have committed, with a firm purpose of sinning no more. Thus a true act of contrition is composed of three acts of the will which form a unity: sorrow, hatred of sin and the intention of avoiding sin in the future.

True sorrow or contrition resides in the will. One does not need to feel contrition in order to have it, but since the human person is a unity of spirit and matter, very often sorrow will overflow into the emotions and sensual part of our human nature. Sorrow can be accompanied by deep feelings and sometimes will be manifested by the shedding of tears. St. Ignatius of Loyola, after his conversion, often shed abundant tears for his past life of sin. In his *Spiritual Exercises* he urges those making a retreat, when they meditate on the evil of sin and their own past sins, to beg God for tears for their past misdeeds. Sensory feelings are not essential to true sorrow, but they do help and are often present.

As is evident from Holy Scripture, without contrition there can be no justification. Just to cite one example, we read in Isaiah 55:7: "Let the scoundrel forsake his way, and the wicked man his thoughts; let him turn to the Lord for mercy; to our God, who is generous in forgiving." Thus, contrition has always been an indispensable condition for the forgiveness of sins. And with the institution of the sacrament of Penance, true contrition must also include the intention of going to confession and doing the penance assigned by the priest.

Since there are various kinds of sorrow, one might ask: "When is sorrow for sin true contrition?" Theologians reply by assigning four qualities to true contrition: it must be interior, supernatural, supreme and universal. Let us briefly consider each of these characteristics.

Sorrow is *interior* when it comes from the heart and not just from the lips. As Jesus says in the Gospel, it is not enough to say "Lord, Lord" in order to be saved; one must also follow God's will and keep the commandments.

Sorrow is *supernatural* when, with the help of God's grace, it springs from motives of faith and not merely from purely natural motives. "Motives of faith" are truths that God has revealed, such as: mortal sin will be punished in hell; sin is an offense against the infinite goodness of God and caused Christ to die.

Sorrow is *supreme* when we hate sin above every other evil, and are willing to endure any suffering rather than offend God in the future by sin. The closer one is to God the more one realizes the evil of sin. Thus we are often astonished to read in the life of a particular saint that he considered himself the greatest sinner.

Sorrow is *universal* when we are sorry for every mortal sin which we have ever committed. When mortal sins are forgiven sanctifying grace enters the soul; if one mortal sin remains, it is impossible for sanctifying grace to take possession of the soul. Therefore, all our mortal sins must be forgiven or none of them is forgiven. When we go to confession, in addition to being sorry for all our mortal sins, we should also try to be sorry for all our venial sins.

42

PERFECT CONTRITION

In the last essay we saw that contrition is "sincere sorrow for having offended God, and hatred for the sins we have committed, with a firm purpose of sinning no more". One might ask at this point whether there is more than one kind of contrition. Catholic tradition and official Church teaching answer in the affirmative. Thus there are two kinds of contrition: perfect and imperfect. Here I will explain the meaning of *perfect contrition*; I will go into *imperfect contrition* in the following essay.

Contrition means sorrow for sin, hatred of it and the intention of avoiding it in the future. Since the Council of Trent in the sixteenth century, a distinction is made between perfect and imperfect contrition according to the motive behind it: Perfect contrition proceeds from the motive of perfect love of God; imperfect contrition proceeds from the motive of imperfect love of God, that is, from any good motive less than from the love of the absolute goodness of God in himself, for example, from the hope of eternal reward or from the fear of hell.

It follows from the variety in the motives that the two kinds of sorrow are different from each other not just in degree but also in kind, that is, they are essentially different.

It is important to stress that the motive of perfect contrition is the perfect love of God, that is, supernatural charity which consists in love for God for his own sake above all. The object of such love is God's goodness in itself.

The love of concupiscence, in which one loves God for one's own advantage, is primarily self-love and therefore only imperfectly love of God. It is a good act but it is not a sufficient motive for perfect contrition.

All Catholics should understand what perfect contrition is and they should strive to make acts of perfect contrition as often as they sin and before every confession. The reason is this: perfect contrition bestows the grace of justification on the mortal sinner even before he or she actually receives the sacrament of Penance. Let me state the same thing in another way: Whoever is sorry for his sins because he realizes that sin is an offense against the absolute goodness of God, is forgiven by God in that instant and restored to his grace.

If that is so, one might ask, then why do I have to go to confession? The answer is that perfect love of God includes the desire to fulfill the will of God and it is God's will, expressed by Jesus Christ and repeated by his Church, that all mortal sins committed after Baptism must be submitted to the authority of the Church; this takes place in the sacrament of Penance. Thus perfect sorrow for sin contains in some way, at least implicitly, the desire for the sacrament.

Although imperfect contrition is sufficient to receive the sacrament of Penance worthily, we should always try to have perfect contrition because it is more pleasing to God. And if we have the misfortune to commit a mortal sin, we should ask God's pardon and grace at once, make an act of perfect contrition and go to confession as soon as we can.

Some Catholics seem to have the idea that we can regain the state of grace by perfect contrition only when we are in danger of death or when it is impossible to go to confession. That is not true. In order to regain sanctifying grace by perfect contrition it is sufficient that we intend to go to confession as soon as we can.

When one has committed a mortal sin and then made an act of perfect contrition, may he receive Holy Communion? The answer is that normally such a person is obliged to go to confession before receiving Holy Communion. The reason is that the state of grace is required for the fruitful reception of Holy Communion. All sorrow for sin, even imperfect contrition, when joined with the sacrament of Penance, certainly restores the state of sanctifying grace. However, when a person has committed a mortal sin and then tries to make an act of perfect contrition, he cannot be certain that his sorrow really proceeds from perfect, selfless love of God. Moreover, the Church prescribes that those who have committed a mortal sin must go to confession before they can receive Communion. There can be exceptions to this norm but they are rare. Explanations of such exceptions can be found in textbooks of moral theology.

43

IMPERFECT CONTRITION

The question I propose to answer in this essay is: What kind of contrition is necessary in order to receive a valid absolution in confession? We have seen that perfect contrition is sorrow for sin that proceeds from an act of perfect love of God. Perfect contrition before confession restores one to the state of grace, provided that the intention of going to confession at the next opportunity is not excluded. Thus, a person who has committed a mortal sin, repents and makes an act of perfect contrition, if he or she should suddenly die in that condition, would be saved.

Not everyone, however, is always capable of perfect contrition. Those who have wallowed in sin for years normally find their way back to God in small stages. Thus, one can be sorry for sin for other reasons besides divine charity. Often people are very repentant because, for one reason or another, they come to see the malice of sin; or they begin to fear the divine wrath and the eternal punishment of hell. Sorrow for sin that proceeds from good motives such as these is called in Catholic theology "imperfect contrition". It is true contrition since it detests sin as the greatest evil, but it does not proceed from the highest motive, namely, the perfect love of God because of his infinite goodness.

Many of our contemporaries seem to think that fear is not a good motive for human actions. Of course, love is a higher motive than fear, but given the weakness of human nature sometimes fear is the best that we can come up with. Just consider a few examples. If we did not have a healthy fear for our physical safety, we could not drive a car for very long: We would crash into another car or perhaps drive over a steep cliff. If we did not have a healthy fear for our personal well-being, we would eat contaminated food or drink poisonous liquids. At that rate we would not long survive. So even though fear is not the highest and best motive, it is still a very good motive.

In the same way, fear for our spiritual well-being is very healthy. The Church teaches that contrition springing from the motive of fear is a morally good and supernatural act. It is often called "imperfect contrition"; in the recent past theologians also referred to it as "attrition". The Council of Trent in the sixteenth century declared that this contrition "is a gift of God and an inspiration of the Holy Spirit, not, indeed, as already dwelling in the soul, but as merely giving an impulse that helps the penitent make his way towards justification." The Council also said that imperfect contrition is "a true and very beneficial sorrow" and that it "prepares a person for the reception of grace", namely, when it is completed by the reception of sacramental absolution in confession to a priest.

That fear of God is a good motive is obvious to those who are familiar with the Bible. The Old Testament repeatedly teaches us to fear God: "The fear of the Lord is the beginning of wisdom." And Our Lord warns us in the same vein: "Do not be afraid of those who kill the body but cannot kill the soul; fear him rather who can destroy both body and soul in hell" (Mk 10:28).

Let us now return to our original question about the kind of contrition necessary for a good confession. The answer is that imperfect contrition, in the sense explained, suffices for the forgiveness of sins in the sacrament of Penance. Thus, even though the sinner might not be motivated by the perfect love of God, if he is sorry for his sins because of their malice or because he fears God's punishments, goes to confession and receives absolution from the priest, he is immediately restored to the grace and friendship of God. On this point Trent declared: "Although attrition without the sacrament of Penance cannot by itself lead the sinner to justification, still it disposes him for the attainment of God's grace in the sacrament of Penance."

The practical value of this teaching is of the highest order. If perfect contrition were required for the valid reception of the sacrament of Penance, we would never really know for sure whether or not our sins had been forgiven. It would also mean that Penance is not a sacrament of the dead but a sacrament of the living, since a person would have to be in the state of grace before going to confession. The power to forgive sins would lose its proper purpose, since mortal sins, instead of being forgiven in the sacrament of Penance, would merely be declared already forgiven. Thus, if we are truly sorry for our sins, even from a motive of fear of God, and make a good confession, we are restored to the grace of God. For this great gift we should rejoice and give thanks to the Lord.

44

IMPORTANCE OF CONFESSION

In order to receive the sacrament of Penance penitents must do certain things: They must be sorry for their sins, confess them to a priest and then carry out the assigned penance. Here I would like to point out a few things about "confession".

The Catechism defines confession as "the telling of our sins to an authorized priest for the purpose of obtaining forgiveness". Actually, "confession" is only one part of the whole sacrament of Penance. The latter is now often referred to as the sacrament of Reconciliation. For decades the Catholic faithful, at least in this country, have been accustomed to calling the sacrament simply "confession". By that they mean the reception of the sacrament. It is interesting to note that both "confession" and "Penance" stress the activity of the penitent, while the name "reconciliation" emphasizes that peace has been restored between God and the sinner.

The Catholic Church requires that each and every mortal sin committed after Baptism must be revealed to a priest in a secret confession. Thus, it is not sufficient to say, "I am sorry for all my sins," or "Please forgive me, Father, for I am a sinner." One must state which mortal sins have been committed and how many times they were committed, along with the important circumstances that change the nature of sin. This is to be done, of course, in a human way—which means to the best of one's ability. Accordingly, often approximations on the number of sins committed are the best that one can do.

When it comes to Church regulations it is important to distinguish between those that are a matter of faith, that is, those that have been ordained by God, and those that have been imposed, for one reason or another, by the human authorities in the Church. Examples of the latter are fasting on Good Friday and abstaining from meat on the Fridays of Lent in honor of the Passion of Our Lord. An example of the former is the obligation to confess our sins to a priest according to species and number. The Church teaches that the sacramental confession of sins is ordained by God; and for all those who have committed a mortal sin after Baptism it is necessary for eternal salvation.

The divine institution of and the necessity for salvation of the individual confession of sins is not explicitly stated in the New Testament, but it is a necessary consequence of the judicial power to forgive sins which Our Lord conferred on St. Peter and the Apostles and their successors (see Mt 16:19; 18:18; Jn 20:23). It is quite obvious that the power of forgiving and retaining sins can only be properly exercised if the possessor of the power of Penance knows both the sins and the dispositions of the penitent. For this the self-accusation of the penitent is absolutely necessary.

The historical testimonies imply that confession is an institution which goes back to divine ordinance. There is no indication that it was started by the Church at some point after the death of Our Lord and the Apostles.

The oldest historical records which mention the self-accusation by the sinner of individual sins committed can be traced back as early as the late second century (St. Irenaeus). One of the most learned of the early Church Fathers, Origen (185–254 A.D.), wrote about the secret confession of sinners to a priest.

As we have all learned from our own experience, individual confession of our sins to a priest is difficult. All have to do it. No one is exempt—not priest, not bishop, not even the pope. Saints have been the most eager penitents.

In the course of history various heretics and false teachers have denied the Catholic teaching about the need for individual confession. The Church strongly reasserted the doctrine at the Fourth Lateran Council in 1215 and again at Trent in 1551. In our own day and age voices are being raised once again against the constant teaching of the Church in this matter. In recent years there has been a drastic falling off in the number of confessions and there have been unjustified uses of the rite for "General Absolution".

Individual confession is difficult and men always seek ways to escape what is difficult. But the Lord has ordained that we confess our sins to the Church through the ministry of the priest. It is difficult but the Divine Healer knows that it is the best remedy both for the soul and for the mind.

45

CONFESSION OF VENIAL SINS

We have considered the importance and necessity of confessing our sins to the Church through the ministry of the priest. In order to cover the matter thoroughly, it might be helpful for many to review precisely what must, by the will of God, be mentioned in confession and what does not have to be mentioned but can be, if the penitent so wishes.

The Council of Trent in 1551 made it very clear, in its official and infallible pronouncement, that all mortal sins committed after Baptism must be told to the priest in a private confession. For the priest must make a judgment on whether to forgive or not to forgive the penitent— and he must also impose a penance; it should be obvious that he cannot reasonably do either if he does not know what the penitent has done. We are talking about sins committed *after* Baptism, since Baptism wipes away all sins, including the eternal and the temporal punishment due to them, committed before its reception.

Trent insisted on another point that has been a part of Catholic teaching on the sacrament of Penance at least since the sixteenth century. The point is that all mortal sins, according to number and kind, must be confessed, if possible. By "number" what is meant is how many times a particular sin was committed. By "kind" what is meant is the class to which they belong, such as blasphemy, disobedience, theft or a sexual sin against the Sixth Commandment. Thus, it is not sufficient to say to the priest, "I committed a sin of impurity." That is too vague. If one is confessing illicit intercourse with another person of the opposite sex, the general circumstances must be mentioned, such as fornication (with a single person), adultery (with a married person) or incest (with a close relative). Priests do not like to have to ask questions of penitents, but often they are forced to do so because the one going to confession does not fulfill the basic requirements.

A venial sin is an offense against God, but it is less serious than a mortal sin and does not separate us from the love of God and divine grace which is necessary for salvation. A sin can be venial either because the matter itself is less serious, such as telling a "white lie" in order to escape some embarrassment, or because there is a lack of complete freedom and knowledge in doing something that is seriously wrong in itself.

Many people wonder whether venial sins must be mentioned in confession. On this point the Church teaches that venial sins do not have to be mentioned in confession at all. Going back to the first centuries of the Church, Christians have recognized that there are other ways to obtain forgiveness from God for venial sins and daily imperfections, such as acts of sorrow for sin, prayer, fasting, works of charity and especially reception of Holy Communion. Also, active participation in the Penitential Rite at the beginning of Mass is a common way to secure forgiveness for our venial sins. Of course, sorrow for our sins is a prerequisite in each case.

However, the Church also says that it is permissible and good to confess our venial sins. It is not necessary but it is recommended. The Church has the power from Christ Our Lord to forgive all sins—mortal and venial. For centuries spiritual directors have recognized the value of confessing venial sins on a regular basis. Some of the benefits are: we receive the grace of the sacrament which helps us overcome our faults; we grow in humility, which is so necessary for growth in the love of God; we become more aware of the evil of sin.

Pope Pius XII often recommended the frequent reception of confession. He called it "the pious practice of frequent confession which was introduced into the Church by the inspiration of the Holy Spirit". He also said in his encyclical letter, *The Mystical Body of Christ* (1943): "Let those, therefore, among the younger clergy who make light of or lessen esteem for frequent confession realize that what they are doing is alien to the Spirit of Christ and disastrous for the Mystical Body of Christ."

Finally, it should be noted that it is also permitted (and often recommended by spiritual directors) to reconfess sins which have been forgiven in the past. This is suitable and acceptable matter for confession. Such a confession is an act of humility and submission to Christ. It results in an increase of grace and a remission of the temporal punishment due to sin. Thus, if a person has little to confess since the last confession, he or she can always mention serious sins of the past which have been forgiven and which are sorely regretted.

46

PUNISHMENT IS NOT POPULAR

In our sensual, self-indulgent, permissive society punishment is not a popular idea. The notion has spread across this land of ours that if a person is truly sorry for his past misdeeds, no matter how heinous, he should be treated mildly and be set free immediately or as soon as possible.

Some Catholics are deeply shocked when they first begin to understand the Church's teaching about how God punishes sinners. I believe it is quite true to say that most Americans do not believe in the reality of hell or, if they believe hell exists, they do not think anyone is there. Surely most of our countrymen of other denominations reject the notion of purgatory—a place of punishment and purifying for those who are saved but have not yet fully atoned for their sins. There are even many Catholics today in America who do not believe in hell and purgatory. Apparently they believe, as most Protestants seem to believe, that all believers at death go immediately and directly to heaven. That is a consoling thought but there is one problem with it: it is not true.

Look at a crucifix and see Jesus hanging there suffering terrible pain in the agony of death. Ask yourself: why did Jesus die like that? The answer is that he was carrying out his Father's will that he suffer and die for the sins of mankind. Jesus *atoned* for our sins; he made *satisfaction* for them. We know from the Bible, both the Old Testament and the New Testament, that there can be no atonement for sins without the shedding of blood, that is, without pain and suffering. Sin brings disorder into being—disorder between man and God and between man and man—and so it must be corrected.

The Church teaches the truth revealed by God that there is a twofold punishment for mortal sin: eternal punishment (= hell) and temporal punishment. Eternal punishment means final and lasting separation from God for all eternity—this is the lot of Satan and his devils.

Temporal punishment means the pain, sufferings and trials that the sinner must still endure after the guilt of his sins has been forgiven. Thus, the book of Genesis relates how Adam and Eve suffered for the rest of their lives as the result of their sin, even though they had repented. Moses was punished for his sin, even though he had repented and had been forgiven by the Lord (Nb 20:11ff.). Even though King David repented of his adultery with Bathsheba and was forgiven by the Lord, he and his descendants were punished because of it (2 Sam 12:13ff.).

For our consideration here on the sacrament of Penance, the point is that sorrow for sin, confession to the priest and absolution are not the end of the matter. Penance must still be done by the one forgiven. It is for this reason that the priest must impose some kind of penance on the sinner who seeks reconciliation with the Church.

As I have mentioned before, in order to make a good confession there are three things required of the repentant Catholic: 1) sorrow for sins committed; 2) confession of all mortal sins committed since the last good confession; 3) satisfaction or atonement for those sins. This latter means that the penitent must perform the penance imposed by the confessor.

Awareness of the need to do penance for one's sins was most intense in the early Church. As a result, severe penances were imposed on sinners for grave sins —and they did not, as a rule, receive the absolution of the bishop or priest until *after* they had performed the penance. Some were required to fast regularly for months or years; some were directed to do charitable works for many months; others were directed to undertake long and arduous pilgrimages to distant shrines. After the completion of the penance, then the penitent would go to the bishop or priest to receive absolution and be reconciled with the Church.

Satisfaction is also due to God as a result of venial sins. Since we are all sinners, this means that each of us has his or her debt to pay to God. Do all Catholics have all these "debts" paid to God at death, so that they go immediately to heaven? I don't think so, and this has not been the belief or practice of the Catholic Church. It is because of the doctrine about temporal punishment due to sin that we offer Masses "for the repose of the souls" of those who die in the Lord. If they died in the grace of God they are certainly saved, but they may have to be purified for a time in purgatory. For this reason we offer prayers and sacrifices for them. In Catholic tradition some of the principal ways of atoning for sin are: prayers, attending Mass, fasting, almsgiving, charitable deeds for others and self-denial of all kinds. Since we are all members of the one Body of Christ we can atone both for our own sins and for the sins of others—either living or dead. Thus, the Church urges us to pray not only for ourselves but also for sinners and for the dead.

47

RECONCILIATION WITH GOD

The Church requires that all Catholics receive the Holy Eucharist at least once a year during the Easter season which lasts from Ash Wednesday to Trinity Sunday. This means, then, that those who have committed a serious sin during the preceding year must also make a good confession and receive absolution. This has been the law of the Church since the Fourth Lateran Council in 1215.

In order to receive the Eucharist worthily a person must be in the state of sanctifying grace. For sinners, the way to regain the state of grace is to receive the sacrament of Penance worthily. The result is that they are reconciled with God. It is for this reason that Penance is now often, since Vatican II, referred to as the "sacrament of Reconciliation".

Reconciliation with God, which is effected by the sacrament, means not only that God forgives the sins confessed, but it also means that he restores the repentant sinner to the state of sanctifying grace. If the one who goes to confession has no serious sins to confess, then through the reception of the sacrament that person receives an increase of grace.

As I pointed out in the discussion of "satisfaction",

the eradication of the guilt of mortal sin through the sacrament of Penance includes the remission of the eternal punishment due to mortal sin. The temporal punishments for sin, however, are not always fully remitted; satisfaction for these must be made either by good works in this life or by the purification of purgatory.

Most Catholics find some difficulty, even embarrassment, in going to confession. In the best of circumstances it is not easy to admit that you were wrong. But at the same time sin and guilt place a heavy burden on the mind and the soul. We have all experienced the profound sense of peace and relief at making a good confession. The joy and peace of reconciliation with God are often experienced by large numbers of penitents at Christmas and Easter.

It is quite obvious that the state of our soul before God affects the way we think—it has a far-reaching psychological effect on us. Guilt produces anxiety, while friendship with God is accompanied by a certain peace of soul. The Council of Trent touched on this point and remarked that the worthy reception of the sacrament of reconciliation "is sometimes followed by peace and serenity of conscience joined to a great consolation of soul". Archbishop Fulton J. Sheen often spoke and wrote about this aspect of the sacrament. Please note that the Council says "sometimes"; it does not say "always". Such feelings may be present, but they are not necessary. For if a person makes a good confession and receives absolution God forgives the sins. So the forgiveness of sins is wholly independent of any subsequent feelings of serenity or consolation.

A further point that might be of help is the question of the necessity of the sacrament of Penance. One might say that Baptism and the Eucharist are sufficient and that there is no real need to receive the sacrament of Penance. Most Protestants seem to hold that position and now, with the drastic decline in the number of Catholics going to confession, one gets the impression that the same notion is gaining ground in the Church.

The Council of Trent, however, drew a close parallel between the necessity of Penance and the necessity of Baptism. Both were instituted by Christ. Baptism is absolutely required for salvation. But Penance is necessary for those who fall into mortal sin after Baptism. For if they lose the grace of God after once having gained it in Baptism, how are they to return to the grace of God? In his mercy the Lord has provided us with the great and consoling sacrament of Penance. If someone never committed a serious sin after Baptism then that person would never have to go to confession, strictly speaking, since the Church does not require the confession of venial sins, which we all commit, as I explained before.

The Fathers of the Church saw a certain similarity between Penance and Baptism, for they are two fundamental ways of gaining the grace of God—passing from a state of wrath to being a child of God. Thus they spoke of it in such terms as "laborious Baptism", "Baptism of tears"; St. Jerome referred to Penance as the "second lifesaver after shipwreck". By that he meant that original sin was the shipwreck for man, while Baptism was the first lifesaver and, after man has been lost, Penance was the second.

48

WHO CAN HEAR CONFESSIONS?

The first time I read a biography of St. Ignatius Loyola, founder of the Jesuit Order in the sixteenth century, I was very surprised to learn that, before going into his last military battle (in which he incurred a serious wound that changed the course of his life), he knelt down and confessed his sins to a comrade in arms who was a layman, not a priest. At the time I was, I believe, about seventeen and had never heard of anyone confessing his sins to a lay person.

A close study of the history of the Church will uncover many strange things. In the early Church great stress was placed on the *satisfaction* connected with the sacrament of Penance, that is, with the performance of severe penances for long periods of time. By the Middle Ages there had been a certain shift of emphasis toward contrition and sorrow for sin. It seems that some considered contrition sufficient for the reception of the sacrament, so that the absolution of the priest could be dispensed with. We know, of course, that perfect contrition with the intention of confessing at the next opportunity secures God's forgiveness and restores a person to the state of grace. In Ignatius' time confession to a lay person in a time of necessity or in danger of death was practiced as a means of stirring up acts of perfect love of God that would restore one to the grace of God. It is not clear whether or not lay persons in such situations presumed to impart some kind of "absolution".

The above account raises the question: Who has the power to absolve from sins in a sacramental way? Even though there may have been some doubt about this in the early Church, there is no doubt about it now and since the Council of Trent in the sixteenth century. For that Council infallibly declared as an article of faith that the sole possessors of the Church's power of absolution are the bishops and the priests. Jesus promised the power of the keys or absolution to the Apostles only (Mt 18:18) and conferred this power on them only (Jn 20:23). That power was passed on from the Apostles to their successors in the priesthood, the bishops and the priests, by the imposition of hands.

It should be remembered that Our Lord established his Church which is a hierarchical community with a variety of functions and powers. Certain priestly powers, such as offering Mass and reconciling sinners, were given to the Apostles and their successors only. In a certain sense, of course, all the faithful are a "priestly people", but there remains an essential difference between the ordained priesthood and the priesthood of all the faithful. Only bishops and priests, therefore, can truly absolve from sins in the sacrament of Penance.

There is another notion connected with the hearing of confessions which many Catholics do not seem to understand. What I am referring to here is what is known as *jurisdiction*. We are familiar with the idea that city police do not have authority outside the city limits. Likewise, state police have authority only in their own state. Therefore, criminals often get out of town or out of the state in order to escape the clutches of the law. There is something similar in Church law.

In order to hear confessions validly and licitly in a given place, a priest must have *jurisdiction* in that place. Jurisdiction is defined as the spiritual power of governing the faithful; and administering the sacrament of Penance is an exercise of spiritual power.

Jurisdiction works like this. The pope and the cardinals have jurisdiction over the whole Church. A bishop who is head of a diocese has jurisdiction over everyone in that territory. Pastors have jurisdiction over their parishes. Those who have spiritual power can often delegate it to others. Thus, when a priest moves into a new diocese, he must receive jurisdiction or "faculties" from the bishop of the place before he can preach and hear confessions.

This is a serious matter, for often the validity of the sacrament depends on whether or not the officiating priest has the proper authorization. Sometimes Catholics are shocked to hear a priest tell them that he cannot hear their confession because he does not have faculties in that diocese. In danger of death, however, and in certain urgent situations, the law of the Church provides jurisdiction to any priest—this is for the spiritual good of the faithful.

49

A SACRAMENT FOR THE SICK

Our Lord instituted the seven sacraments to assist us in our journey to heaven. If you reflect on them for a moment, you will see that they are associated with the critical moments in each person's life: for example, birth (Baptism), personal awareness on attaining the age of reason (Penance and the Eucharist), choosing a spouse (Matrimony). There is also a sacrament for intense suffering and the danger of death. This sacrament formerly was called "Extreme Unction", meaning "the last anointing". It is now called "Anointing of the Sick".

The new name is more appropriate and more correctly describes the sacrament, since it is not necessary to be at the very point of death in order to receive the spiritual strengthening imparted by the sacred anointing. Since the Second Vatican Council this holy rite has come into more common use among the faithful. Now it is often given to the elderly during a service in church and to those who are about to undergo surgery. Before the Council many people were reluctant to call a priest in a serious sickness to administer "the last rites" either because they did not want to admit that their loved one was really dying or because they did not want to frighten the sick person to death.

For some years now the Church has striven to instruct the faithful on the true meaning of this great and consoling sacrament. All should realize that when a person is seriously sick or about to undergo major surgery he or she has a right to the sacrament and should receive it if at all possible.

The holy anointing of the Church is the sacrament of the sick. Sickness, pain and death have always been a heavy burden for man and a mystery for his mind. All men have to suffer—there is no escape. We come into this world in suffering; our days are dotted with physical and mental sufferings; we go out of this world in suffering.

The Christian suffers just like the rest of mankind but with a difference: The Christian has faith and by faith in Jesus Christ he is able to understand at least some of the dimensions of the mystery of suffering and death. The Christian knows that Jesus, the Sinless One, freely suffered and died, not for his sins, but for the sins of the whole world. He knows that Christ calls him to follow him in suffering and death. The Christian knows that he is a sinner and that by obedient acceptance of his sufferings he can atone for his own sins and for the sins of others.

We know from revelation that sickness, suffering and death are the result of original sin. They were not intended by God for man, but Adam and Eve brought them upon the whole human family. So sickness is not necessarily the punishment for personal sin, as we know from John 9:3. Jesus himself was sinless, yet he suffered much and was finally nailed to a cross.

In his mercy the Lord has not left us defenseless

in the face of sickness, pain and death. He has given us a powerful spiritual weapon in the sacrament of the Anointing of the Sick. It may be defined as the sacrament in virtue of which the sick Christian by the anointing with oil and the prayer of the priest receives the grace of God for the supernatural salvation of his soul and often also for the natural healing of his body.

Though denied by Protestants, the Church teaches that the Anointing of the Sick by the priest is a true and proper sacrament which was instituted by Christ. The Council of Trent rejected the Protestant contention that this sacrament is a human invention—either of the Fathers of the Church or of those who came after them.

The biblical basis of the sacrament is found in Mark 6:13 where Jesus sends out the twelve to preach the Good News and to drive out devils. St. Mark says also that they "anointed many sick people with oil and cured them". But the principal scriptural text in support of the sacrament is James 5:14–15: "If one of you is ill, he should send for the elders of the church, and they must anoint him with oil in the name of the Lord and pray over him. The prayer of faith will save the sick man and the Lord will raise him up again; and if he has committed any sins, he will be forgiven."

In the above passage from James we find all the elements of a true sacrament: 1) an outward sign of grace, consisting of anointing with oil and of the prayer of the priest over the sick person; 2) an inner operation of grace through the communication of grace and the forgiveness of sins; 3) institution by Christ, since the Apostles regarded themselves merely as "ministers of Christ and dispensers of the mysteries of God" (1 Cor 4:1).

50

HEALING FOR SOUL AND BODY

The four Gospels inform us that Jesus, in his ministry in Galilee and Judea, was very solicitous for the sick and infirm. Most of his miracles were directed to curing the blind, the lame, the possessed and those with impaired hearing. He gave his disciples power to heal the sick. Thus Jesus stands out as a healer. It is not surprising, therefore, that in his permanent legacy to his Church he bequeathed a sacred rite or sacrament for the sick. That sacrament is called the Anointing of the Sick.

The ancients saw in oil, especially olive oil, a sign of strength and health. They believed that oil contains restorative and medicinal powers, so they used it abundantly in treating the sick. For example, they used oil to wash open wounds. Since sacraments are visible signs of invisible grace, as we have seen, it is fitting therefore that Jesus should choose anointing with oil as the visible "sign" for the sacrament of the sick.

In order to administer the sacrament correctly, the priest must normally anoint the sick person with oil on the forehead and hands and pray over him/her in the manner prescribed by the Church. Until 1972 it was necessary to use olive oil blessed by the bishop on Holy

Thursday. In his new directives for the renewal of the sacrament, Pope Paul VI decreed that olive oil is still to be preferred, but he also declared that a suitable oil from other plants may be used in those areas where olive oil is not available or very difficult to acquire.

The anointing on forehead and hands must be accompanied by the prayer of faith, as St. James says: "Is there anyone sick among you? Let him call for the elders of the Church, and let them pray over him and anoint him in the name of the Lord. This prayer, made in faith, will save the sick man. The Lord will restore his health, and if he has committed any sins, they will be forgiven" (5:14–15).

The prayer which the priest must say while he is anointing the sick person is as follows: "Through this holy anointing may the Lord in his love and mercy help you with the grace of the Holy Spirit. May the Lord who frees you from sin save you and raise you up." If, for one reason or another, it is not possible to anoint a dying person on the forehead or hands, then it is permissible to anoint him/her on any major portion of the body which is accessible.

What are the effects of the sacrament of Anointing of the Sick? According to St. James and the teaching of the Council of Trent, the effects are twofold: salvation of the soul and healing of the body.

The spiritual effects of the sacrament include the bestowal of sanctifying grace, forgiveness of sins, comfort in sickness and strength against the temptations of the devil as death approaches, preparation for immediate entrance into heaven by the remission of venial sins and the cleansing of the soul from moral weakness and indifference caused by original and actual sin.

Since Anointing of the Sick is a sacrament of the living, normally it presupposes the state of sanctifying grace in the person who receives it. Thus it should be preceded by a good confession, if at all possible. However, if a person in mortal sin is unconscious and not able to go to confession, he may receive the sacrament of Anointing. In this case the sacrament forgives his sins and restores him to the state of grace, provided that he has turned away from sin and has in some sense made an act of imperfect contrition before falling into unconsciousness.

Sometimes this sacrament brings about the restoration of bodily health. As we noted above, St. James says, "This prayer, made in faith, will save the sick man. The Lord will restore his health. . . ." The Council of Trent put it in the following way: "This anointing occasionally restores health to the body if health would be of advantage to the salvation of the soul." Thus, at times the sacrament works a bodily cure, but only if it contributes to the salvation of the soul of the person.

When health is restored through the sacrament it is not produced directly in a miraculous manner, but indirectly by the fact that, because of the intimate connection between the soul and the body, the spiritual strengthening of the soul brings about the restoration of the body to health. So the sacrament presupposes the possibility of natural healing.

These truths about the sacrament of Anointing of the Sick should be pondered seriously. The sacrament is a great gift of the Lord and certainly we need all the help we can get in order to save our souls and finally reach God. I would ask each person who reads this to make the intention right now to receive the sacrament when seriously ill and especially at the hour of death. And we should do all in our power to get a priest for those who are dying: For their eternal salvation may depend on receiving this sacrament.

51

WHO SHOULD BE ANOINTED?

Who can legitimately receive the Anointing of the Sick? The Second Vatican Council said that it "is not a sacrament for those only who are at the point of death. Hence, as soon as anyone of the faithful begins to be in danger of death from sickness or old age, the fitting time for him to receive this sacrament has certainly already arrived" (Sacred Liturgy, no. 73). Thus sickness or old age that involve some danger of death are sufficient requirements in the one who is to receive the sacrament. Obviously the person must also be baptized and have attained the use of reason. Since the anointing is the culmination of the sacrament of Penance, and since it can forgive personal sins, it cannot be administered to infants who have not yet attained the use of reason.

It is very important to note that one does not have to be at death's door in order to be ready for the sacrament. A prudent or probable judgment about the seriousness of the sickness is sufficient. The general rule is that one may receive the sacrament only once during the same sickness. However, if, after having received the sacrament, a person recovers considerably and then has a relapse, he may be anointed again.

Also, a sick person should be anointed before surgery whenever a dangerous illness is the reason for the surgery. Thus, those about to undergo major surgery should be anointed beforehand, since they are sick and there is always the possibility that they might die either during or after the operation.

A healthy development in thinking about the Anointing of the Sick concerns its administration to old people. The revised rite for the sacrament says: "Old people may be anointed if they are in weak condition although no dangerous illness is present." Accordingly, many parishes now schedule special Masses for the elderly at which the sacrament is administered to them. A few years ago I took a group of pilgrims to the shrine of Our Lady at Knock, Ireland. Every day a special Mass is celebrated at 3 P.M. and during the Mass the elderly and infirm are anointed. We saw hundreds of the faithful at that service and many of them approached the priests to be anointed.

Since the sacrament requires faith and the proper dispositions, it may not be administered indiscriminately. Thus, there must be some indication that the sick person wishes to receive it. Those who are conscious can ask for it, and should be urged to do so. Also, those who are unconscious may be anointed if, as Christian believers, they would have asked for it were they in control of their faculties. If they had faith and wanted to die as Catholics, that is sufficient.

The sacrament may not be administered to one who is certainly dead. Often, however, there is doubt about whether a person is dead or not. When there is doubt, the priest may anoint the person conditionally. By this is meant that the priest says, before administering the sacrament, "If you are alive . . ." or "If you are capable of receiving the sacrament. . . ." Evidence points to the probability that the soul does not leave the body immediately when the signs of life cease. Thus one can anoint an apparently dead person for a number of hours afterwards. Many moralists would extend the time up to three hours.

Who can administer the sacrament of Anointing? St. James says that "the elders of the Church" should do it. The tradition of the Church and the decree of the Council of Trent interpret this to mean the bishop and priests. Normally it will be the pastor of the place or the chaplain of the hospital where the sick person is staying. In a case of necessity any priest can hear the confession of a dying person and also anoint him or her.

The Church wants all of her children to receive this sacrament before they face their eternal judge. She urges priests to be diligent in administering the sacrament. In the new official Rite for the sacrament we read: "In public and private catechesis, the faithful should be encouraged to ask for the anointing and, as soon as the time for the anointing comes, to receive it with complete faith and devotion, not misusing this sacrament by putting it off. All who care for the sick should be taught the meaning and purpose of anointing."

52

THE MEANING OF HOLY ORDERS

So far in this series of essays on the sacraments we have considered the special acts of Christ which pertain to the sanctification of the individual person—Baptism, Confirmation, Holy Eucharist, Penance and Anointing. There remain two Sacraments—Holy Orders and Matrimony—which look to the spiritual welfare of the Christian community. The former provides for the spiritual growth of the Church, while the latter assures that husband and wife can mature in Christ and continue the Church in history by adding new members. We will now reflect on the main truths connected with the sacrament of Holy Orders.

One might ask, "Why is the sacrament that constitutes deacons, priests and bishops called 'Orders'?" Or, "What does the priesthood have to do with 'order'?" This is an important point, since it touches on the role and function of the priest in the Catholic community. In this context we should recall that Jesus Christ founded a hierarchical society. Through Baptism, of course, we are all children of God and heirs of heaven. However, a well-ordered community with thousands and millions of members requires different functions of leadership, teaching and sanctifying. In order to achieve this goal there must be a proper relationship between all the parts or members; there must be some *order*. By the institution of Christ himself, the members of the Christian community who provide and secure this *order* are those who have received special powers from the Apostles through the imposition of hands, namely, bishops, priests and deacons. Therefore the sacramental rite or sacred sign that imparts that special power in the community is called "Holy Orders".

Holy Orders is defined as that sacrament in which a spiritual power is conferred on one of the faithful by the imposition of hands and the prayer of the bishop, together with the grace necessary to exercise this power in a manner pleasing to God.

It is the official teaching of the Church, sanctioned by the Council of Trent in the sixteenth century and often repeated by the popes (also by Vatican II), that Christ Our Lord himself instituted Holy Orders. For, on the same first Holy Thursday on which he instituted the Eucharist, Jesus also conferred the priesthood on his Apostles and said, "Do this in remembrance of me" (Lk 22:19–20). On Easter Sunday evening he appeared to his Apostles. Breathing on them—a sign of imparting the Holy Spirit—he said: "Receive the Holy Spirit. For those whose sins you forgive, they are forgiven; for those whose sins you retain, they are retained" (Jn 20:22–23).

We read in the Acts of the Apostles that they established deacons by praying and imposing hands on them (6:6). Paul and Barnabas appointed elders (or priests) in the various churches they founded: "In each of these churches they appointed elders, and with prayer and fasting they commended them to the Lord in whom they had come to believe" (Acts 14:23). St. Paul wrote to his disciple

Timothy: "That is why I am reminding you now to fan into a flame the gift that God gave you when I laid my hands on you" (2 Tim 1:6).

Thus we see from the New Testament that acceptance into the Church's hierarchy took place by a religious rite of prayer and the imposition of hands, started and perpetuated by Jesus' Apostles. The Fathers of the Church testify to this rite and the Church has always taught that there is an essential difference between the ordained priesthood and the priesthood of the laity which is praised in 1 Peter 2:9.

By the external rite of ordination a spiritual power or office among the people of God is conveyed to the one ordained and interior supernatural grace is communicated to him. Thus the sacrament of Holy Orders confers grace. But only God or the God-Man Jesus Christ can causally associate the communication of inward grace with an outward rite like the imposition of hands. This shows that Jesus instituted the sacrament of Holy Orders and that the Apostles carried out his most holy will.

Let us listen to St. Gregory of Nyssa who compares the consecration of priests with the consecration of the Eucharist: "The same power of the word makes the priest also sublime and venerable, marked off from the crowd by the rarity of consecration. Yesterday and the day before yesterday he was one of many, one of the crowd. All at once he becomes a leader, an overseer, a teacher of piety, a perfector of the concealed mysteries. And this without changing body and form. As to the outside he remains the same as he was, but by an invisible power and grace his invisible soul has been changed for the better."

53

HOLY ORDERS COMES IN THREE STAGES

Priesthood is intimately related to sacrifice. Thus, if there were no sacrifice of the Mass in the Church, there would be no need for priests. Holy Orders is a sacrament which was instituted by Christ Our Lord to continue until the end of the world the priestly office which he committed to his Apostles. The role of the Apostles is to be servants of Christ and stewards of the mysteries of God (see 1 Cor 4:1). The "mysteries of God" that pastors have charge of are the Eucharist and the other sacraments.

We know from Scripture and the tradition of the Church that priests are primarily concerned with the administration of the sacraments and the proclamation of the Good News of salvation in Jesus Christ. In the long history of the Church priests have done many other things—we see much evidence of that today—but their primary concern has been and is the Sacraments and the Word of God.

One thing that distinguishes Holy Orders from the other six sacraments is that it must be received in stages, or in parts, or in degrees, since there are three "orders" to the one Holy Orders, namely, bishop, priest and deacon. It should be remembered, as I have stressed before, that Jesus instituted *seven* sacraments and only seven. Holy Orders, therefore, is just one sacrament, even though it consists of three levels or three degrees, bishop, priest and deacon.

Ordination on each level involves the reception of the Holy Spirit and the reception of certain spiritual powers for the good of the faithful. The fullness of the sacrament is found in the ordination of a bishop, since to him is communicated the power not only to consecrate the Eucharist and forgive sins but also the power of *communicating to others the power* of consecrating the Eucharist and forgiving sins. In short, a bishop has the sacred power of ordaining others to the priesthood while the ordinary priest does not have that power. The bishop is also the ordinary minister of the sacrament of Confirmation; priests have the spiritual power to confirm but are allowed to do so only in certain circumstances.

The sacrament of Holy Orders is also conferred on the priest and the deacon. The priest, through his ordination, receives the power from Christ to consecrate bread and wine into the Body and Blood of Christ. He also receives the power to forgive sins and to administer the other sacraments, with the exception of Holy Orders.

The lowest degree of Holy Orders is conferred on the deacon who is ordained to assist the priest and the Christian community. He can help at the altar; he is allowed to handle the Body of Christ and to administer the Cup. He is empowered to preach the word of God from the pulpit, to baptize and to assist at marriages.

We are all aware of the fact that our bishops, in union with and under the leadership of the Holy Father (who is bishop of Rome), rule and guide the Church. The Church teaches infallibly in the Council of Trent (1563) that bishops are superior to priests. According to Vatican II, they are the successors of the Apostles and so direct the Church by the will of Christ. They are not in any sense usurpers. Their preeminence resides in the fact that they are the successors of the Apostles, that they can communicate the power of the priesthood to others and so perpetuate the eucharistic sacrifice until the end of time, that they have the power of jurisdiction over those under their pastoral care.

Thus, in a very special way bishops take the place of Christ for the faithful and for that reason deserve the respect due to their office.

54

SACRED RITE OF ORDINATION

The ordination rite in the Catholic Church—whether for a deacon or a priest or a bishop—is a beautiful and inspiring ceremony. Most Catholics, perhaps, have never assisted at such a service. I would urge all those who have not witnessed an ordination to make every effort to do so at the next opportunity.

To ordain someone means to invest him officially with ministerial or priestly authority. As we have seen, according to the will of Christ there are three levels or degrees of the sacrament of Holy Orders—diaconate, priesthood and episcopate. The conferral of Holy Orders on the man judged worthy by the bishop takes place through an external, sacred sign. Also, the minister of the sacrament of Orders is the bishop and only the bishop.

Actually, the ceremony or sacred rite of ordination is quite simple. It consists of two main parts: 1) the ordaining prelate must impose or lay his hands on the head of the one being ordained. This he does in silence, but of course he must have the intention of ordaining or conferring the power of orders and the grace of the Holy Spirit; 2) next the ordaining bishop must pray over the candidate, using the prescribed words or formula of the "Order Preface" as prescribed by the Holy See. When those two actions have been completed, namely, the imposition of hands and the proper prayer said by the bishop, the candidate (deacon, priest or bishop) is duly ordained in the Catholic Church.

The imposition of hands for the conferral of an office in the Church, as we have seen, goes back to the Apostles. Thus when the first community in Jerusalem had selected seven men to be deacons, "They presented these to the Apostles, who prayed and laid their hands on them" (Acts 6:6). And St. Paul said to his disciple Timothy: "You have in you a spiritual gift which was given to you when the prophets spoke and the body of elders laid their hands on you" (1 Tim 4:14). The same gift is not to be conferred lightly: "Do not be too quick to lay hands on any man" (1 Tim 5:22), and it is to be carefully guarded: "I am reminding you now to fan into a flame the gift that God gave you when I laid my hands on you" (2 Tim 1:6).

From a historical and theological point of view it is clear that the imposition of hands has always been an essential part of the ordination rite. This is true both for the Eastern Church and for the Roman Catholic Church. The Church has officially defined in the Council of Trent that the sacrament of Holy Orders was instituted by Christ. Our Lord conferred the full priesthood on his Apostles at the Last Supper when he said to them, "Do this in memory of me."

There is some dispute among theologians as to whether Jesus specifically told his Apostles to impose hands with a special prayer in order to confer the sacrament, or whether he just gave them more general directions to continue the priestly office in the Church and left it up to them how that office would be transmitted from generation to generation. The more common opinion among theologians is that Our Lord told the Apostles specifically what to do in this matter.

From the Middle Ages until 1947 there was some dispute among theologians about the matter and form of the sacrament. In that year Pope Pius XII settled the question once and for all with his Apostolic Constitution, *Sacramentum Ordinis*. In that document he decreed: "The matter of the holy orders of diaconate, priesthood, and episcopate, is the imposition of hands and that alone; and the form (likewise the only form) is the words determining the application of this matter. . . ." As he did in so many other instances, Pius XII clarified the question, resolved doubts and set consciences at ease.

55

ONCE A PRIEST ALWAYS A PRIEST

I explained the meaning of the rite of ordination to the diaconate, priesthood and episcopate. We saw that two things are involved: The ordaining bishop must impose his hands on the head of the one being ordained and then he must pray over him, using the Church's prescribed formula for this rite. That is a brief explanation of the external rite of ordination, visible to all present at the ceremony.

But what, if anything, happens to the man who is ordained according to the norms of the Church? Is ordination merely an external rite which designates an individual to perform certain functions, similar to the President's naming someone to a position in his cabinet or to be the U.S. ambassador to France? The Church replies that the sacrament of Orders has two interior, spiritual effects on the person who receives it: sanctifying grace and the sacramental "character" which I explained previously in connection with the sacraments of Baptism and Confirmation.

First of all, it is an article of divine faith that the seven sacraments, properly administered, confer sanctifying grace. Since Holy Orders is one of the sacraments instituted by Christ it must, therefore, effect an increase of grace. St. Paul said in his second letter to Timothy 1:6: "I admonish you to stir up the grace of God which is in you by the laying on of my hands." The purpose of the grace of Holy Orders is twofold: to enable the recipient worthily to perform the functions of deacon or priest or bishop and to help him lead a holy life in accordance with his sacred office.

It should be obvious that Holy Orders is primarily a divine gift for the good of the community, since the priest is there to proclaim the saving word of God and to administer the sacraments. Secondarily, Orders is a special means of sanctification for those who receive it.

If you reflect for a moment you will note that some sacraments can be repeated while others cannot. From apostolic times it was the practice of the Church never to repeat Baptism, Confirmation and Holy Orders. St. Augustine seems to be the first Church Father to explain clearly the reason for this. He referred to the action of Christ on the soul as stamping us "with his seal", as it is expressed by St. Paul (2 Cor 1:21–22; Eph 1:13–14 and 4:30). Augustine called this seal the sacramental "character", in the sense of a mark or brand.

A sacramental character is defined as a permanent spiritual quality, inhering in the soul, which gives the one who receives it a special position in the Church. The Council of Trent taught infallibly in 1563 that Holy Orders imprints a character "which can neither be blotted out nor taken away". Thus, a consequence of ordination is: once a priest always a priest. And we usually sing at the ordination ceremony: "You are a priest forever according to the order of Melchizedek."

In recent years we have witnessed the sad spectacle of thousands of priests leaving the active priesthood and returning to the lay state. Most of them are now married. What has happened to their priesthood? Because of the permanent character received in ordination, they remain priests forever but, if they are legitimately "laicized" by Church authority, they are dispensed from the obligations of the priesthood (especially celibacy and the requirement to pray the Divine Office each day) and are forbidden to function as a priest in preaching and administering the sacraments. But even a laicized priest can hear the confession of someone who is dying, provided that another priest is not available.

Bishops, priests and deacons have certain spiritual powers which are rooted in the sacramental character of ordination. These powers are especially directed to the Sacrifice of the Mass and the Holy Eucharist. By reason of ordination, the deacon can baptize, witness marriages, preach and assist the priest at Mass; the priest receives the power to consecrate bread and wine into the Body and Blood of Christ and to absolve from sins; the bishop receives the power of ordination. Of course, a higher grade of Orders contains all the powers of the lower Orders.

The Second Vatican Council stressed that all the faithful share in the priesthood of Christ, but not all in the same way. There is therefore an essential difference between the priesthood of the faithful and the ordained priesthood. A practical consequence of this is that only bishops and priests have the sacred power to celebrate the Eucharist and to forgive sins.

56

WHO CAN ORDAIN AND WHO CAN BE ORDAINED?

Because of the agitation of a few laywomen and radical nuns who are demanding to be ordained to the priesthood in the Catholic Church, there is now more than usual interest in all aspects of the sacrament of Holy Orders. Given the rare, even sensational, feature of women wanting to be Catholic priests, the media have given extensive and supportive coverage to the issue. Accordingly, I now propose to present the basics of Church teaching on who can confer Holy Orders and who can receive them.

It has always been Catholic teaching that the bishop is the ordinary minister of the sacrament of Holy Orders by divine institution, that is, only a validly consecrated bishop can ordain a baptized male to the Orders of diaconate, priesthood and episcopate. This teaching was solemnly proclaimed by the Council of Trent; it is legislated by canon law; Holy Scripture indicates only bishops as the ministers of sacred Orders (Acts 6:6; 13:3; 1 Tim 4:14; 5:22; 2 Tim 1:6). Ancient liturgical and canonical writings testify that this has been the traditional practice of the Church.

For his own personal spiritual good, the ordaining bishop should be in the state of sanctifying grace and he should act according to the norms of the Church as prescribed by canon law and the special directives of the Holy See. In order validly to confer the sacrament he must impose hands on the candidates and offer the prescribed prayer (= the necessary matter and form). The ordaining bishop must also have the interior intention of conferring the sacrament. Thus if, as an unlikely example, an ordaining bishop properly performed all of the external rites but internally did not have the intention of conferring the sacrament, the candidates for the priesthood would not be ordained. As in all of the sacraments, the minister must at least have the intention to do what the Church does in such situations.

In order to insure that only worthy candidates will be ordained to preach the word of God and administer the sacraments, over the centuries the Church has developed a rather strict code for admittance to ordination.

The first condition is that only a baptized male is a capable subject of valid ordination. Also, candidates must have the intention to receive the sacrament of Orders. In her law, the Church has added a number of other conditions. For example, candidates for the priesthood must have a vocation from God for celibacy and the clerical life; they must have certain physical, intellectual and moral qualities. With regard to education, canon law requires that diocesan seminarians must be well into their fourth year of theological studies before they can be ordained. The age established by law for the various Orders is: twenty-two for the diaconate, twenty-four for the priesthood and thirty for the episcopacy.

Intimately connected with ordination, of course, is the

whole question of a "vocation" to the priesthood. Even though the Church has always recognized a vocation to the priesthood only in Catholic men, now we read in the newspapers that certain women are claiming that they have a "vocation" to the priesthood.

A true vocation is a divine interior call of grace. It presupposes both natural and supernatural gifts that will enable the one called to be a worthy minister of the Church for the good of the faithful. Traditionally, the real validation of a "vocation" comes when ecclesiastical authority accepts a candidate for the priesthood and allows him to proceed along the established route toward Holy Orders.

Church law also establishes a number of impediments (such as the marriage bond or being a recent convert) and what are called "irregularities" (such as illegitimacy, serious physical defects such as blindness and insanity). These are all obstacles to ordination. The mere passage of time will take care of some of them, while others may require a dispensation from the competent authority.

Since Holy Orders is a sacrament of the living, it should be received in the state of grace. In order to insure that only holy and learned men will be ordained, the Church has wisely established many requirements. The system is not absolutely foolproof—nothing human is. But since the time of the Council of Trent the diocesan seminaries, for the most part, have served the Church well. Good seminaries have an importance for the Church that is hard to exaggerate.

57

WHY WOMEN CANNOT BE ORDAINED

The media have made all of us very much aware of the fact that a few nuns and laywomen are demanding that the Catholic Church admit women to the sacrament of Holy Orders. In concluding our treatment of Orders it might be worthwhile to present some of the reasons why women cannot be ordained priests (or priestesses). We will pass over other questions which could be taken up in connection with this sacrament, such as vocation to the priesthood, celibacy and the "laicization" of priests who do not wish to continue in the active ministry. These pertain to Church discipline and are important, but they do not touch directly the nature of the sacrament.

It is common knowledge that women are not and never have been admitted to the Catholic priesthood. In the early Church some heretical groups did ordain women, but that was just one more sign that they had broken communion with the apostolic Church of Christ. It is simply an historical fact that women have never been ordained priests (or priestesses) in the Catholic Church —either in the West or in the East. The heart of the present dispute does not concern that fact but rather whether it is theologically possible to ordain women and, given the possibility, whether women actually should be ordained to serve in the active ministry as priests and bishops—proclaiming God's word and administering the sacraments to the faithful.

Many years ago Protestants admitted women to the ministry—to the chagrin of many, but since the Protestants never admitted that Holy Orders was a sacrament instituted by Christ, they saw no basic problem with it. Since 1971 various segments of the worldwide Anglican communion have ordained women. In 1974 the first eleven in this country were "ordained" in Philadelphia. In recent years this issue has led to severe strain in the Episcopal church in America and to further division.

In response to agitation in the Catholic Church for the ordination of women, on January 27, 1977, the Vatican Congregation for the Doctrine of the Faith issued its "Declaration on the Question of the Admission of Women to the Ministerial Priesthood". The Declaration reaffirms the traditional teaching and practice of the Church and says that "the Church, in fidelity to the example of the Lord, does not consider herself authorized to admit women to priestly ordination" (Introduction). After thus stating the position of the Catholic Church, the Declaration then proceeds to present the arguments for it from the attitude of Christ himself, from the practice of the Apostles and from the constant tradition of the Church.

The main argument of the proponents of women's ordination is that Jesus' selection of twelve men to be Apostles—men only without the inclusion of women —was merely an acquiescence on his part to a relative, time-conditioned, changeable cultural situation. With a change in woman's social status, they argue, this restriction to males can and must be lifted. They also argue that the Church has power over the sacraments and therefore can change the canonical and traditional norm that only baptized males can be ordained.

The Declaration briefly states these objections to Church teaching and tradition and then lucidly answers them. The document points out that Jesus went against many of the social customs of his time, such as publicly conversing with women, allowing sick women to touch him, allowing the public sinner to anoint him with perfume and so forth. Fundamentally, the Declaration rejects the validity of the argument from social and cultural change.

Further, the document points out, with regard to the Church's power over the sacraments, that her power is limited to the *accidentals* of the sacraments. What has been instituted by Christ, such as bread and wine in the Eucharist, cannot be changed to hamburgers and Coke by the Church. The point the Congregation makes in this regard is that it is the will of Christ—therefore a divine positive command—that only men can serve as priests.

It seems to me that the crucial argument in this question is a theological one; it has nothing to do with sociology or anthropology or cultural differences. The priest takes the place of Christ and Christ was a man, not a woman. The sacraments use *natural signs* to signify spiritual realities. Holy Orders is a sacrament—therefore it is a sign. When the priest says, "This is my body . . ." or "I absolve you from your sins" he is taking the place of Christ. Only a man can do that. If a woman tried to act as a priest, the sign value of the sacrament would be lost.

We should not neglect the Scriptural evidence of a *nuptial relationship* between God and his people. God is portrayed as the groom and Israel as the bride. The New Testament continues the same imagery (for example in Ephesians 5). Between the glorified Christ and his Church there is an intimate bond similar to the marriage bond, but he is the groom and she is the bride. Thus, if a woman could serve as a priest this "natural resemblance", as the Declaration calls it, would be lost.

For these and other reasons women cannot and therefore never will be ordained priests (or priestesses) in the Catholic Church. Scripture is against it; tradition is against it. Why? Because it is against God's will and therefore a theological impossibility.

58

GOD CREATED THEM MALE AND FEMALE

Having treated six sacraments, it now remains to present, as simply and clearly as possible, the Church's teaching on the holy sacrament of Matrimony. Today there is an immense amount of material available on marriage and the family. Much of it, however, approaches the subject from the points of view of sociology, psychology and anthropology.

We are all aware of the alarming breakdown of the American family. For every ten marriages there are over four divorces. In a large city like New York the figures are even higher. During 1977 in Washington, D.C., the nation's capital, there were more abortions than live live births. Teenage pregnancies average annually in the neighborhood of one million.

These problems, of course, are not restricted to the United States; they are common in much of the free world. Aware of this fact, the Holy Father selected the whole problem area of "marriage and family" as the topic for the world synod of bishops in Rome in 1980.

The task I set before myself is the modest one of presenting and explaining the fundamentals of Catholic doctrine on Christian marriage. With absolutely no claim of being exhaustive, I will attempt to explain the basics that every Catholic with some religious education should know.

The first point to clear up is what we mean by Christian marriage or the sacrament of Matrimony. The following will serve as a working definition: "Christian marriage is that sacrament in which a baptized man and a baptized woman enter into a permanent communion of life and love by mutual agreement for the generation and education of children, and in which they receive God's grace to help them grow in holiness and fulfill the duties of their state." In the present short essay I cannot possibly explain all of the ramifications of this definition of Christian marriage. But in the following essays I will develop it part by part.

Before we get into the definition it might be helpful to point out that marriage as a natural society was not instituted by man, but by God. This follows logically from the fact of creation and is stated explicitly in the Bible: "God created man in the image of himself, in the image of God he created him, male and female he created them" (Gen 1:27). Sexual differentiation into male and female was willed by God and is ordered to reproduction, as we see from the very next verse in Genesis: "God blessed them, saying to them, 'Be fruitful, multiply, fill the earth and conquer it.'"

In Genesis 2 the sacred author says that Adam was alone and needed a "helpmate", so God "made the man fall into a deep sleep. . . . Yahweh God built the rib he had taken from the man into a woman and brought her to the man" (verses 21–22). Immediately Adam sees in her an equal and a companion: "The man exclaimed, 'This at last is bone from my bones, and flesh from my flesh! This is to be called woman, for this was taken from man.' This is why a man leaves his father and mother and joins himself to his wife, and they become one body" (verses 23–24).

Given the contemporary obsession with sex—which leads to the glorification, sometimes even the divinization of it—you might be surprised to discover that certain groups in the past have looked upon marriage as evil and therefore as something to be totally shunned. They arrived at this conclusion because of a false view of the world in which they claimed that there are two sources of reality—a good one called "God" and an evil one sometimes called the Devil. For them, man's spirit and all things spiritual proceed from the good principle, while the body and all material things proceed from the evil principle. Since marriage involves sexual intercourse and since sex requires the body (which, in their view, is evil), they concluded that marriage was evil. In the early Church the Gnostics and the Manichaeans held views similar to these; in the Middle Ages the Cathari (a sect which has not completely died out in Europe) embraced this type of dualism. The Catholic Church has always rejected Manichaean dualism, asserting that matter is good because God created it, and that therefore marriage is good and lawful.

In his famous 1930 encyclical "On Christian Marriage" the great Pope Pius XI clearly stated the Catholic teaching on this question:

> First of all, let this remain the unchanged and unshakable foundation: Matrimony was neither established nor restored by man but by God. It has been protected, strengthened, and elevated not by the laws of men, but by those of God, the author of human nature, and of Christ who restored that same nature. Consequently, these laws cannot be changed according to men's pleasure, nor by any agreement of the spouses themselves that is contrary to these laws. This is the teaching of Sacred Scripture (see Gen 1:27; 2:22f.; Mt 19:3ff.; Eph 5:23ff.); this is the constant, universal tradition of the Church; this is the solemn definition of the holy Council of Trent, which in the words of Sacred Scripture teaches and reasserts that the permanent and indissoluble bond of matrimony, its unity and strength, have their origin in God.

59

CHRISTIAN MARRIAGE IS A SACRAMENT

The point I want to make here is that marriage is a sacrament. In the last essay we saw that God created man "male and female", so God himself is the author of marriage on the natural plane. It is therefore good and holy.

Before Jesus elevated marriage to the level of a sacrament, it was a natural contract between a legally competent man and woman. Although surrounded by different rites according to the culture, marriage results from the free consent given and received by the contracting parties. So there is no doubt that marriage is a contract. But what kind of contract is it? Is it fundamentally the same as a commercial contract to buy an automobile or a new home?

Most of the Protestant churches and, so far as I know, all non-Christians hold that marriage is a natural contract between a man and a woman. Such contracts are products of man's free choices and, by mutual agreement, can be terminated at any time. It is for this reason that most Protestants and non-Christians hold for the moral liceity of divorce when partners cannot continue to live together in harmony.

Soundly based on Holy Scripture, on the teaching of the Fathers and on tradition, the Church teaches that marriage between two baptized Christians is more than a purely natural contract, such as agreeing to purchase a piece of land. As a result of the positive will of Christ, marriage is now something holy and supernatural—it is in fact one of the seven sacraments of the Church.

Since marriage is a sacrament, this means that it confers sanctifying grace in a way similar to the other sacraments such as Baptism, Penance, Eucharist and so forth. What this means is that when Christian lovers exchange their marriage vows they are God's instruments in the sanctification of each other. Not only do they receive divine grace on the wedding day, but, since they enter into a *permanent state* of holy Matrimony, the Lord will continue to give them the graces they need at every stage of their married life. In short, the sacrament confers a special title to these ongoing graces.

In opposition to the Protestants of the time, the Council of Trent in 1563 taught clearly and infallibly that Matrimony is a sacrament. At one point the Council said:

> Christ himself, who instituted the holy sacraments and brought them to perfection, merited for us by his Passion the grace that brings natural love to perfection, and strengthens the indissoluble unity, and sanctifies the spouses. The Apostle Paul intimates this when he says: "Husbands, love your wives, just as Christ also loved the Church, and delivered himself up for her" (Eph 5:25); and he immediately adds: "This is a great mystery—I mean in reference to Christ and to the Church" (Eph 5:32).

In the Old Testament some of the prophets daringly spoke of the love of God for his people as similar to the amorous love between spouses. At that time marriage was primarily a civil affair, though the Sixth Commandment guaranteed the sanctity of the institution.

In the New Testament St. Paul stresses the religious character of marriage by demanding that it be contracted "in the Lord" (1 Cor 7:39), and by proclaiming its indissolubility in virtue of the Lord's command (1 Cor 7:10–11).

In order to grasp St. Paul's view of the dignity, sanctity and indissolubility of Christian marriage, it is necessary first to consider the relationship of Christ with the Church. For Paul, the relationship of husband to wife is a reflection and symbol of the love relationship between Jesus and the Church. For Paul, Jesus is the groom and the Church is his bride. He loved her totally and sacrificed himself for her; now in his glory, he is indissolubly united to her in love.

In like manner, in the thinking of Paul, a husband should love his wife "just as Christ loved the Church, and delivered himself up for her" (Eph 5:25). So in some sense Christian marriage mirrors the heavenly relationship between the glorified Christ and his Church. And since it is an image of Christ's association with his Church, Paul sees great dignity and sanctity in Christian marriage. (The more detailed thinking of St. Paul on marriage will be found in chapter seven of 1 Corinthians and chapter five of Ephesians.) Later the Church came to see that Christian marriage is indeed one of the seven sacraments.

60

WHAT IS THE PURPOSE OF MARRIAGE?

In previous essays I have shown that God is the author of marriage and that marriage between baptized Christians is one of the seven sacraments instituted by Christ. It follows from the above, then, that marriage is a natural institution willed by God; for Christians, moreover, it is a supernatural state, since it is a sign and cause of divine grace.

The next question to answer is this: What is the purpose of marriage? God, being infinitely wise, does not act or create anything without some purpose in view. Since he is the author of the conjugal union between husband and wife, what purpose or purposes did he establish for that union?

When we ask this question we are concerned with the objective purposes of marriage itself and not with the subjective intentions of this or that person who decides to get married. Young and old enter into Matrimony for hundreds of different reasons, for example, to have children, to escape an unpleasant home situation, for money, for security, for social position, for political advantage and so forth. The point I wish to make here is that the institution of marriage itself, since it was ordained by God and willed by him, has its own finality which is independent of the subjective motivation of various individuals.

The Church has been very clear in answering the question about the purpose of marriage. She has stated the following in the Code of Canon Law (repeated by Pope Pius XI and often by Pius XII): The primary purpose of marriage is the generation and education of children; the secondary purpose is the mutual assistance of the spouses and the morally regulated satisfaction of the sex urge.

With regard to the primary purpose: The meaning of a valid marriage contract is that an eligible man and woman give and receive the right to use the body of the other person for sexual acts that of their nature are ordered to the procreation of children. If this right is not given the marriage contract is simply invalid. And there is more to marriage than just the generation of children, since infants require the love and care of both father and mother for many years before they can survive in this world on their own. Consequently, parents have the primary right and duty to *educate* their children to the best of their ability so that the children can eventually stand on their own and then begin their own families.

The primary purpose of marriage is clearly expressed in Genesis 1:28: "God blessed them, saying to them: 'Be fruitful, multiply, fill the earth and conquer it.' " This purpose may not be uppermost in the minds of young people when they get married. That does not affect the validity of the marriage provided that they do not positively exclude it by a special act of the will.

With regard to the secondary purpose: "Mutual assistance" includes all the things that pertain to a community of life and love between spouses, such as sharing material goods, living together in the same house, eating together and sleeping together, helping each other to grow physically, morally, psychologically and spiritually to full human maturity. Satisfaction of the sex urge, which is stronger in some than in others, is naturally provided for by fulfilling the primary purpose of marriage. In a sense too the sex drive is tamed and sublimated in personal love of the other.

It is very important to note that both purposes, primary and secondary, are *essential* to a true marriage. The Church has never said anything like this: "You parents, you are obliged to have as many children as you can, but it doesn't matter whether you love each other and have a happy life together." When the Church says "secondary" it does not mean "unimportant". The secondary end is just as important as the primary one, and it is often uppermost in the minds of married people. The point is that in philosophical terms the secondary purpose is *subordinate* to the primary purpose and cannot be attained without the latter.

The secondary purpose is expressed in Genesis 2:18: "The Lord God said, 'It is not good that the man should be alone. I will make him a helpmate.' "

In an effort to stress the personal dimension of marriage, some Catholic writers in the past forty years have attempted to downgrade or even to reject the "primary/secondary" emphasis of official Church teaching. In recent years much has been made of the fact that the Second Vatican Council did not use this terminology. It is true that Vatican II avoided those words, but in the Constitution on the Church Today, numbers 48 to 50, the same reality is affirmed. The Council tried to stress that both purposes are essential to marriage and omitted (but did not reject) the customary distinction between primary and secondary ends of marriage. Emphasis is given to marriage as a community of love, but the essential role of children is brought out forcefully. Thus the Fathers say in paragraph no. 50 of the same document: "Marriage and conjugal love are by their nature ordained toward the begetting and educating of children. Children are really the supreme gift of marriage and contribute very substantially to the welfare of their parents."

61

WHAT'S WRONG WITH POLYGAMY?

Christian sacramental marriage was ordained by the Lord Jesus Christ for one man and one woman. Thus the Catholic Church, from the time of Christ himself, has always condemned as contrary to nature and God's law polygamy (a multiplicity of wives), polyandry (a multiplicity of husbands) and divorce/remarriage.

In her teaching on marriage the Church stresses, after its sacramentality and primary/secondary purposes—which we have already treated—its *unity* and *indissolubility*. These are called in Catholic theology the "essential properties" or "distinguishing marks" of a sacramental marriage. In this context unity refers to one husband with one wife, and indissolubility concerns the permanence of marriage until the death of one of the parties.

Why does the Church forbid polygamy and polyandry? It seems to me that there are basically two reasons for this opposition: 1) they are opposed to the explicit teaching of the New Testament, especially that of Jesus and St. Paul, and 2) they are opposed to the primary and/or secondary purposes of marriage.

We see in the Old Testament that God instituted marriage between Adam and Eve as a monogamous institution (Gen 1:28; 2:24). Mankind, however, soon lapsed from the original ideal of monogamy when

Lamech took two wives (Gen 4:19). Polygamy was widely practiced by the Israelites, as we see in the case of the Patriarchs, Saul and David. There were even regulations covering it in the Jewish Law (Dt 21:15ff.), which implied some kind of divine dispensation or at least toleration.

Christ, however, on his own divine authority, restored marriage to its original purity and unity. This is evident from his exchange with the Pharisees on the question of divorce in Matthew 19. For in answer to their question about whether or not divorce could ever be justified for any reason, Jesus said: "Have you not read that the creator from the beginning 'made them male and female' and that he said: 'This is why a man must leave father and mother, and cling to his wife, and the two become one body'? They are no longer two, therefore, but one body" (verses 3–6). Jesus also said that divorcing one's wife and marrying another is adultery (Mt 19:9). The same teaching is also found in St. Mark and St. Paul (cf. Rom 7:3; 1 Cor 7:2; Eph 5:32ff.).

The second reason for the condemnation of polygamy and polyandry is that they are opposed to the essential ends of marriage, namely, the generation and education of children, and the mutual assistance and love of the spouses.

When one man has several wives there is occasion for much domestic strife, as is evident from the former practice among the Chinese and the current practice among Moslems who are allowed by the Koran to take up to four wives. Polygamy allows for a limited attainment of the primary end of marriage in that children can be generated, but many problems arise with regard to their education, inheritance, social position and so forth. But in this system it is difficult, if not impossible, to attain the secondary end of marriage. There is always the problem of jealousy among the many wives and what happens in the concrete is that the wives tend to be more servants to the man than his equals and helpmates.

Polyandry is even more opposed to the ends of marriage than is polygamy; also, it is found usually among the most primitive of human societies. One woman living simultaneously with several men finds the sexual demands on her impossible. If she should bear a child, the enforced sexual abstention by her several husbands before and after birth might prove impossible. The child of such a mother might be totally deprived of a father's love and support because of doubt about who the real father is. Likewise, it is hard to imagine true interspousal love in such an arrangement.

The Council of Trent in 1563 strongly defended monogamy and pronounced an anathema on anyone who says that "it is lawful for Christians to have several wives at the same time, and that it is not forbidden by any divine law".

Pope Pius XI beautifully summed up the Catholic teaching on monogamy:

> Conjugal faith demands in the first place the complete unity of matrimony which the Creator himself laid down in the marriage of our first parents when he wished it to be not otherwise than between one man and one woman. And, although afterward this primeval law was relaxed to some extent by God, the supreme lawgiver, there is no doubt that the law of the Gospel fully restored that original and perfect unity, and abrogated all dispensations, as the words of Christ and the constant teaching and action of the Church show plainly. With reason, therefore, does the sacred Council of Trent solemnly declare: "Christ our Lord very clearly taught that in this bond two persons only are to be united and joined together when he said, 'Therefore they are no longer two, but one flesh.' "

62

THE QUESTION OF DIVORCE

We now live in a post-Christian society in which easy divorce is widely practiced and accepted. It was not always so. According to recent figures, four out of ten marriages end up in divorce. The rate for teenage marriages is something like eight or nine out of ten. It is bad enough that this is true of our society in general; it is even more distressing to learn that there is little difference between Catholics and non-Catholics in this regard.

It is well known that the Catholic Church forbids divorce in the case of a sacramental marriage between baptized Christians. Until the time of Luther in Germany and Henry VIII in England in the sixteenth century this was the universal law in Christian lands. For the most part Protestants maintained this tradition until the twentieth century. Since 1900 divorce has become easier with each decade so that now we have come to the stage of "no-fault divorce".

The Catholic Church's prohibition of divorce is based on the revelation of Jesus himself and the practice of the early Church. Jesus' attitude is quite uncompromising on this subject, in marked contrast to the laxness of the Law of Moses which Jesus explicitly intended to correct.

If you want to know what the Lord thinks about divorce consider the following:

> Some Pharisees came up to him and said, to test him, "May a man divorce his wife for any reason whatever?" He replied, "Have you not read that at the beginning the Creator made them male and female and declared, 'For this reason a man shall leave his father and mother and cling to his wife, and the two shall become as one'? Thus they are no longer two but one flesh. Therefore, let no man separate what God has joined." They said to him, "Then why did Moses command divorce and the promulgation of a divorce decree?" "Because of your stubbornness Moses let you divorce your wives", he replied; "but at the beginning it was not that way. I now say to you, whoever divorces his wife (lewd conduct is a separate case) and marries another commits adultery, and the man who marries a divorced woman commits adultery." (Mt 19:1–9; cf. also Mt 5:32; 1 Cor 7:10–16; Eph 5:32).

A certain laxity had crept into the Mosaic Law and tradition and Jesus intended to correct that. This is clear from the Sermon on the Mount in Matthew 5 to 7.

Jesus' prohibition of divorce is usually referred to as the indissolubility of Christian marriage. This means that once a truly sacramental bond of marriage is present it cannot be broken either by the marriage partners or by the Church. The Council of Trent in 1563 declared that the marriage bond cannot be dissolved "by reason of heresy, domestic incompatibility, or wilful desertion by one of the parties". The same Council also stated officially that the Church does not err when she has taught and teaches that, according to the doctrine of the Gospels and the Apostles, the bond of matrimony cannot be dissolved because of the adultery of one of the parties.

Theologians dispute the meaning of the "exception

347

clause" in Matthew 19:9—"lewd conduct is a separate case." A few of the Fathers interpreted this to mean that adultery by one of the parties would dissolve the marriage, but this opinion was never generally accepted. The exact meaning is still contested. One possible explanation that is widely accepted is that it refers to incestuous unions that are prohibited by the natural law and therefore are invalid.

In addition to Jesus' prohibition of divorce, it is possible to adduce other reasons for the indissolubility of marriage. Thus, we argue, divorce is opposed to both the primary and the secondary ends of marriage. For unbreakable marriage is the best guarantee of the physical and moral education of the children; it protects the marital fidelity of husband and wife; it contributes immensely to the welfare of the family and society. And as St. Paul says in Ephesians 5, it is a reflection of the indissoluble union of Christ with his Church.

There is no such thing as "Catholic divorce" once a truly sacramental marriage has been entered into and it has been consummated by sexual union. The annulment of some marriages, which has become more common since the Second Vatican Council, is not properly a "divorce", that is, a *breaking* of the marriage bond; rather, it is a declaration from the Marriage Tribunal that a true marriage bond never existed. Therefore, the parties are declared to be free to separate and to enter into a sacramental union.

The so-called "Pauline Privilege" refers to the teaching of St. Paul in 1 Corinthians 7:12–16. This privilege refers to a valid, consummated marriage between two unbaptized persons. Paul says that such a marriage can be dissolved by the Church, if one party to the marriage is baptized and the other party refuses to live with him or her peacefully in the married state. In such a case the Church exercises power over the natural bond of marriage in order to support the faith of the converted person.

63

THE MARRIAGE CONTRACT

We have seen that Christian marriage is a sacrament. By that we mean that it is a *sacred sign*, instituted by Christ himself, to signify sanctifying grace and also to confer it. The question I propose to treat here is: In the marriage ceremony, what precisely constitutes the sacrament of Matrimony? Or, at what point do the bride and groom actually receive the sacrament and the grace that accompanies it?

This question has been pondered for centuries by profound Catholic thinkers and the results of that effort are incorporated into the teaching of the Church as it is found in various Councils, the writings of such popes as Leo XIII and Pius XI, and in the Code of Canon Law. The latter summarizes the tradition in Canon 1012: "Christ Our Lord elevated the very contract of marriage between baptized persons to the dignity of a sacrament.

Therefore it is impossible for a valid contract of marriage between baptized persons to exist without being by that very fact a sacrament."

Marriage is always and by its very nature a *contract* between an eligible man and woman. It is an exclusive agreement by which a man and a woman mutually give and accept a right over their bodies for the purpose of acts which are in themselves suitable for the generation of children. Catholic authors also stress that it is a *sacred contract* because God the Creator willed and established marriage as the natural means of propagation for immortal human persons who are destined to be with God for all eternity.

According to Catholic teaching, Matrimony is a sacrament. This means, then, that Christ our Lord elevated the natural state of marriage to a sign that imparts divine grace and life. Since marriage is essentially a contract, it follows that the outward, visible sign of the sacrament is the contract. Thus, in the Nuptial Mass it is the exchange of marriage vows between the bride and the groom that causes the marriage to come into existence.

What, then, is the role of the priest? His presence is required by canon law as an official witness for the Church. It is important to note that the priest does not confer the sacrament on the two parties; rather, they confer it on each other and so are rightly called the ministers of the sacrament. In addition to being an official witness, the priest also confers special blessings on the newlyweds, but these are not essential to the contract and the sacrament.

There are a number of interesting consequences of this teaching. Thus, a priest is not absolutely required. For a good reason the bishop can dispense a Catholic from the requirement to be married before a priest; he can delegate someone else to perform the ceremony, such as a Protestant minister, rabbi or civil judge. The law also provides certain cases in which a valid marriage can be contracted before two witnesses.

Since a valid contract of marriage between baptized persons is a sacrament, it follows that the marriages of properly baptized Protestants are sacraments, even though they do not teach or believe that Matrimony is a sacrament. However, the Church exempts them from certain prescriptions of canon law such as certain impediments and the requirement that they be married before a Catholic priest.

It is obvious that marriages between unbaptized persons are not sacramental, since only a baptized person can validly receive a sacrament. If a man and a woman convert to the Church and receive Baptism, then their marriage becomes sacramental too. If one person is baptized and the other is not, the common opinion among moral theologians is that the baptized person enters into a natural contract of marriage but that he or she does not receive the sacrament. Of course, there are also those who dispute this and argue that the baptized party alone receives the sacrament.

On this matter Pope Leo XIII said in 1880: ". . . It is certain that in Christian marriage the contract cannot be separated from the sacrament. And therefore it is impossible for the contract to be genuine and lawful, unless it is at the same time a sacrament. For Christ the Lord enhanced matrimony with the dignity of a sacrament."

In his important encyclical letter on Christian marriage, *Casti Connubii* (1930), Pope Pius XI repeated the same teaching: "Since Christ has made the valid matrimonial consent between the faithful a sign of grace, the essence of the sacrament is so perfectly identified with Christian marriage that there can be no true marriage between baptized persons 'that is not at the same time a sacrament.' "

64

RELIGIOUS CONSEQUENCES
OF MATRIMONY

Christian marriage is a sacred sign, a covenant of love, a symbol of the perpetual union between Christ and his Church. We can ask in this context what the religious consequences are for the baptized man and woman who enter into the holy and sacramental state of matrimony.

What I propose to discuss here are the *religious* effects of receiving the sacrament of Matrimony. There are many consequences in the secular and human order, such as the economic, psychological, social and familial changes that take place in the lives of newly wedded couples. Though important, they are not the object of our consideration here.

As far as our Catholic faith goes, then, what are the major consequences of receiving the sacrament of Matrimony? There are two principal ones: 1) the marriage bond, and 2) the grace of the sacrament.

By the marriage bond is meant the perpetual, indissoluble union between husband and wife that is forged by the reception of the sacrament. In recognition of this indissoluble bond Adam, our first parent, under the influence of the Holy Spirit said, "This now is bone of my bones, and flesh of my flesh. . . . Wherefore a man shall leave father and mother, and cleave to his wife: and they shall be two in one flesh" (Gen 2:23f.; see Eph 5:31).

Jesus clearly taught that the nature of the marriage bond was unbreakable. Referring to the words quoted above as spoken by God he said, "Therefore now they are no longer two, but one flesh" (Mt 19:6). Immediately after this, with the words, "What therefore God has joined together, let no man put asunder" (Mt 19:6; Mk 10:9), he confirmed the stability of that same bond which had been declared by Adam so long before.

The marriage bond is something like the mark on the soul effected by Baptism: It cannot be repeated. This is absolutely true in the case of Baptism. The marriage bond is indissoluble during the lifetime of the two partners, whether they live together or not. When one of the parties dies, then the surviving party is free to marry again if he or she is so inclined. In a previous essay I explained that an annulment is a declaration on the part of the Church that a true bond of marriage never existed, even though the man and woman thought it did. In the Pauline Privilege the Church breaks the natural bond of marriage between two unbaptized persons so that one of the partners may become a Catholic and enter into a sacramental marriage. These are only apparent exceptions. The Church herself says that, when a couple is married sacramentally in the Lord and has expressed their union by sexual intercourse, no power on earth can break that bond, not even the Church. For true Christian marriage is a reflection and image of Jesus' eternal, indissoluble union with his bride, the Church. You may recall that the Pope defended this teaching against Henry VIII of England when he wanted a divorce from his wife Catherine. Eventually England was lost to the Church because the Church would not capitulate to a lustful king.

The second effect of receiving the sacrament of Matrimony is an increase of sanctifying grace. All sacraments, as we have seen, both signify and confer divine grace. Since Matrimony is a sacrament, it produces an increase of grace in the souls of those who receive it. This should be a very consoling teaching for all married Catholics. The married state is a sacramental state that has certain graces attached to it. Not only is an increase of grace granted on the wedding day; the sacrament also guarantees that throughout one's married life God will confer on husband and wife those actual graces that they need in order to fulfill the ordinary duties of their state in life. So the sacrament helps spouses both to grow in love of one another and also to grow in the love of God.

Pope Pius XI said in this regard:

> When the faithful give their sincere matrimonial consent, they open up for themselves a vast treasure of sacramental grace from which they may draw the supernatural strength to fulfill the duties of their state with fidelity, holiness, and perseverance until they die.
>
> If men do not place any obstacle, this sacrament increases for them the permanent source of their supernatural life, sanctifying grace; and it gives them special additional gifts, good inspirations, and seeds of grace, at the same time augmenting and perfecting their natural faculties. Thus husband and wife can have more than an abstract appreciation of all that pertains to the goals and duties of their married state; they can have an

internal realization, a firm conviction, an efficacious will, and an actual accomplishment of it. Finally, this sacrament gives them the right to ask for and receive the help of actual grace as often as they need it to fulfill the duties of their state.

65

THE CHURCH'S POWER
OVER MATRIMONY

Our final consideration on the sacrament of Matrimony concerns the power of the Church to regulate it. Since marriage is not only a sacrament but also affects civil society and therefore the state, there is a certain overlapping of authority. This means that both the Church and the state have rights over marriage.

As a natural society, that is, one created and willed by God, marriage pertains to civil society or the state. In recognition of this, the Church does not claim authority over the unbaptized nor does she claim jurisdiction over the marriages of those who are not Christians. Accordingly, it is up to the state to regulate marriages with regard to age, public order, health and so forth, provided that it does not command something that is contrary to the divine law. Obviously, a human law that mandates something contrary to the law of God is null and void and must not be obeyed.

Marriages, however, between Christians or between

a Christian and an unbaptized person are a different matter. You will recall that Jesus raised marriage between Christians to the level of a sacrament: It is a sacred sign of Christ's perpetual union with his Church—a sign which not only signifies grace but also confers it on husband and wife. The state has nothing to say about the sacraments; they come exclusively under the authority of the Church.

Since marriage between Christians is a sacrament it follows that the Church alone possesses the right to regulate the matrimonial affairs of baptized persons, at least insofar as these affect the sacrament. This means that it is in the competency of the Church to legislate with regard to all those things that concern the sacrament, such as establishing impediments to marriage and also dispensing from the same, prescribing the proper form, providing for witnesses, judging the possibility of nullity of the marriage and so forth.

In this country we are blessed in that the state does not interfere with the Church, for the most part, in her regulation of marriages between Catholics. The state requires a license, which it has the right to do, and may require some sort of health certificate (a requirement which varies in the different states). But the state recognizes the right of the Church to preside over marriages between her members and therefore deputes the ministers of the Church as legitimate witnesses of the ceremony.

Things are much different in some countries where there is opposition between Church and state. In countries such as Belgium and France, for example, the state does not recognize Church marriages and the Church does not recognize state weddings. What are Catholics to do in such a situation? As a practical solution, couples first go through a civil ceremony in order to satisfy the law. The Church regards such civil marriages not as real marriages, but merely as legal formalities. The couple must then go to the Church in order to receive the sacrament of Matrimony and to be really married. Occasionally stories about this situation appear in the newspapers when prominent Catholic Europeans get married.

There are certain merely civil effects of marriage, even for Christians, which are within the province of the state to regulate. These would include such things as the right of the wife to her husband's name, property rights, her right of inheritance and so forth.

What about the case of a Catholic who is married to an unbaptized person? It is commonly held by Catholic moralists that such marriages are not a sacrament, because an unbaptized person cannot receive any sacrament except Baptism. However, there is a natural bond of marriage created by the contract and one of the parties to that contract is a member of the Church. Therefore the Church has power over such marriages and the right to regulate them by establishing the norms that must be followed in order to contract a truly valid natural marriage.

In the past, secularist opponents of the Church in Europe have claimed that the state alone has power over the contract of marriage and that the sacrament is not the contract, but the blessings and rites that follow it. The Church rejects that view. For example, in 1880 Pope Leo XIII firmly opposed that opinion and said: ". . . It is certain that in Christian marriage the contract cannot be separated from the sacrament. And therefore it is impossible for the contract to be genuine and lawful, unless it is at the same time a sacrament. For Christ the Lord enhanced Matrimony with the dignity of a sacrament."

It follows, then, that the Church has exclusive authority over the marriages of Christians and the right to regulate them in all things pertaining to the sacrament.

PART IV

ESCHATOLOGY

I

THE LAW OF DEATH

We will now take up another important area of Catholic teaching, namely, the doctrine of the "Last Things" or, as it is often called by theologians, "eschatology". At the conclusion of our reflections it seems to me appropriate to spend some time thinking about the last things—death, judgment, heaven, hell, purgatory and the end of the world.

The first subject we will consider is death. We have all known what death is from a very early age, and we all fear it. Death is not a popular subject for discussion at social gatherings, except perhaps for the brief statement that someone has "passed away", a very common euphemism for the harsh, cold reality of death.

But what is death? Death is the cessation of life by the separation of the soul from the body. Some of the signs of death are: cessation of movement, cessation of breathing, radical dismemberment, corruption of the flesh. Death means the end of human life in the flesh as we know it. All of us, with the exception of some young children, have had the experience of loved ones and friends dying. The dead are no more. Their bodies are buried in the ground; we can visit the cemetery and see the spot where their bodies were placed. We erect a small plaque or monument in their memory, but physically they are no longer with us. When we die their memory will die with us.

It is a sad reality. And there is something in us which says that things should not be that way. We instinctively resist death and all that it implies. The Bible teaches, as you know, and the Church teaches that death is a punishment for sin. The Council of Trent says that by his sin Adam became subject to death and transmitted death to all of his descendants (*Denzinger* 788ff.).

Because man is composed of material parts which can be separated, he is by nature mortal, just as all other living material beings are mortal. But in the beginning, as we know from the Bible, God endowed man in Paradise with the preternatural gift of bodily immortality. Thus, in their original state Adam and Eve were exempted from the law of death. As a punishment for their disobedience, however, they were made subject to the death that God had warned them about. For God had said: "Of the tree of the knowledge of good and evil you are not to eat, for on the day you eat of it you shall most surely die" (Gen 2:17). And in the same book we read: "With sweat on your brow shall you eat your bread, until you return to the soil, as you were taken from it. For dust you are and to dust you shall return" (3:19).

St. Paul teaches very clearly that death is a result of Adam's sin: "As through one man sin entered into the world and through sin death, and thus death has passed into all men because all have sinned" (Rom 5:12). But for those who die in the state of sanctifying grace death is not so much a punishment as it is a consequence of sin. Since Our Lord and his Blessed Mother were free from original sin, death for them was not a result of sin; it was rather a consequence of life in a material body.

According to Genesis, St. Paul and Trent, all human beings, as descendants of Adam and Eve, are subject to original sin (excluding Jesus and Mary); therefore they are all subject to the law of death. This teaching is based especially on Romans 5:12ff. St. Paul also says in Hebrews 9:27, "It is appointed to men once to die and after that comes judgment." There is some disagreement among theologians about whether or not the persons living at the end of the world will have to die. St. Paul seems to say that they will not (see 1 Cor 15:51; 1 Th 4:15ff.).

Human life on this earth is the time of trial, temptation and merit. Death is the dividing line. During life one can perform good or evil deeds; one can merit eternal life or lose it; one can be a sinner for a time and then go through a conversion. With death these kinds of changes cease. As one is at the moment of death, so one remains for all eternity. There is no possibility of merit, or repentance, or sin, or conversion after death. Contrary views, as we have seen, have been repeatedly condemned by the Church. Thus, those in hell cannot attain heaven, just as those in heaven cannot sin and so lose their blessed state. We find confirmation of this truth in many places in the Bible. For example, Paul says: "For all the truth about us will be brought out in the law court of Christ, and each of us will get what he deserves for the things he did in the body, good or bad" (2 Cor 5:10; see also Mt 25:34ff.; Lk 16:26; Jn 9:4).

2

THE PARTICULAR JUDGMENT

In the Creed we proclaim our belief that Jesus "will come again in glory to judge the living and the dead". This refers to the general judgment at the end of the world. We will have more to say about that in a future essay.

But most human beings will have already died before the Second Coming of Christ. What happens to them between the moment of their death and the general judgment, which for very many involves thousands of years? Basing herself on the words of Jesus in the Gospel and also on certain statements of St. Paul, the Church gradually came to the conclusion that there is a "particular judgment" of each individual at the moment of death. There is no explicit mention of this judgment in the New Testament, but the implication is there. It was drawn by some of the Fathers of the Church and eventually accepted by the teaching authority of the Church.

Accordingly, most of us learned in our catechism lessons that immediately after death the particular judgment takes place, in which the eternal fate of the deceased person is decided by the Divine Judge. The expression "particular judgment" refers to that act of God by which the soul of man at death is either numbered among the elect in heaven or is rejected by God for all eternity.

The teaching of the Church on the particular judgment is directed against various sects and heresies which have maintained that the souls of the dead are held in some type of suspended animation until the end of the world and the Second Coming of Christ. These individuals and groups denied that those who die in Christ attain the Beatific Vision right now. For them judgment does not take place until the general judgment.

That there is a particular judgment of each person at the moment of death is not a defined dogma of the Catholic Church, but it is clearly implied in other dogmatic statements. Thus, two ecumenical Councils, Lyons II and Florence, declared that the souls of the just, free from all sin and punishment, are immediately assumed into heaven, and that the souls of those who die in mortal sin descend immediately into hell; those who die in the state of grace but still need purgation must first be cleansed in purgatory before they can be admitted to heaven.

Likewise, Pope Benedict XII in the fourteenth century taught officially that the completely pure souls of the just, immediately after death or after their purgation, enter heaven and enjoy the immediate vision of God, while the souls of those who die in mortal sin descend immediately into hell (*Denzinger* 530ff.).

The Bible implies the existence of the particular judgment by teaching that immediately after death the departed souls receive their reward or punishment. The clearest and most frequently cited text is that of the parable of the rich man and Lazarus (Lk 16:19–31). Immediately after death Lazarus is taken into the bosom of Abraham and the self-indulgent rich man goes immediately to hell for punishment. There is no hesitation and no waiting for the end of the world. Also, Jesus said to the thief on his right on Calvary, "I assure you: This day you will be with me in paradise" (Lk 23:43). For St. Paul death is the gateway to heaven and to personal communion with Christ: "I desire to be dissolved and to be with Christ" (Phil 1:23). These and similar texts gave rise, already in the second century, to the Christian reflection that some sort of judgment of each person takes place at the moment of death. Thus each deceased person learns immediately after death what his or her eternal destiny is. Thus all those who have died before us know exactly how they stand with God—they do not have to wait for the general judgment in order to discover that.

It is fruitless to try to imagine what the particular judgment is like. We just cannot adequately picture these transcendent realities. The image of a judge and tribunal has often been used in Christian art, and it does serve some useful purpose. But we should not think that such representations are accurate. The particular judgment involves a most intimate relation between the human person and the divine Judge. But there will be no witnesses, cross-examination, accusers, defenders and so forth. For in a very true sense we have already judged ourselves, depending on how we have made use of God's grace during this life. Our merits and demerits go with us. We appear before God immediately at the moment of death bearing in our hands our good deeds and our sins. Those who die in the state of mortal sin have already judged themselves; they have rejected God and God lets that rejection stand firm forever. Those who die in the state of sanctifying grace have chosen to believe in God and to serve him in this life. After death, adorned with grace and good works, they are admitted into the eternal kingdom as children of God and co-heirs with Christ. That is their particular judgment.

3

PERFECT HAPPINESS

Having considered death and the particular judgment, we will now reflect on what the Church says about *heaven*. Heaven is defined as the place and condition of perfect supernatural happiness. It is a "place" because Jesus and Mary are there with their resurrected bodies, even though it is not the same kind of place that we inhabit. It is a "condition" because it involves a modification of the human mind and will so that there is direct knowledge and love of God.

In this life heaven is very mysterious to us. St. Paul stresses the mysterious character of heaven when he says, "Eye has not seen, nor ear heard, nor has it entered into the heart of man what things God has prepared for those that love him" (1 Cor 2:9).

The Church's teaching on heaven is very consoling. She says that the souls of the just which in the moment of death are free from all guilt of sin and free from the punishment due to sin (that is, they do not have to go to purgatory) enter immediately into heaven.

We profess our belief in this revealed truth when we say in the Apostles' Creed, "I believe . . . in life everlasting," and when we say in the Creed at Sunday Mass, "We look for the resurrection of the dead, and the life of the world to come."

Heaven, as a place and state of eternal bliss, is often referred to by most people even in daily conversation; the words "heaven" and "hell" and the ideas behind them keep cropping up in our language in various ways —seriously, thoughtlessly or merely in jest. This shows, it seems to me, that the possibility of eternal happiness or eternal horror is very much on the minds of most people.

In the Gospels Jesus speaks clearly about heaven. He vividly paints the happiness of heaven in the image of a wedding feast (see Mt 25:10) and calls it eternal life. One attains life everlasting through the knowledge of God and Christ: "Eternal life is this: to know you, the only true God, and Jesus Christ whom you have sent" (Jn 17:3).

St. John the Apostle stresses in his writings that one attains eternal life by believing in Jesus, the Messiah and Son of God (see Jn 3:16; 20:31; 1 Jn 5:13). He also says that eternal life consists in conformity to God and in the direct vision of God: "We shall be like him because we shall see him as he really is" (1 Jn 3:2).

The basic human acts which are involved in heavenly bliss are *knowledge*, *love* and *joy*; it does not consist in eating, drinking, having money and clothes and engaging in sexual activity. Since the Middle Ages there has been a dispute between various schools of Catholic theologians on whether knowledge or love is the primary act. That dispute arose from different philosophies. Its resolution, however, is not necessary for a proper understanding of the Catholic teaching about heaven.

Many people wonder about whether or not they will know their parents, relatives, spouse, children and friends in heaven. On this point most Catholic theologians have taught that the blessed in heaven, in addition to the vision of God, also enjoy the companionship of the saints and their loved ones. There will also be an increase of glory and joy at the end of the world when the souls of the just are united forever with their resurrected and transfigured bodies.

Can the blessed in heaven commit sin and so lose their eternal happiness? In the early Church some theologians proposed this view, but the Church has consistently rejected it. In fact, in a solemn dogmatic statement Pope Benedict XII in the fourteenth century declared: "The vision and this enjoyment (of the Divine Essence) continues without interruption or diminution of the vision and enjoyment, and will continue until the general judgment and thenceforth for all eternity" (*Denzinger* 530).

Those who attain heaven, therefore, can never lose that blessed state. Because of the face-to-face vision of God they see themselves clearly as they are and so are morally incapable of sin. Thus, Jesus compares the reward for good works with treasures in heaven which cannot be lost (Mt 6:20; Lk 12:33); and St. Paul calls eternal happiness in heaven "an incorruptible crown" (1 Cor 9:25).

Are all of the saved equal in the sense that they all have the same degree of enjoyment of the Beatific Vision? It is an infallible teaching of the Catholic Church that the level of participation in the Beatific Vision granted to the saved is proportioned to each one's merits. For the Council of Florence declared in the fifteenth century that the saved "see clearly the Triune God himself, just as he is, *some more perfectly than others* according to their respective merits" (*Denzinger* 693). Thus, Jesus promised that he will "render to every one according to his works" (Mt 16:27). In the same vein St. Paul writes that "each will duly be paid according to his share in the work" (1 Cor 3:8). Jesus' words about the "many rooms" or "mansions" in his Father's house have often been interpreted, in Catholic tradition, as affirming the inequality of rewards, depending on each one's merits (see Jn 14:2).

4

HELL IS NO JOKE

It is indeed curious that so many people like to use the word "hell" often in their daily conversation, but do not want to think about what it means. There must be a certain fascination in the subject, however, for otherwise the word would not be so popular. The word even crops up in the name of a well-known group of motorcyclists.

There is another curious dimension of the very frequent use of the word "hell", and that is that perhaps most of the people who employ the word regularly do not believe in the reality of hell at all. If they really believed in the existence of hell, they would not be so flippant in their use of the word.

What do we mean by "hell"? Hell is the place and state of eternal punishment for the fallen angels and human beings who die deliberately estranged from the love of God. The existence of hell, as the everlasting abode of the devils and those human beings who have died in the state of mortal sin, is a defined dogma of the Catholic Church. Anyone who denies this truth simply refuses to accept the clear words and parables of Jesus about this reality as true.

The important fifth century Athanasian Creed says that, when Christ comes in glory, all will have to give an account of their lives and "those who have done good deeds will go into eternal life; those who have done evil will go into everlasting fire" (*Denzinger* 40).

Pope Benedict XII declared in 1336: "We define that, according to the general decree of God, the souls of those who die in actual mortal sin go down into hell soon after their death, and there suffer the pains of hell" (*Denzinger* 531).

The above teaching of the Magisterium is clearly based on the Bible. The New Testament mentions hell more than thirty times. Jesus often threatens sinners with the punishment of hell, if they do not repent. Thus, he calls it "eternal fire" (Mt 18:8), "the hell of fire" (Mt 18:9), "everlasting fire" (Mt 25:41), "unquenchable fire" (Mk 9:43). St. Paul says of sinners that "it will be their punishment to be lost eternally, excluded from the presence of the Lord and from the glory of his strength" (2 Th 1:9).

Catholic theologians distinguish a twofold punishment in hell: *the pain of loss* and *the pain of sense*. The pain of loss, which is the essence of the punishment of hell, consists in exclusion from the Beatific Vision or eternal rejection by God. This is indicated by those powerful words of the Eternal Judge, "Depart from me, you cursed, into the eternal fire prepared for the devil and his angels" (Mt 25:41).

The pain of sense consists in the suffering which is caused by outside material things. The Bible describes hell vividly as a place where there is wailing and gnashing of teeth, a place of sorrow, intense suffering and despair.

Some of the Fathers of the Church understand the "fire" of hell in a metaphorical sense as a symbol for purely spiritual pains; others think that it is an actual physical fire, but say that there is a difference between this fire and ordinary fire. The Church has given no official decision on this matter, so you can hold either opinion.

The punishment of hell is eternal. This is clear from the repeated warnings of Jesus in the New Testament. The Fourth Lateran Council (1215 A.D.) declared that the wicked "will receive a perpetual punishment with the devil" (*Denzinger* 429). The word "eternal" is not to be understood in the sense of "a very long time, but finally coming to an end", since there is a clear contrast between everlasting punishment and everlasting life in Matthew 25. Just as we believe that heaven will never end, so also will hell be everlasting.

The existence of hell is in accordance with divine justice. The damned witness to God's justice, since he respects human freedom, and those who are lost really condemn themselves by resisting God's abundant grace. The reason why the damned cannot repent is that their wills are hardened in evil and hatred of God; in such a state they cannot repent and God refuses all further grace to the damned. The time of grace and merit is during this life, as we have seen.

It is the common opinion of theologians that the punishment of the damned is proportioned to each one's guilt. The Second Council of Lyons in 1274 said that "the souls of those who die in mortal sin . . . soon go down into hell, but *there they receive different punishments*" (*Denzinger* 464).

Hell is an unpleasant subject because it is an unpleasant reality. Remembering hell will keep us humble and it can also be a great help to us in staying out of mortal sin. Pope John XXIII used as a motto for his whole life the following, entitled "Four Future Things":

Death, than which nothing is more certain;
Judgment, than which nothing is more strict;
Hell, than which nothing is more terrible;
Paradise, than which nothing is more delightful.

(Journal of a Soul, Appendix 6)

5

YES, THERE IS A PURGATORY

Some years ago Frank Sheed said that, since the Second Vatican Council closed in 1965, every article of Catholic faith has been either challenged or denied by some theologian. This has given rise to much confusion among the Catholic faithful. Certainly one Catholic doctrine that has been and is often denied is the reality and existence of *purgatory*. In this essay I will set forth briefly what the Church teaches on this point.

The most important thing to note about purgatory is that its existence is an article of Catholic faith. This means that anyone who doubts or denies the existence of purgatory has departed from Catholic orthodoxy. Purgatory is defined as the place or condition in which the souls of the just are purified after death and before they enter heaven.

Because of the holiness of God nothing unclean can enter into his presence. After death there are, we know from revelation and the teaching of the Church, only two eternal and irrevocable possibilities: heaven or hell. Those in the state of sanctifying grace who have no taint of sin on their souls go directly to heaven, while those unfortunate ones who die in the state of mortal sin go directly to hell, as we have seen.

But there is a third possibility: those who die in the state of sanctifying grace but carry with them unrepented venial sins or the temporal punishment due to forgiven mortal sins for which satisfaction has not yet been made by prayer and penance. Since they are "unclean" they cannot enter into heaven; since they possess sanctifying grace they do not deserve hell. The Catholic Church says that they must spend a certain amount of time in purgatory—a place or state of temporal punishment or cleansing. As soon as they have made adequate satisfaction for their sins they go directly to heaven and enjoy forever the Beatific Vision with Mary, the angels and all the saints.

Since the Middle Ages there have been many who have denied the reality of purgatory. Luther, Calvin and most of the Protestant Reformers in the sixteenth century denied the existence of purgatory because of their erroneous view of justification.

The Second Council of Lyons in 1274 clearly affirmed the traditional Catholic teaching on purgatory: "If those who are truly penitent die in charity before they have done sufficient penance for their sins of omission and commission, their souls are cleansed after death in purgatorial or cleansing punishments" (*Denzinger* 464). The same doctrine was repeated by the Council of Florence (1438–45), the Council of Trent (1545–63) and the Second Vatican Council (1962–65).

The biblical evidence for the existence of purgatory is, for the most part, indirect, but it does admit the possibility of purification in the next world. Thus, Judas Maccabaeus ordered sacrifices to be offered in the temple in Jerusalem for the souls of his men killed in battle that their sins might be forgiven (see 2 Macc 12:42–46). Many Fathers of the Church interpreted the words of Jesus in Matthew 12:32 as referring to purgation in the next life: "Anyone who says a word against the Son of Man will be forgiven; but let anyone speak against the Holy Spirit and he will not be forgiven either in this world or in the next." Similar indirect references to purgatory, often cited by Catholic theologians, are found in Matthew 5:26 and 1 Corinthians 3:12.

The souls in purgatory, after their particular judgment, know for certain that they are saved; in this they rejoice. But since they need cleansing, they are separated from God for a time. This separation is most painful to them, since their whole being longs to be united with God.

We are not certain about the nature of the punishment of purgatory. The Church does not teach dogmatically that it is a "physical fire", even though many preachers and some catechisms speak of "the fires of purgatory". The official declarations of the Councils speak only of "purifying punishments", not of purifying fire. Whatever it is, it is painful.

The souls in purgatory are purified by atoning for the temporal punishments due to sin by their willing acceptance of the suffering imposed by God. It should also be noted that the sufferings in purgatory are not the same for all, but are proportioned to each one's degree of sinfulness.

Through the constant practice and belief of the Church we know that the sufferings of the poor souls can be alleviated by the prayers and penances of faithful Christians on earth. That is why we are urged to pray for them, to suffer for them, and to offer up Masses for them. Also, the pains of purgatory are accompanied by great peace and joy because the poor souls love God and know for certain that they will eventually reach heaven.

6

COME, LORD JESUS!

So far we have considered those aspects of the "last things" that pertain to the individual and his or her personal relationship to God: death, particular judgment, heaven, hell and purgatory. Deep down most human beings are intensely interested in these matters because they concern them intimately.

There is another aspect, however, to the last things which has to do with the future of the whole human race. From this point of view eschatology reflects on such questions as the Second Coming of Christ, the resurrection, the general judgment and the end of the world. We will now take up each of these points, beginning with the Second Coming of Christ. It is also often referred to as the "Parousia", which means his "presence" or "arrival".

The "first" coming of Christ occurred at the Incarnation when God became man in Jesus Christ. During his earthly life Jesus founded his Church, suffered and died for us, rose from the dead on Easter Sunday, ascended into heaven where he now reigns gloriously at the right hand of the Father.

Now is the age of the Church. Now is the time of salvation for all those who believe in Jesus, keep his commandments and die in his grace. But the history of the Church or the story of the Church will not go on forever. There is a time limit for it; history as we know it will come to an end. That will happen when Jesus comes "again in glory to judge the living and the dead" as we pray in the Creed at Sunday Mass. So according to the faith of the Church, at the end of time there will be a Second Coming of Christ when the glorified Lord will establish his eternal kingdom, rewarding the good and punishing the evil.

Jesus clearly foretold that he would come again at the end of the world. "Then the sign of the Son of Man will appear in heaven . . . and they will see the Son of Man coming on the clouds of heaven with power and great glory" (Mt 24:30); "For the Son of Man is going to come in the glory of his Father with his angels, and when he does, he will reward each one according to his behavior" (Mt 16:27); "If it is my will that he [John] remain until I come, what is that to you?" (Jn 21:23); "This Jesus . . . will come in the same way as you saw him go into heaven" (Acts 1:11).

The New Testament offers certain "hints" or "signs" that will be an indication that the end of the world is near. One must be very careful in trying to interpret these signs too literally. In the past many Christians thought they saw them fulfilled in events during their own time and predicted that the end was near. They were mistaken. There are those who say that the signs are evident in our time. Such assertions should be treated with a great deal of reserve.

Jesus said that before the end of the world comes the gospel "will be proclaimed to the whole world as a witness to all the nations" (Mt 24:14). Has that already happened with radio and TV? Maybe, but there are still hundreds of millions of people in China, India and other parts of the world who have not yet heard the good news of salvation in Jesus Christ. St. Paul writes that before the end "all Israel" will be converted and saved (Rom 11:25–32). That has not happened and seems to be far off in the future.

In the time before the end there will be false prophets who will lead many astray (Mt 24); St. Paul says that before the Lord's Second Coming there will be a great "schism" and many will fall away from the true faith. This seems to be verified in our time, but similar apostasies have occurred in the past.

Before the end the Antichrist will appear. He is the "man of sin", the "rebel" who will oppose God and claim to be God. He will lead many astray but "the Lord . . . will annihilate him with his glorious appearance at his coming" (2 Th 2:8). Jesus foretells that there will be

378

wars, famines, persecutions and natural catastrophes before the end (see Mt 24).

When the Parousia will take place no one knows but the Father (Acts 1:11), nor is there any clear indication in Scripture just how it will be accomplished.

To the early Christians the Second Coming of Jesus, which was understood as the climax of salvation history, was not something to be feared. Rather, it was hoped for, longed for. They fervently prayed, "Come, Lord" (1 Cor 16:22). The next to last sentence of the whole Bible reflects this longing, first by quoting Jesus and then by adding a prayer: " 'Surely I am coming soon.' Amen. Come, Lord Jesus!" (Rev 22:20). As followers of Jesus Christ that should be our prayer too.

7

THE RESURRECTION OF THE BODY

At the end of the world, Jesus will come again. God has revealed to us through the life, teaching and Resurrection of Jesus Christ that all the dead will rise again on the last day with their bodies. Now let us reflect for a few moments on some of the astonishing truths connected with the resurrection of the dead.

It is a solemn truth of the Catholic faith that all men and women, both good and evil, will rise from the dead at the end of the world, just as Jesus rose from the dead on Easter Sunday. The term "resurrection" means the return to life in the body of a dead human being; it means taking on a completely new existence in God. Thus, the souls of all those who have died will be reunited to their bodies.

When we pray the Apostles' Creed we profess, "I believe in . . . the resurrection of the body." In the Nicene Creed that we say at Sunday Mass we proclaim, "We look for the resurrection of the dead."

In the Gospels Jesus speaks clearly and often about the resurrection. He rejects as an error the Sadducees' denial of the resurrection (see Mt 22:29ff.). He teaches not only the resurrection of the just (Lk 14:14), but also the "resurrection" of the wicked who will be cast into hell with their bodies (Mt 5:29ff.). Jesus goes so far as to say of himself, "I am the Resurrection and the life" (Jn 11:25). He promises the resurrection on the last day to those who believe in him and eat his flesh and drink his blood (see Jn 6).

Belief in the resurrection was an integral part of the early preaching of the Church. It occupies a large part in Peter's first sermon on Pentecost (Acts 2); it is an essential part of the good news of salvation in Jesus Christ as proclaimed by Peter, Paul and the other Apostles (see Acts 3, 4, 5, 10, 17, 24, 26). It will take place at the end of the world—a day that is known only to the Father (Mk 13:32).

It is also a point of Catholic belief that the dead will rise again with the same bodies as they had on earth. The Bible implicitly affirms this when it speaks of the resurrection or "re-awakening" of the body. Also, St. Paul says in 1 Cor 15:53, "Our present perishable nature must put on imperishability and this mortal nature must put on immortality." Speaking to the same point, the Fourth Lateran Council in 1215 said: "And all these will rise *with their own bodies which they now have* so that they may receive according to their works. . ." (*Denzinger* 429).

When the Church says "same bodies" she does not mean that in a chemical or scientific sense. Since all of the matter in our bodies changes about every five years, obviously we will not have exactly the same atoms and molecules that we now have. But our soul will inform matter in such a way that we will have the same body in full maturity and perfection. We will look the same and we will retain our sexual differentiation. The integrity of the body in the resurrection requires the organs of vegetative and sensitive life, but the vegetative functions will no longer take place.

It is a common opinion in theology that both the saved and the damned will rise again. The bodies of the lost will share in incorruption and immortality, but they will not be transfigured and glorified (see Mt 18:8–9).

Jesus himself is the "first fruits" from the dead, as St. Paul said. The Blessed Virgin Mary was also assumed body and soul into heaven. Jesus went first, and we follow. This means that we will be transformed into a glory similar to his.

The Gospels record a number of amazing qualities in the body of the resurrected Lord. He suddenly appeared and then disappeared; he passed through walls; his body seemed to be the same as it was before, but it was also very different; he even changed his appearance so that his disciples did not recognize him (see Lk 24).

Catholic tradition holds that the resurrected bodies of the saved will be transfigured according to the pattern of the risen Christ. St. Paul said, "It is sown in corruption;

it shall rise in incorruption. . . . It is sown a natural body; it shall rise a spiritual body" (1 Cor 15:42–44).

Reflecting on the scriptural accounts of the resurrected Christ, theologians in the past have distinguished four special gifts of the risen body. It possesses: 1) impassibility, that is, freedom from physical evils of all kinds, such as sickness and death; 2) subtility, that is, the spiritualization of the body so that it is completely dominated by the soul; 3) agility, that is, the ability of the soul to move the body with the greatest ease and rapidity; 4) clarity, that is, freedom from all defects and endowment with great beauty and radiance.

To godless materialists the resurrection of the dead is utter foolishness. To those who believe in Jesus Christ, who said "I am the Resurrection" (Jn 11:25), his bodily Resurrection is a divine pledge of our own personal resurrection and triumph over death.

8

THE LAST JUDGMENT

We have already seen that each person is judged by God right after his or her death. In Catholic teaching that prompt sentence is called "the particular judgment". Scripture is very emphatic in asserting that there is also a general judgment of all mankind at the end of the world. In that dread moment Christ will come again in glory, the dead shall rise from their graves and they will all stand before Jesus Christ, the Eternal Judge, to await his decision.

Belief in the general judgment is an integral part of the Catholic faith. It is prominent in both the Apostles' Creed and the Nicene Creed, which affirm that Christ now "sits at the right hand of God the Father almighty and will come again in glory to judge the living and the dead".

In the Gospels Jesus frequently speaks about the "day of judgment". He gives his listeners, including us, plenty of advance warning. He assures us that he will execute the judgment: "For the Son of Man is going to come in the glory of his Father with his angels, and, when he does, he will reward each one according to his behavior" (Mt 16:27). The Father has handed over all judgment to the Son: "The Father judges no one; he has entrusted all judgment to the Son, so that all may honor the Son as they honor the Father. . . . The Father . . . has appointed him supreme judge because he is the Son of Man" (Jn 5:22–27).

St. Peter affirms of Jesus that "God has appointed him to judge everyone, alive or dead" (Acts 10:42). St. Paul makes the same point when he says: "According to the good news I preach, God, through Jesus Christ, judges the secrets of mankind" (Rom 2:16). St. John describes the final judgment in terms of rendering an account of all one's deeds which are written down in a book. The examination of deeds written in a book is meant to be an image or symbol of a spiritual process that takes place all at once (see Rev 20:11–15).

Jesus paints a vivid, memorable picture of the last judgment in the parable found in Matthew 25:31–46.

The Son of Man, escorted by his angels, will take his seat on the throne of glory. "All the nations will be assembled before him and he will separate men one from another as the shepherd separates sheep from goats. He will place the sheep on his right hand and the goats on his left" (verses 32–33). The basis of his judgment will be how generously people responded to the needs of others during their lifetime. Jesus identifies himself with those people and their needs.

While the particular judgment is individual and personal, the general judgment answers to the social side of humanity. So on the last day we will be judged not only as individuals but also as members of society. In this way God will reveal to all his justice in those he condemns and his mercy in those who are saved.

There is also the matter of the body sharing in the final reward or punishment. The saved and the damned are now deprived of their bodies. At the general judgment, when they have risen from the dead and the body is rejoined to the soul, the whole human person, body and soul, will share in the final punishment or reward.

Another reason for the final judgment is that a full and public verdict with regard to each person cannot be reached while history is still running its course. Both our good deeds and our evil deeds can and do have far-reaching effects. The good example of St. Francis still motivates many people to imitate his virtue. Parents live on in their children; how they have raised them affects others. So only on the last day, when all of our deeds have attained their final effect, can a truly definite judgment be made.

At the last judgment nothing will escape the notice of the Eternal Judge. He will judge us on the basis of our good deeds and our evil deeds, on our external actions and the desires of our hearts. As with the Second Coming of Jesus and the resurrection, no one knows, except the Father in heaven, when it will take place. According to St. Thomas Aquinas, it is very probable that the judgment will be in the form of a spiritual enlightenment of all and will take place in an instant. We should not imagine it to be like a series of trials in a courtroom, one after the other, going through the billions of human beings who populated the earth. God will make known immediately, and to all, the merits and the demerits of each person.

We do not know for certain where the last judgment will take place. The prophet Joel speaks of the "Valley of Jehoshaphat" (Joel 4) as the place of judgment. This is the area around Jerusalem and near the Mount of Olives where Jesus ascended into heaven. The place is probably to be understood symbolically.

9

THE END OF TIME

Our final reflection on the "Last Things" will center on the Christian belief that the world as we know it will come to an end. The Bible instructs us that the present world will be destroyed on the last day. It is not part of revelation that our world or universe will be *annihilated*, that is, reduced to nothingness, so that the only reality left would be God, the angels, and resurrected men—but no material universe. The main thrust of the biblical statements about the end of the world is that the material universe will be *renewed*. Thus, St. John writes: "Then I saw a new heaven and a new earth," and "Then the One sitting on the throne spoke: 'Now I am making the whole of creation new' " (Rev 21:1, 5).

The idea of the end of the world is rather common in Christian literature. Our belief in the "new world" is expressed in the Nicene Creed: "We look for the resurrection of the dead, and *the life of the world to come*. Amen." At the conclusion of the great commission in St. Matthew's Gospel Jesus says to his disciples, "And know that I am with you always; yes, *to the end of time*" (28:20). In another context Jesus says, "Heaven and earth will pass away, but my words will never pass away" (Mt 24:35).

On the last day God will raise all men from death to eternal life—the just to glory and the wicked to punishment. In a certain sense the material world will participate in the triumph of the just. It too will experience a "death" or destruction that leads to a rich renewal. St. Peter brings out this aspect when he writes: "The elements will be dissolved with fire, and the earth and the works that are upon it will be burned up" (2 Pet 3:10). But, in order to show that he is talking about a miraculous transformation of the material universe, he then adds: "We wait for new heavens and a new earth" (verse 13; see Is 65:17; 66:22).

The idea of the destruction of the world by fire can be understood as a mode of expression, borrowed from the Jewish apocalyptic literature, which means that the present world will be dissolved by divine power and a new world will come into existence. That new world will be adapted to the eternal, incorruptible nature of the resurrected body. It will not be characterized by the material change of generation and corruption that is an essential part of the world as we now know it.

It is impossible to say, in more precise terms, what the new heavens and the new earth will be like. It will be a world of peace and happiness. Jesus says that everything will be "made new": "I tell you solemnly, when all is made new and the Son of Man sits on his throne of glory, you will yourselves sit on twelve thrones to judge the twelve tribes of Israel" (Mt 19:28). St. Paul says that the material creation will share in the triumph of God's mercy: "The creation itself will be set free from its bondage to decay and obtain the glorious liberty of the children of God" (Rom 8:21).

St. Thomas Aquinas argues for the renewal of the world from the fact that it was created to serve mankind. Since the resurrected human person no longer needs the food, drink, oxygen and so forth that the world now provides, and that are now necessary for his human existence, Aquinas reasons that the material universe will also undergo a radical change that adapts it to the new, transfigured state of the resurrected human being. He thinks that the transfigured eye of the blessed will see the glory of God in the operations of the renewed physical world, in the body of Christ and in the bodies of the saints.

Thomas also argues, from hints in Scripture, that the heavenly bodies will emit new and greater light; there will be no more conception, birth and death in the plant and animal kingdoms. He is of the opinion that the new

387

world will not contain plants and animals, because their existence depends on generation and corruption and that type of change will no longer exist. Presumably the perfections of God that we now perceive in plants and animals will be shown to us in a more brilliant way when God makes all things new.

The end of the world and its restoration bring to a conclusion the redemptive work of Christ. When all of his enemies have been overcome, he will hand over the kingdom to his Father (1 Cor 15:24–28) without surrendering his own lordship which flows from the Hypostatic Union.

The end of the world will break suddenly upon us. It will mark the beginning of God's perfect lordship over all creation, having destroyed the power of Satan. The glorious kingdom of God is the ultimate goal of all creation and it gives final intelligibility to all human history—from Adam, through Christ, to the last human being.